Is **Rock** Dead?

Is Rock Dead?

Kevin J. H. Dettmar

 Routledge
Taylor & Francis Group
New York   London

Published in 2006 by
Routledge
Taylor & Francis Group
270 Madison Avenue
New York, NY 10016

Published in Great Britain by
Routledge
Taylor & Francis Group
2 Park Square
Milton Park, Abingdon
Oxon OX14 4RN

Printed in the United States of America on acid-free paper
10 9 8 7 6 5 4 3 2 1

International Standard Book Number-10: 0-415-97033-4 (Hardcover) 0-415-97034-2 (Softcover)
International Standard Book Number-13: 978-0-415-97033-4 (Hardcover) 978-0-415-97034-1 (Softcover)
Library of Congress Card Number 2005026752

Library of Congress Cataloging-in-Publication Data

Dettmar, Kevin J. H., 1958-
   Is rock dead? / Kevin J. H. Dettmar.
        p. cm.
   Includes bibliographical references and index.
   ISBN 0-415-97033-4 (hardback : alk. paper) -- ISBN 0-415-97034-2 (pbk. : alk. paper)
   1. Rock music--History and criticism. I. Title.

ML3534.D48 2005
781.66--dc22   2005026752

Taylor & Francis Group
is the Academic Division of Informa plc.

Visit the Taylor & Francis Web site at
http://www.taylorandfrancis.com

and the Routledge Web site at
http://www.routledge-ny.com

For Bill Richey, 1956–2003

Thank you for the days ...

CONTENTS

ACKNOWLEDGMENTS

This book is better than it otherwise would have been, owing to the patient indulgence of a number of friends and colleagues—a technical distinction that means little at times like these. Together, Bill Richey and I learned how to talk, think, and write about the music we loved in common; when I write today, I hear his voice. This book is, more than anything else, the result of a long and ongoing conversation with Bill. If there's a rock & roll heaven, well you know they got a helluva man. Conversation over the years with Jon Levin has helped me expand my notions of what ought to count as rock & roll. Michael Coyle and Ed Brunner—one of whom abandoned rock for jazz in what I like to think was a kind of midlife crisis, the other of whom fell in love with jazz early and never progressed as far as rock—have together provided a model, if (for me) an unattainable one, of thoughtful, interdisciplinary, American-studies-inflected thinking about American popular music.

I've benefited as well, in ways too numerous and various to delineate, from the support of my colleagues in the International Association for the Study of Popular Music (IASPM), U.S. chapter, especially (but by no means only) Bernie Gendron, Fred Maus, Norma Coates, and Rob Walser. Stephanie Graves, Humanities librarian at Morris Library, Southern Illinois University Carbondale, was a tremendous resource during a hectic time: hats off to you, Stephanie. I'm grateful to Jeff Abernathy, late of Illinois College, for an invitation to speak on the putative "death of rock" at an opportune moment. Jeff invited me because he'd seen a piece I had published in the *Chronicle of Higher*

Education; and this book, too, is a direct result of that *Chronicle* essay, which Richard Carlin at Routledge read and wrote me to ask, "Are you working on a book?" To which my response, of course, was an immediate "No … er, I mean, Yes! Yes I am!" That *Chronicle* essay benefited greatly from my long-standing editorial relationship with Jean Tamarin, and before her Jenny Ruark; together, they have taught me more than anyone else has about how to write in public. And Richard Carlin, in his turn, has been a paragon of patient, good-humored support as this narrative of death labored to get itself born.

A shout-out to Dettmars in the house: my children Emily, Audrey, Esther, and Colin have taught me a tremendous amount about the narrowness of the paradigm of rock & roll I grew up under and have shown me through their example a whole range of ways to use music very differently from the way my friends and I taught ourselves in high school. They've been patient mentors, always, and gentle with their old man. They even, at times, pretend to like "my" music, while surreptitiously teaching me to love theirs.

And finally, Robyn. Not really "rockin' Robyn," truth be told; not, finally, a huge fan of much of the music that makes me melt, but my muse and the true music of my life. As Lou Reed sings to Suzanne at the end of "Coney Island Baby," Robyn, I swear, I'd give the whole thing up for you. And yet the most amazing thing: you'd never ask me to.

Portions of this book have appeared, in somewhat different form, in the *Chronicle of Higher Education* and *CEA Critic.* I am thankful to the editors for the opportunity to try out these ideas in those venues and for their permission to reprint them here.

PREFACE

I'm conscious of having lured you here under false pretenses because the question in my title, "Is rock dead?", is less honest than even a rhetorical question. Indeed, from where I sit, it's a quite preposterous question. Moreover, it is not a question that we will end up spending very much time trying to wrestle with here. So if you're interested primarily in an answer, you can skip directly to the book's last paragraph. It's a bit anti-climactic, I'm afraid, but I suspect you already knew the answer.

No, this isn't a book that most importantly seeks to answer the question of its title; rather, it's a book that investigates the question, the puzzle really, of why we as a culture have so consistently asked that particular question, for fifty years now. This is a book not so much about rock & roll per se but about the ways we write, talk, and think about rock & roll; not about what rock & roll *is* so much as about the various ways we use and abuse rock & roll, about the ways we find to talk about the music, more than about the music itself. And, I suppose it must be said, this is also a book about rock's stunning ability to withstand the very worst we can throw at it.

Because my real topic here is how we tend to talk about rock & roll—to paraphrase Raymond Carver, "what we talk about when we talk about rock"—this is a rather citational book. More often than is my custom, I've turned the writing over to others, those who would attempt to persuade us, for whatever reason, that rock is dead; it is my conviction that, as we listen to them, as we would the narrator of a Poe story or a Browning poem, they make clear their own agendas, more trenchantly than I could ever hope to do.

"Is rock dead?" There's only one appropriate answer to this query, I think: "I don't know. Why do you ask?"

Much of the impulse to declare rock & roll dead is generational, as well as structural: the parents (of whatever generation) hate their children's music, and pronouncing it dead is a comforting, if not finally efficacious, way of staying its menace. Those of us who grew up in the rock era do precisely the same thing as our parents, it turns out: across the nation, even now, hippie parents who met at Woodstock are grimly shaking their heads at the music coming out of their children's bedrooms, cars, and iPods.

Because I believe much of this response to be generational, or at least affected by generational issues, I feel the need to say a thing or two about my own positioning amid the music I write about; again, as will become clear in what follows, I'm not sanguine about the ability of any of us to rise above our own affective investments when it comes to popular music. Nor, truth be told, do I regret this state of affairs. For those of us to whom rock & roll matters, it often matters quite irrationally, and sometimes illogically; hence we're bound to make mistakes, to declare as fact what are in fact mere matters of taste. I'm sure I have in *Is Rock Dead?*: if I knew where, I would try to fix it. But the least I can do, it seems to me, is to declare at the outset what my own generational affective investments in rock & roll might be.

I'm a late baby boomer, what John Strausbaugh, in *Rock 'Til You Drop*, calls a "tail-end boomer": late enough that I had just turned one year old when the '60s started and was not yet a teen when they finished. The oldest of three children, I had no big brother or sister (as has the fortunate William, in Cameron Crowe's film *Almost Famous*) to clue me in to the secret ways of youth culture: I was not just eleven, then, but a very young eleven, when the '60s ended. I grew up in a conservative, upper-middle-class, professional, Republican household: I remember coming home from school one day in the fifth grade with a peace sign innocently doodled on the back of my hand—I genuinely had no idea what it represented, but they were everywhere!—and it was quickly and unceremoniously scrubbed off of me with Comet. Ours was not a very rock & roll household.

While my slightly older boomer colleagues were hanging out at Woodstock, in the summer of 1969, I was in Belfast, Northern Ireland, on an extended family visit with my grandfather; I watched the Apollo 11 moon landing on the fuzzy black-and-white TV in my auntie's living room. Certainly I don't remember hearing or seeing anything about three days of peace and music; the first reference to Woodstock I can remember, in fact, was Snoopy's avian friend in Charles Schultz's *Peanuts,* an allusion with (for me) no real-world referent. Yeah, I know; it embarrasses me, too.

All of which is to say that, in the generational battles that sometimes rage between boomer rock critics and those following on (and biting at) their heels, I feel strangely displaced; though technically a boomer, born between 1946 and 1964, my musical consciousness is in some ways that of Generation X. When the Beatles broke up, I was in sixth grade; I remember my friend Hugh coming to school with the news, crying, and I had no idea why. (Hugh, it should be said, had a very cool big brother.) I hadn't, so far as I was aware, ever heard a Beatles song. My first "rock & roll memory," from 1967, is (perhaps appropriately) a secondhand one: we had a teenaged babysitter named Sue (great rock & roll name!), and she was just "crazy" for rock & roll; she brought her transistor radio with her to the babysitting gig and kept it on all night waiting for the biggest AM rock station in the Los Angeles area, 93 KHJ, to cycle through the top ninety-three songs and get to her favorite and the current number one, the Doors' "Light My Fire." And not just any "Light My Fire," mind you: the grandiloquent, seven-minute album version, not the bowdlerized, three-minute pop radio hit. We were given to understand that its playing would be a tremendously significant moment; the activities of the evening were scheduled around its estimated time of broadcast.

The first pop record I ever owned I won during the middle of the night in a call-in contest on Los Angeles's big MOR ("middle of the road") station, KFI; it was the 45 of Bette Midler's "Boogie-Woogie Bugle Boy" (1972). A swingin' record—especially for someone whose musical memory didn't include the Andrews Sisters' version, of which Midler's is a bloodless reproduction—but it certainly didn't rock. The first two records (*albums*, we used to call them) that I ever bought—and I can no longer remember which might have come first—were the Carpenters' greatest hits collection *Singles 1969–1973* and Bachman-Turner Overdrive's *Not Fragile* (1974). (It would be some years before I recognized the insult, in the latter's title, to an album that came in time to mean a great deal more to me, Yes's *Fragile* [1972].)

Having rehearsed for you this inglorious early chapter in the development of my rock aesthetic, it should be clear that I'm in no position to condescend. The era that critics like Nik Cohn call "the golden age of rock" is no part of my birthright: it's all been makeup work for me, nights and weekends, rather than the music of my own youth, absorbed by osmosis. That seems to me a neutral fact: I don't feel especially proud of the fact that *Achtung Baby* (1991) was the first U2 album I'd ever heard or owned, but it's no less true for all that (or for the fact that I first heard about it not from friends, or even in the alternative rock press, but on National Public Radio's "Morning Edition"). In musical terms I have, as Robert Christgau's title has it, "grown up all wrong"; but obviously I believe that, wrong though it might have been, my musical upbringing and training haven't completely disqualified me from writing about the music I've not grown up with but instead grown to love.

I'll make this further, bold claim: having grown up without any real music in my life until midway through high school means that, in some ways, I'm perhaps better suited to stand back and take a hard look at some of rock criticism's hoary myths than are many of my peers. I'm perhaps more resistant than most to rock & roll nostalgia (from the Greek, literally, an aching to return home), for "home" and youth were pretty rock-free until I first started driving. James Joyce's short story "Clay" ends with a very drunk, middle-aged man, Joe Donnelly, declaring too loudly that "there was no time like the long ago and no music for him like poor old Balfe, whatever people might say"; Michael William Balfe was the composer of mid-nineteenth-century sentimental light opera, and Joe's full of shit.[1] This is musical nostalgia.

To be sure, I've voluntarily, gleefully, strapped on blinders of my own in the years since my deprived musical upbringing: I didn't discover Neil Young until 1975, for instance, but you'd best not now try to take him away from me. Gina Arnold opens her book on the late-'80s–early-'90s indie scene, *Route 666: On the Road to Nirvana*, with a heartbreaking confession: "I grew up thinking that everything had already happened.

The Beatles, the Beach Boys, Beethoven, Bread."[2] Immersing herself in the alternative music scene that burgeoned in the '80s and '90s, Arnold is able to shake off that feeling; although perhaps I should have, I never *had* that feeling. I didn't know enough to be embarrassed; I didn't know what I had missed, and I had no one telling me I'd missed it. Music always seemed there for the taking, and once I began consuming, I devoured it hungrily, idiosyncratically. Rock never seemed dead—how could it? For once I'd discovered it, it made me—makes me—feel so very alive.

A Note on Terminology

Along with all the other silly things that popular music critics quarrel about, there's very little agreement about how best to refer to the object of our criticism and adoration. Reading the criticism of blues-based, country-inflected, popular music from 1951 to the present, one will see it referred to, by turns, as the following:

>
> rock n' roll
>
> rock 'n' roll
>
> rock'n'roll
>
> rock-'n'-roll
>
> rock and roll
>
> rock-and-roll
>
> rock
>

And there are doubtless other permutations; this list, for example, strategically leaves to one side the vexed question of capitalization (Rock 'n' Roll!).

One early journalist called attention to these orthographic high jinks, complaining,

> Up in Boston where they once staged a tea party of considerable renown, revolt has erupted again. This time the Puritans are in revolt against rock 'n' roll. (Hereinafter referred to for purposes of brevity as rock and roll. Those apostrophes stick in my teeth.)[3]

The different naming conventions (already becoming pronounced in 1956) might thus be brushed off lightly (as, indeed, the writer quoted above goes on to dismiss the music with similar flippancy). On the other hand, orthographic differences have sometimes been made to bear more significance than they can easily sustain, as in this well-known pronouncement from the opening of Charlie Gillett's pioneering study *The Sound of the City* (1970):

> In tracing the history of rock and roll, it is useful to distinguish *rock 'n' roll*—the particular kind of music to which the term first applied—both from *rock and roll*—the music that has been classified as such since rock 'n' roll petered out around 1958—and from *rock*, which describes post-1964 derivations of rock 'n' roll.[4]

Gillett makes an important point here but sounds almost like a self-parody; this is the kind of thing that gives intellectuals a bad name. These different formulae are inflected differently, it is true, but even the same term can be understood differently in different contexts, by different writers: none can carry the stable (and exceedingly fine) discriminations of meaning with which Gillett wants to imbue them. It may be *rock* to you, but it's still *rock 'n' roll* to me. Yet a writer has no choice but to settle on one—or else, as Lawrence Grossberg has, to invent one's own term (in his case, the punning "rock formation").[5] Although surely he was not the first to employ it, ever since reading Anthony DeCurtis's collection *Present Tense: Rock & Roll and Culture,* that ampersand has seemed to me to say something important about the music and strikes me as the natural and logical solution to our terminological quandary: rock & roll.

The ampersand turns "rock & roll" from just a description into a logo, almost a wordmark: it's got style. It's both casual and decisive: a piece of shorthand with a kind of hieroglyphic authority. Most important, the ampersand is not just inclusive: it's downright voracious. Rather than disappearing into the mix, the ampersand rises magisterially above the component terms it joins: like rhythm & blues and country & western, the individual components are powerful, but the synergy the ampersand creates is what makes the music magic. So rather than glossing over it, or picking it from our teeth, let's lay the emphasis on the ampersand: Rock & Roll. It stands for inclusivity, incorporativity—rock & roll's most important features. The Russian literary theorist Mikhail Bakhtin, writing under Soviet oppression that often turned his literary criticism in the direction of political allegory, described the novel as the genre of greatest incorporative ability; and rock is the popular music genre that, in this respect, most closely parallels the novel. "The stylistic uniqueness of the novel as a genre," Bakhtin writes in "Discourse in the Novel" (1934–35),

> consists precisely in the combination of … subordinated, yet still relatively autonomous, [compositional-stylistic] unities (even at times comprised of different languages) into the higher unity of the work as a whole: the style of a novel is to be found in the combination of its styles; the language of a novel is the system of its "languages."[6]

This power for inclusivity in the novel Bakhtin calls "heteroglossia":

> Authorial speech, the speech of narrators, inserted genres, the speech of characters are merely those fundamental compositional unities with whose help heteroglossia can enter the novel; each of them permits a multiplicity of social voices and a wide variety of their links and interrelationships. … This is the basic distinguishing feature of the stylistics of the novel.[7]

In his introduction to the volume that collects this essay, Michael Holquist writes that Bakhtin "posits a novel defined by what could be called the rule of genre inclusiveness: the novel can include, ingest, devour other genres and still retain its status as a novel, but other genres cannot include novelistic elements without impairing their own identity."[8] This same spirit, emblematized by the ampersand, is the animating force behind the best of rock & roll; like the novel, rock & roll operates by means of heteroglossia, the free and democratic mixing of a wide variety of voices, and that openness to other traditions, genres, sounds, worlds, is both what's best and what's most challenging about the rock & roll that matters. Given the available options, then, this book is about rock & roll.

1

THE BRIEF LIFE
AND PROTRACTED DEATH
OF ROCK & ROLL

They give birth astride of a grave, the light gleams an instant, then it's
night once more.

—**Pozzo,** *Waiting for Godot*

The history of modern art, in whatever genre we might wish to examine,
is (or imagines itself to be) a history of outrages: a chronicle of insults
done to the reigning style in the name of "the new," and the greater
mimetic or expressive potential of the art form. In fiction, for instance, the
genial omniscient Narrator of the Victorian novel is replaced with the
limited, unreliable first-person narrator so prevalent in modernist fiction;
we end up with psychic wrecks like Charlie Marlow (Joseph Conrad's
Heart of Darkness) and John Dowell (Ford Madox Ford's *The Good
Soldier*), and narcissistic poseurs like Stephen Dedalus (James Joyce's
A Portrait of the Artist as a Young Man)—and the "gentle reader" used to
the guiding hand of a Charles Dickens or a George Eliot feels utterly
alone: abandoned in the Congo mists rather than nimbly led through the
London fog. Thus does modernist narrative experimentation "kill off" the
well-made Victorian triple-decker. After the outrages of Henry James,

1

William Faulkner, Virginia Woolf, and Gertrude Stein, the nineteenth-century novel is left for dead.

In the visual arts, the *Salon des Refusés* kills off the Paris Salon, just as surely as Duchamp puts an end to certain notions of the artist as godlike *ab nihilo* Creator; in Stravinsky and Diaghilev's *Le Sacré du printemps,* it is the classical ballet tradition that is sacrificed, much as T.S. Eliot, in the words of an admiring James Joyce, "ended the idea of poetry for ladies" by publishing *The Waste Land.*[1] In each of these instances—and many more like them—art history now records that something important was struggling to be born; but contemporary reaction more frequently believed that something irreplaceable was dying, was being killed. In the modern era, the birth of new art is always greeted by the cry that "art is dead."

Nowhere is this more obviously the case than in popular music. In June 1929, the Paris-based bilingual arts magazine *Tambour* ran an album review under the title "MORT DU JAZZ?" because the slight fare issuing forth from American jazz labels suggested to the reviewer that jazz had run its course. When Bob Dylan, famously, plugged in his electric guitar at the Newport Folk Festival in 1965, traditional music fans imagined him swinging his axe at the very root of what we would now call roots music.[2] Muddy Waters similarly muddied the pristine waters of the blues when he moved up to Chicago and transformed his sound from acoustic to electric, from rural South to urban North. Even classical music is improbably believed by some traditionalists to have died, a topic pursued in Norman Lebrecht's 1996 book, first published with the sensationalistic title *When the Music Stops: Managers, Maestros, and the Corporate Murder of Classical Music* and then issued in paperback under the more generic name *Who Killed Classical Music?*. More recently, *New York Times* music critic Joseph Horowitz published a new book with the symptomatic title *Classical Music in America: A History of Its Rise and Fall.* Popular music, it seems, has always already been dying.

It's amazing, when you stop to look at it, how many still vital, still evolving art forms have been declared dead over the years. The novel has a long history of being declared dead; the most famous modern manifesto on this seemingly ageless topic is American novelist John Barth's "The Literature of Exhaustion" (1967). The death he announced, needless to say, hasn't prevented Barth from publishing a whole string of novels in the wake of the novel's wake. "If you were the author of this paper," Barth playfully suggests, "you'd have written something like *The Sot-Weed Factor* or *Giles Goat-Boy:* novels which imitate the form of the novel, by an author who imitates the role of Author."[3] In a recent piece in the *New Yorker*, Louis Menand organized a review essay of three books on popular cinema around the "death of cinema" metaphor:

> The cinema, like the novel, is always dying. The movies were killed by sequels; they were killed by conglomerates; they were killed by special effects. *Heaven's Gate* was the end; *Star Wars* was the end; *Jaws* did it. It was the ratings system, profit participation, television, the blacklist, the collapse of the studio system, the Production Code. The movies should never have gone to color; they should never have gone to sound. The movies have been declared dead so many times that it is almost surprising that they were born, and, as every history of the cinema makes a point of noting, the first announcement of their demise practically coincided with the announcement of their birth.[4]

The things we love, it seems, are always dying; Gerald Marzorati even wrote a much-discussed article in the *New York Times Magazine* in 1998, arguing that the rock & roll album as a conceptual space was dead, "played out": "Culturally speaking, the ambitious rock album is where it was in the early 1960's of Top 40, the 'Peppermint Twist' and the Singing Nun: Nowhere."[5]

The titles of a handful of books for popular audiences may suggest the ongoing rhetorical power of the "death" trope; on my own music bookshelf alone, apart from my rock & roll titles, I see Henry Pleasants's *Death of a Music? The Decline of European Tradition and the Rise of Jazz;* Donald Clarke's *The Rise and Fall of Popular Music;* Nelson George's *The Death of Rhythm & Blues;* and Mike Read's *Major to Minor: The Rise and Fall of the Songwriter.* But if the death (or the ever-popular formula, derived from Edward Gibbon's famous history of the Roman Empire, "rise and fall") of various forms of popular music swirls like a rumor across the criticism, it seems almost an established fact within rock & roll writing. Books on the death of rock & roll nearly balance out those tracing its birth; again, on my own shelves, I find Steven Hamelman's *But Is It Garbage? On Rock and Trash;* Bruce Pollock's *When the Music Mattered: Rock in the 1960s;* Martha Bayles's *Hole in Our Soul: The Loss of Beauty and Meaning in American Popular Music;* Joe S. Harrington's *Sonic Cool: The Life and Death of Rock 'n' Roll;* Fred Goodman's *The Mansion on the Hill: Dylan, Young, Geffen, Springsteen, and the Head-On Collision of Rock and Commerce;* James Miller's *Flowers in the Dustbin: The Rise of Rock and Roll, 1947–1977;* Jeff Pike's *The Death of Rock 'n' Roll: Untimely Demises, Morbid Preoccupations, and Premature Forecasts of Doom in Pop Music;* and John Strausbaugh's *Rock 'Til You Drop: The Decline from Rebellion to Nostalgia.* And again, this list doesn't exhaust the books about the death of rock & roll: they are merely those that feature the trope (or a related one) in the book's title, right there on the cover. (The most significant of these, as well as other writings exploiting the death trope, are the focus of chapters 3 and 4.) At the very least, we might begin to suspect that arguments for the death of rock & roll help to sell books.

A quick case study in the "death" of jazz—based largely on Gary Giddins's suggestive essay, "How Come Jazz Isn't Dead?"—may help to illustrate how very similar this rhetoric sounds across different musical genres. There's enough resemblance, in fact, to suggest a nearly identical MO in the deaths of jazz and rock & roll—and enough to make us suspect foul play. "Jazz coroners have been hanging crepe since the 1930s," Giddins points out; "Armstrong, they alleged, sounded the first death rattle when, in 1929, he adapted white pop from Tin Pan Alley." But "at the dawn of its second century," he suggests, jazz "affirms a template for the way music is born, embraced, perfected, and stretched to the limits of popular acceptance before being taken up by the professors and other establishmentarians who reviled it when it was brimming with a danger-ous creativity." Rock & roll, at the dawn of its second half-century, has already traced a very similar trajectory with fans and critics:

> For half a century, each generation mourned anew the passing of jazz because each idealized the particular jazz of its youth. Countless fans loved jazz precisely *because* of the chronic, tricky, expeditious jolts in its development, but the emotional investments of the majority audience—which pays the bills—quickly metamorphosed from adoring into nostalgia.[6]

Although Giddins does not mention him in the essay, no better (or more articulate) example of this tendency can be found than the British poet Philip Larkin, who between 1961 and 1971 reviewed new jazz releases for the *Daily Telegraph;* his dismissive attitude toward nearly all post–World War II jazz is handily summed up in the title of one collec-tion of his music writing, *All What Jazz.*[7] More to our purposes here, Giddins realizes that the word *jazz* in the preceding quotation, and indeed throughout most of his essay, could easily be replaced with the phrase *rock & roll,* without the argument losing any of its validity.

According to the helpful model that Giddins develops, jazz has gone through four distinct "stations" in its first century; more than simply describing the stages of jazz history, however, Giddins sees himself as describing a structure that is nearly universal in the life cycle of popular music genres. Narratives of the life and death, or the equally popular "rise and fall," of musical genres are thus to some degree what literary critics call "overdetermined": the narrative has a logic and a momentum, we might even say a "mind," of its own, and inconvenient facts are often trampled in its path; conclusions are quite predictable from the outset. As structuralist thinkers as far back as Claude Lévi-Strauss have emphasized, these large cultural narratives often tell us more about the societies that deploy and perpetuate them than they do about their ostensible objects of analysis. That the "rise and fall" of rock & roll so closely mirrors the "rise and fall" of jazz might conceivably tell us something about the great degree of similarity among the life cycles of all forms of popular music; but it might also tell us something about the compulsion to discover this pattern, about our need as a culture to kill off new musics "brimming," as Giddins has it, "with a dangerous creativity." When used to describe a form of high or popular art, "death" is of course always a metaphor and as such is hardly available to confirmation or rebuttal.

The first station in the life cycle of jazz and other popular musics Giddins dubs the "native": "Every musical idiom begins in and reflects the life of a specific community where music is made for pleasure and to strengthen social bonds."[8] In rock & roll narratives, this community is usually the African American community, and its idiom the blues—although rock & roll is always acknowledged to be a mongrel of quite various pedigree. Hence the fetishization, in rock writing, of the concept of "authenticity": rock & roll matters, justifies its existence (according to this model), to the degree that it can establish its solid connections to an organic community. So Bruce Springsteen, to pick a popular example, makes music that matters because his songs grow out of, and continue to speak to, the real concerns of real working Americans.[9]

Succeeding this first stage, according to Giddins, is the "second and most important," the "sovereign," which in jazz had taken over by 1940; "here," Giddins writes, "music ceases to be the private reserve of any one place or people."[10] For rock & roll, as for jazz, this is the most significant, but also the most dangerous, of stages: for here, having at first wielded a myth of authenticity to argue for its primacy, rock & roll is challenged to tell the more complicated truth about its genealogy, to admit that mongrel pedigree. Rock & roll has no pure source but, having won a degree of legitimacy, it can now begin to come clean on the subject of its illegitimate birth.

However, as much as rock & roll embraces its ampersand, and celebrates the multicultural, interracial, generically hybrid condition of its existence, there have always been, and continue to be, audience members more distressed than pleased by this eclecticism. "When jazz became capacious enough to include Dixieland, boogie-woogie, swing, and modern jazz (or bop), the word *jazz* grew too large for the comfort of most listeners," Giddins writes.[11] Likewise, in the case of rock & roll, the tangled family tree from which rock arises, as well as the varied offspring to which it has given birth (sometimes bearing little or no family resemblance), push the imagined community "united" by rock & roll to the breaking point. The allmusic.com website, for instance, lists 175 "musical styles" under the heading "rock"; there is of course a good deal of overlap and hairsplitting involved here (one would be hard pressed, for instance, to explain the difference between "shoegaze" and "emo"), but the list, manic and obsessive though it may be, suggests something important about the variety that rock & roll comprehends. As the website says by way of prologue, "For most of its life, rock has been fragmented, spinning off new styles and variations every few years, from Brill Building Pop and heavy metal to dance-pop and grunge. And that's only natural for a genre that began its life as a fusion of styles."[12] Interestingly, given questions we take up in chapter 6, this mother of all rock lists doesn't include rap as a rock & roll style (listed separately, rap is further broken down into twenty-seven musical styles).

When the list gets too long—when jazz, or rock & roll, comprehends such a diversity that the centrifugal forces threaten to overpower the centripetal, and "the center cannot hold"—we arrive at the music's third station. This is when rock & roll—or jazz, or alt-country, or disco, or shoegaze—is most in danger of being declared dead. Again, Giddins illuminates the situation with regard to jazz:

> The widening gap between jazz and the public's understanding of it … [suggests that] jazz was now sweeping inexorably toward the third station, which might be called "recessionary." This occurs when a style of music is forced from center stage…. Yet it's a mistake to think that the distancing of jazz from the commercial center resulted in a great decline in popularity. "Recessionary" means a retreat from marketplace power but not bankruptcy.[13]

Depending, again, on whether one considers rap a style of rock & roll, rock may have reached this recessionary station in 1991, when rap for the first time outsold more traditional rock & roll: the same year that saw the runaway success of Nirvana's *Nevermind* also saw the first gangsta rap album reach number one in the *Billboard* charts, NWA's *Niggaz4life*. Both signified, to some, the death of rock & roll.

Jazz has arrived at Giddins's fourth station, and it seems just possible that rock & roll has, too. "The situation in which jazz is presently found," Giddins writes of "the fourth and final station,"

> might be called "classical," not to denote an obeisance to orthodoxies and traditions (though, yes, there's plenty of that), but because even the most adventurous young musicians are weighed down by the massive accomplishments of the past.... For the first time, a large percentage of the renewable jazz audience finds history more compelling than the present.... In a sense, the "classical" station is defined by the question: Who will inherit the music—the classicists or the renegades?[14]

The ubiquity of the term *classic rock*—an oxymoron that has become so naturalized that its oddness no longer even bothers us—perhaps suggests that rock & roll too has reached this station; fending off the challenge posed first by disco and later by rap, "classic rock" radio stations, proudly playing only "rock that really rocks," represent the canonizing impulse within the rock & roll audience, who want rock & roll to stop changing and to become instead, like classical music, a standard repertory, a completed and surveyable body of work (and, perforce, one that the fan can master). In an irony lost on those who declare rap the illegitimate offspring of rock & roll, it is arguably rap that has most successfully dealt with the burden of tradition: through sampling. In a stylistic move made popular by the literary figures of high modernism, rap alludes, by means of samples, to the "canon" to redeploy it in a new context; at its best, sampling acknowledges its debt to, achieves an accommodation with, and sometimes even manages to breathe new life into the works of the tradition. It's a dynamic that T.S. Eliot described well in his essay "Tradition and the Individual Talent," suggesting that the intervention of the truly new work necessitates a virtual reordering of the texts of the tradition:

> The existing monuments form an ideal order among themselves, which is modified by the introduction of the new (the really new) work of art among them. The existing order is complete before the new work

arrives; for order to persist after the supervention of novelty, the whole existing order must be, if ever so slightly, altered; and so the relations, proportions, values of each work of art toward the whole are readjusted; and this is conformity between the old and the new.[15]

This may seem a highfalutin way to talk about the way the Beastie Boys's use Led Zeppelin's "The Ocean" on their track "She's Crafty," but the point remains: in its own fourth station, rock & roll seems equally divided between those on the side of the tradition and those on the side of innovation. And to those on the side of the tradition, innovation, perversely, always looks like death.

Giddins closes his essay with the hopeful observation that "the notion that jazz is dead or could die in the foreseeable future is predicated on one of two ideas: it is a narrow musical style with fixed parameters, or it is a passing fashion that has had its day. A century of development puts paid to both."[16] Although based on just a half-century of rock & roll history, it would be nice to put an end to the persistent rumors of rock's death, too: that, in short, is the burden of the pages that follow.

Like the death of jazz in Giddins's narrative, or the death of the movies in Menand's, the death of rock & roll is a perdurable narrative structure, and one that, seemingly, can bend just about any event in rock & roll history to support its thesis. In the next chapter we will look in much more detail at the history of the death of rock & roll, but it is worthwhile here at the outset to consider briefly the ways in which the story of rock & roll—the history of rock & roll, the story of its "rise and fall"—is always haunted by rumors of its death. The story of rock & roll is, we might say, the story of the death of rock & roll: there is, seemingly, no way to tell the one without the other.

The exact moment of rock's birth is of course a topic of some debate, and one to which we return later; but whichever early-'50s date we choose for the birth, the first symptoms of rock's imminent demise were not long in coming. In an unfortunate (and unpremeditated) coincidence, the selection of Bill Haley's "(We're Going to) Rock Around the Clock" as the musical theme for the sensationalist 1955 Hollywood blockbuster *Blackboard Jungle* seemed to have doomed rock & roll before the form was properly launched, linking rock & roll inexorably to juvenile delinquency (we explore this connection in more detail in chapter 5). The 1957 Senate hearings investigating the role of rock-oriented upstart music publisher BMI in polluting the nation's airwaves evolved almost seamlessly into the very public scandal over payola, which ultimately brought down deejay Allan Freed, the man who more than any other is responsible for putting the term *rock 'n' roll* in front of the American (and world) public. In the midst of all this controversy, the king of the previous generation of crooners, Frank Sinatra, declared, "Rock 'n' roll smells phony and false. It is sung, played and written for the most part by cretinous goons and by means of its almost imbecilic reiteration, and sly, lewd, in plain fact dirty, lyrics … it manages to be the martial music of every side-burned delinquent on the face of the earth."[17]

A further late-'50s event that served an important symbolic function for those who wished to find evidence of rock & roll's death was the crash of the plane carrying Richie Valens, Buddy Holly, and the "Big Bopper" in 1959; because that event has been famously memorialized in Don McLean's song "American Pie," I deal with it in some detail in chapter 5. With no disrespect intended to the dead, I think equating the death of rock & roll with the death of one or more of its stars is far too simple an equation; it suggests that one's understanding of rock & roll's importance is anchored firmly to an individual, and rock & roll is bigger than even giants like Elvis, John Lennon, and Kurt Cobain. When people talk about the death of rock & roll, of course, it's only a metaphor: to attach it too closely to the death of these or other individuals is to make a fundamental, even ontological, error. Nonetheless, within a short time of that crash, Chuck Berry was in prison for violating the Mann Act, Jerry Lee Lewis was in disgrace after marrying his thirteen-year-old cousin, and Elvis was in the army. Rock & roll appeared to some observers to be, if not quite dead, certainly contained for the time being.

Limping into the 1960s, against all odds, rock & roll was gaining momentum and cultural legitimacy. In spite of the work of bloodless cover artists like Pat Boone, rock & roll received an infusion of new energy, new life, and new creative blood with the successive waves of Beatlemania and the British Invasion. One of the most important contemporary influences on the Beatles, at the same time, seemed to some to have betrayed his gifts and calling when Bob Dylan famously plugged in his electric guitar at Newport on July 25, 1965. This is one of rock history's legendary moments, of course, and we have many firsthand accounts of the reaction of folk music purists to Dylan's sacrilege. A similar moment occurred during Dylan's "Royal Albert Hall" concert of May 17, 1966.[18] In the quiet of a break between songs, an audience member famously shouted out, calling Dylan "Judas," and after a stunned silence, Dylan responded, "I don't believe you…. You're a liar." Turning then to his band, as they launched into the show's last song, "Like a Rolling Stone"—the song that had introduced his electric music to a popular audience—Dylan barked, "Play it fucking loud." In the history of rock & roll, Dylan's denunciation by his "folk" fans is perhaps the first occasion on which rock & roll was widely declared dead not because it was without merit, or because some of its principals were dead, but because it had begun to change—to grow, even. When growth is equated with death, we know that a strange cultural calculus is at work.

Sometimes the declaration is made that rock & roll is dead owing to some dramatic public event. One such event was the Altamont Free Festival organized by the Rolling Stones for December 6, 1969; the idea was to create a West Coast response to that summer's Woodstock Music Festival in upstate New York. Unfortunately, however, the Stones "hired" the Hell's Angels to provide security for the concert and paid them in beer; by the end of the night, four audience members were dead, one of them killed when the Angels attacked with leather boots, knives, and pool cues. To many—including, notably, journalist and novelist Hunter S. Thompson, whose nonfiction novel *Fear and Loathing in Las Vegas* (first published serially in *Rolling Stone* magazine in 1971) is haunted by Altamont—the violence seemed to signal both the end of the '60s and the death of rock & roll. Thompson's was not the first active intelligence to see in Altamont evidence that something beautiful and fragile had died; indeed, it has become one of the hoary clichés of rock writing about the '60s.

Although it has done yeoman's service in rock histories to date, the Woodstock–Altamont pairing is surely a bit too reductive; Altamont wasn't nearly as evil, or Woodstock as innocent, as it has sometimes been convenient to pretend. At Altamont, an African American man, Meridith Hunter, with a white girlfriend, was brutally murdered by the Hell's Angels—but he was no angel; the footage captured during the Stones's performance in the Mayles's brothers film *Gimme Shelter* (1970) makes it clear, for instance, that Hunter was brandishing a handgun and seemingly was rushing the stage.

Furthermore, the documentary suggests that Mick Jagger was not quite the inhuman monster he was made out to be by the mainstream media; although the urban legend grew up that Hunter had been murdered during "Sympathy for the Devil," a myth that suited certain interests, in fact he was stabbed during "Under My Thumb," and no one onstage could see just what was happening. As Jagger struggled to finish "Under My Thumb" above the offstage confusion, he sang, with real concern written all over his face, not "Baby it's all right," the words he had written and sung on the 1966 single, but instead "I pray that it's all right." In footage included by the Mayles of Jagger in the editing room, watching Hunter's murder in slow motion—really seeing it for the first time—he realizes for certain that things definitely weren't all right. But the film also makes clear that Jagger was out of his depth in this situation, overpowered by forces beyond his control: hardly a provocateur unmoved by or uninterested in the violence taking place in the audience, hardly the "Satan laughing with delight" that Don McLean was to conjure three years later in "American Pie."

Woodstock, earlier that summer, had been documented in far greater detail in Michael Wadleigh's film; the DVD reissue restores even more footage to the original theatrical release—a total, in the director's cut, of nearly four hours. But arguably, in the public imagination, a four-minute AM radio hit had a bigger impact and was more successful in writing the narrative of Woodstock—one without mud and without bad, brown acid. Joni Mitchell's folk-rock standard "Woodstock" might seem a textbook case of the kind of remorse for the death of rock & roll sometimes captured in rock songs, as well as the fragile hope that it will persevere. This anthem of the Woodstock generation has, however, been shrouded in myth, mystification, and misunderstanding—and the rather inappropriate role it has been made to play in the public imagination might serve as an object lesson in the persistence of rock & roll nostalgia in general and the triumphalist vein of rock history promulgated by baby-boomer critics in particular.

Leaving mere facts to one side for a moment, then, let's rehearse the generally accepted story of Mitchell's "Woodstock" and that magical summer for which it's meant to function as a sound track. For those who know the song and its history well, a certain suspension of disbelief will be required: the myth bears little resemblance to the more mundane realities of the song's material production. For now, just play along.

In Mitchell's telling, the Woodstock Music and Art Festival is a parable of Innocence & Experience—or perhaps Innocence alone, which even Experience cannot sour. Turning William Blake's terms on their heads, Mitchell's road of excess leads not to the palace of wisdom but back to a lost and primal Eden—"And we've got to get ourselves back to the garden." For those familiar with the concert film, the muddy slough of Max Yasgur's farm is hard to mistake for a garden, but never mind that, for now.[19]

Caught up in the optimistic spirit of the moment, on her way to the festival ("three days of peace and music"), Mitchell penned the song as a celebration of a newly revitalized youth culture in which the artificial barriers between artist and audience melted away. Mitchell's song represents more than just a tribute to Woodstock, and more than just a hopeful (and preemptive) sound track to the great gathering of the hippie nation; it is rather a real-time souvenir, both a product and a memento of one of rock & roll's most magical moments. Fortunately Mitchell was able to get people singing along with her version before the terrible events of Altamont, in December of that year, or of the 1970 Isle of Wight Festival, which Mitchell was to dub the "Hate the Performer" Festival. When Mitchell first sang "Woodstock" to the Woodstock audience—a slight young woman cradling her huge acoustic guitar, before those hundreds of thousands of people—the horrors of Altamont were unimagined, unimaginable; although, to the discerning ear, when Crosby, Stills, Nash and Young released their cover of "Woodstock," which turned Mitchell's gentle acoustic version roughly electric, some of the dark energies of Altamont and after could almost be heard in the mix. Already, the stardust had begun to fade.

For those who don't already know how far off the mark this fanciful narrative wanders, it's time to interrogate this story. To begin with, Joni Mitchell never appeared on the Woodstock stage; like Chaucer's great poem, Mitchell's song narrates a pilgrimage she never made, and the song's first-person protagonist is a narrative contrivance. On Saturday, August 16, 1969, Mitchell shared the bill in Chicago with her friends Crosby, Stills, and Nash; they all then made their way to New York, along with Neil Young, and all were scheduled to appear on the closing day of Woodstock, on Sunday, August 17. The lads made it, although they were, as Stephen Stills said to the assembled crowd, "scared shitless." Young, opposed to the making of the film, refused to appear in it, and all the CSNY shots are cropped close; the band turned, in effect, back into CSN. It's an instability that has plagued the band throughout its troubled career.

But Mitchell chose the mainstream over the counterculture: she was scheduled to appear on the Dick Cavett show in Manhattan on Monday evening, and her manager was nervous that, had she gone, with the traffic bottleneck at Woodstock, she wouldn't have made it back in time for her appearance. Thus Mitchell "became one of the fans that missed it, which is an interesting perspective," she later remarked. "I don't think the song would've been born if I had been there backstage." An intriguing suggestion: Mitchell has called Woodstock a "modern miracle," but Mitchell's own Woodstock documentary couldn't have been made had she been there to document the goings-on. Instead, Mitchell watched the proceedings on TV in Manhattan with David Geffen. (In the event, her manager's concerns about logistics were misguided; Crosby and Stills managed to get into Woodstock and back to Manhattan in time to share the Cavett bill with Mitchell and Jefferson Airplane).

Another misconception: CSNY's noisy version of "Woodstock" isn't a cover. It's in some weird sense the original, or else what Jean Baudrillard calls a "simulacrum," the cover that precedes the original: "The simulacrum is never that which conceals the truth—it is the truth which conceals that there is none."[20] The song was recorded first by CSNY and released on their March 11, 1970 album, *Déjà vu;* Mitchell in fact wrote the song for them, and her version first appeared on her April 1970 album, *Ladies of the Canyon.* In the public imagination, the song speaks to a nostalgia for a purer experience of the youth culture, one whose broadest hopes were symbolized by Woodstock; in the public imagination, I would venture to suggest, the CSNY version of the song is heard as the raucous remake of Mitchell's folky acoustic original, first performed at Woodstock in 1969. If not a declaration of the death of rock & roll, Mitchell's "Woodstock" certainly reflects a concern about its vitality; it reiterates, in unvarnished fashion, the most central of Western myths, the story of the Fall. In the song, Woodstock represents if not the death of a certain segment of rock & roll culture, at least the opportunity for rebirth and renewal, ritual baptism and cleansing. If we've got to get back to the garden, it means that we've already been expelled.

For those who, in spite of Woodstock and Altamont, believed that rock & roll had lived on into the '70s, anecdotal evidence of its death was suddenly seemingly everywhere: the rise of disco,[21] the triumph of corporate rock and arena concerts, the ascendancy of hair metal, *Frampton Comes Alive* (the joke, at the time [1976], was that the last seven million bought it to find out why the first million had bought it), and Ken Russell's

Tommy and Robert Stigwood's *Sgt. Pepper's Lonely Hearts Club Band* (not to mention *The Wiz*). Elvis died; the Sex Pistols exploded then imploded; the Stones, with a wink and a nudge, titled their greatest hits compilation from the decade *Sucking in the Seventies*.

Opening the '80s, Bruce Springsteen scored his first top-ten single with the overproduced and bloodless "Hungry Heart"—a song that, rather improbably, he had written for the Ramones, before his manager Jon Landau persuaded him to keep it for himself. Something other than the Boss's vaunted "authenticity" seemed to propel that record up the charts and out of car radios. The launch of MTV on August 1, 1981, caused many a rock & roll purist's brow to furrow; the network kicked off, famously, with the Buggles's "Video Killed the Radio Star," itself a somewhat more complex response to the changing conditions of rock & roll production than has usually been acknowledged. In suggesting a structural homology between worries that sound would ruin motion pictures in the 1920s and fears in the '70s and '80s that video would ruin rock & roll, the Buggles helped to point up the somewhat predictable nature of these protests, although none at the time seemed to register the critique. In 1984, Christopher Guest & Co. punctured hair-metal pretension with *This Is Spinal Tap;* two decades later, the movie stands as an irrefutable indictment of either rock & roll's bankruptcy or its unquenchable ability to laugh at itself: "Seen now, in the period of rock's long decline," the *New Yorker's* tone-deaf David Denby wrote, "the 1984 *Spinal Tap*, in which the band's American tour slides into disaster, appears as a tragicomic epitaph for an art form that succumbed to its own unfulfillable ambitions."[22]

In retrospect, for some, Schoolly D's "PSK What Does It Mean?" (1985), inaugurating gansta rap, hammered a nail in rock & roll's coffin. Schoolly's self-titled debut album also contained the track "I Don't Like Rock and Roll": "All you rock and roll lovers, we're knocking you out, / Because that is what rap's all about." For the first time in its thirty-year history, rock & roll might have seemed not to be dying of natural causes but instead to be under attack by a predatory new form: rap, in Schoolly D's track and others, is the new kid on the block who'll uncrown rock & roll. As Andrew Ross notes, it didn't take long for rap, in its turn, to be declared dead:

With the rise of hip hop, a fully popular black music form has been held up to the highest scrutiny for the integrity, authenticity and independence that were found wanting in the rock counterculture. It was only a matter of time before an organ of record, in this case *The Source,* announced the "death of rap" (after Ice-T's 1992 decision to pull "Cop Killer" from Warner's *Body Count* album), with the same sense of indignation that had accompanied countless previous declarations about the "death of rock," a genre in its own right.[23]

The decade ended just as inauspiciously as it had started, with the ersatz dance–pop stars Milli Vanilli having their Grammy for Best New Artist rescinded in 1990 when it was discovered that they had only lip-synched their multiplatinum album *Girl You Know It's True.* One half of the duo, Rob Pilatus, died by his own hand in 1998.

Another category of symptoms often seized on to argue that rock & roll is dead has to do with the sudden popularity of a previously little-known, but highly regarded, band or performer. When, in an example mentioned earlier, Bruce Springsteen's song "Hungry Heart" became his first top-ten single in 1980, many of his fans and critics cried sellout and were forced to conclude that rock & roll was dead. The best example of this phenomenon to date—popular success equated with the demise of rock & roll—surrounds a record that first brought "alternative rock" to a wide audience, Nirvana's *Nevermind.*

Nevermind is a record that announces, as critic Anthony DeCurtis has written, both the beginning of one era in rock & roll and the end of another.[24] With its familiar cover photo of a naked baby boy swimming toward a dollar bill dangling from a fish hook, *Nevermind* marks the coming of age of alternative rock and the death of some cherished and deep-seated beliefs about authenticity, selling out, and the artistic purity of the rock & roll underground. Or at least it should have meant these things: one of the morals to be gleaned from the rise and fall of Nirvana and their charismatic front man Kurt Cobain is that the romantic attempt to divorce "art" from "commerce" is alive and well, thriving, of all places, in the backwater called alternative rock. Meanwhile, the rest of the popular music scene has moved on, moved beyond.

The story of *Nevermind's* breakthrough success has been well rehearsed in the rock media. In 1989, Nirvana's first LP, *Bleach,* was recorded for $606.17, a sum indie fans seem to have committed to memory. That debut record, on the then-obscure Seattle label Sub Pop, was widely admired but, given the very limited distribution and marketing muscle of

Sub Pop, sold only about 35,000 copies in its first two years. (By way of contrast, Nirvana's *MTV Unplugged in New York*, the first album to be released after Cobain's death, shipped 310,500 copies in its first week of release.) Still, while the sales of *Bleach* were modest—perhaps *because* sales were modest—the record was cheaply produced and the band was able to keep its artistic integrity intact. And, in the world of indie rock, integrity, or street cred or authenticity—however one chooses to describe the refusal to sell out—is the ultimate working capital. In alternative rock, nothing succeeds like failure.[25]

The success/failure of *Bleach*—artistic success resulting in (or evidenced by) commercial failure—serves to illustrate, in small, the foundational contradiction at the heart of indie rock. Cobain, bassist Krist Novoselic, and drummer Dave Grohl took as axiomatic the do-it-yourself, no-non-sense ethos of punk rock: "punk rock is freedom," Cobain was fond of say-ing. Yet not, apparently, the freedom to succeed: indeed, bands put themselves in the no-win position of having to prove the purity of their artistic vision by selling few records and fewer tickets to their shows. [26] According to this logic, the perfect indie album would be more-or-less self-published and purchased by practically no one—a dogma articulated most fiercely by Calvin Johnson, a member of the group Beat Happening and founder of the Olympia, Washington, label K Records, and his aptly named followers, the Calvinists. In the tenets of "Calvinism," no sin is more heinous than leaving the obscurity of an independent record label like K Records, Sub Pop, Kill Rock Stars, or SST for one of the corporate "majors," like MCA/Universal or the label Nirvana signed with for *Never-mind*, Geffen. (David Geffen, remember? The one who watched "Wood-stock" on the TV news with Joni Mitchell; the one indistinguishable from the anti-Christ in Fred Goodman's *The Mansion on the Hill* [see chapter 3]; the one who produced the Broadway musical *Cats*.) According to the credo of alternative rock, the greater a record's sales, the greater per-force the artist's compromise with the public taste. As David Fricke wrote in his *Rolling Stone* review of the band's 1993 release *In Utero*, "This is the way Nirvana's Kurt Cobain spells *success:* s-u-c-k-s-e-g-g-s."[27]

Nevermind was to be an entirely different beast from *Bleach*. To begin with, *Nevermind* overran its initial $65,000 budget by almost 100 percent, which meant, according to the inscrutable logic of indie/punk rock, that it was about two hundred times lamer than their $600 first record. *Never-mind* hit number one on the *Billboard* chart the same day the band appeared on *Saturday Night Live*, January 11, 1992. To date it has sold more than ten million copies—in part because it's a trenchant, painfully beautiful, brilliantly produced, uncannily timed record, and in part no doubt because of the deep pockets and promotional clout of Geffen Records. A multiplatinum sales figure like this is next to meaningless for most of us who live in the "real" world; to put it in perspective, on the one hand, it took Bob Dylan's *Blonde on Blonde* thirty-three years to sell its first million copies, while, at the other end of the spectrum, the Eagles' 1976 *Greatest Hits* compilation has sold more that twenty-eight million, making it the best selling rock & roll album of all time. (*Nevermind* sits, respectably, at number seventy-five—right next to the sound track for *The Lion King*). According to *Billboard* magazine, Nirvana wasn't among the ten top-selling artists of the '90s, a list dominated by the divas in heavy rotation at my dentist's office: Mariah Carey, Celine Dion, Whitney Houston, Michael Bolton, and Toni Braxton. If we can for purposes of argument posit the existence of a category of popular music called "challenging rock"—"difficult listening," a friend of mine used to call it, as opposed to the EZ listening that pervades the RIAA charts—well, such challenging rock & roll ordinarily goes all but unrepresented in surveys of the best-selling pop albums.

Like a private citizen in seventeenth-century New England, a rock musician in the Pacific Northwest in the late '80s and early '90s could hardly afford to break openly with orthodox Calvinism. Yet one of the real revelations of Charles R. Cross's powerful biography of Cobain, *Heavier Than Heaven,* was that Cobain coveted and actively cultivated the very fame that he was required publicly to abhor. Cobain's home record collection was full of power-pop and pop-metal records, like *Get the Knack!,* while before going onstage, he made his own "Flipper" T-shirt with a Marks-a-Lot. Painting oneself into a corner seems altogether too polite a metaphor for this artistic catch-22, and Cobain's private journals, to which Cross was allowed unprecedented access, make it clear both that Cobain wanted to sign *Nevermind* with a major label for the very best of reasons—*so that his music would be heard*—and that he knew he must publicly disavow any such desire. Neither was Cobain above playing to the romantic fantasies of his fans: another of the revelations of the Cross bio is that the well-worn story of Cobain living under a bridge in Aberdeen, Washington, the story told in "Something in the Way," *Nevermind*'s official closing cut (all but the earliest pressings of the CD also have a "hidden" track, popularly known as "Endless, Nameless," that begins about ten minutes after "Something in the Way" ends), is a fiction.

Cobain never lived under a bridge, but wasn't it romantic to think so? Most significant, he retailed that story to Michael Azerrad, who wrote about the band a number of times for *Rolling Stone,* as well as the definitive study of Nirvana and their music, *Come As You Are: The Story of Nirvana.*

The physical artifact that is *Nevermind*—the CD in its jewel case, the LP in its sleeve—bears throughout the impress of the irreconcilable demands of this complexly contradictory posture. The cover photo, of course, playfully suggests that we're all chasing after the almighty dollar; the back cover, on the other hand, features a dark and disturbing photo collage of Cobain's own making. Fold the jewel case open, and you're greeted by a photo of the band on the inside sleeve—and Kurt's angrily giving you the finger. Having opened the CD, you've become complicit in the popularity that will of necessity ruin Nirvana and prove them to be sellouts. You bought our record? Fuck you, man!

The album opens with two tracks that speak of Cobain's disdain for his audience. "Smells Like Teen Spirit," the album's biggest single, features a chorus in which audience members sing with one voice, "I feel stupid, and contagious…." "In Bloom" follows hard on its heels, a track on which the band sings of a typical fan, he "likes all the pretty songs / And he likes to sing along…." Pretty strong stuff for a band that, at the time the tracks were laid down, hadn't in two years sold as many records as 'N Sync used to sell on a good day. Not to put too fine a point on it, Nirvana (and especially Cobain) were disgusted with the enormous success of *Nevermind* long before it had enjoyed any—before, seemingly, it had been released. Surely this suggests that their rejection of fame is structurally, rather than experientially, determined.

Later, as *Nevermind* was climbing the charts, Cobain and Novoselic were interviewed on the heavy-metal-oriented MTV program "Headbanger's Ball"; Cobain wore a yellow organza dress and dark sunglasses, so things got off to a pretty nervous start. The show's host observed, "Everywhere you go, in all different types of the music scene, people really seem to be getting into Nirvana." "Everyone wants to be hip" was Cobain's snide response, while Novoselic offered, sensibly, "Maybe they like the record."[28] When the band was selected for the ordinarily coveted cover of *Rolling Stone* for the April 16, 1992, issue, Kurt wore a homemade T-shirt with the motto CORPORATE MAGAZINES STILL SUCK emblazoned across the front in black marking pen (simultaneously incensing the bourgeoisie and, by a nudging reference to the SST slogan "Corporate

Rock Still Sucks," sharing an in-joke with the hip kids). In another photo from the session, Cobain flips *Rolling Stone* readers a PG-13 version of the bird, with his ring finger.

In a 2001 interview with David Fricke of *Rolling Stone,* Dave Grohl refers to these and other gestures as manifestations of "that punk-rock guilt. Kurt felt, in some way, guilty that he had done something that so many people had latched onto. The bigger the shows got, the farther we got from our ideal."[29] When producer Butch Vig was asked whether Cobain's disavowal of *Nevermind* bothered him, he responded in much the same terms: "I know the band loved it when it was done. But I expected that to happen. When you're hanging out with your punk friends, and all of a sudden you go Number One, you can't go, 'God, I love that album, I'm glad it sold 20 million copies.' It was hard for them to embrace it."[30]

What, then, is the enduring legacy of *Nevermind?* If ever an album's title suggested that it ought not to leave a legacy, this is it: and yet, in terms of opening up commercial markets for challenging music, bands that run the musical gamut from power pop to punk to nu-metal to hip-hop to the progressive-rock revival are to different degrees in Nirvana's debt. Perhaps most important, *Nevermind* demonstrated—although it was a demonstration Cobain didn't heed, couldn't heed—that very good records sometimes sell very well in spite of themselves, and that artistic quality isn't always inversely proportional to commercial success. Clearly, as such polar examples as Dylan and the Eagles suggest, sales figures can't be linked in any simplistic way with artistic importance: many master-pieces sell miserably, and some pretty forgettable pop records sell like hotcakes.

One band that has picked up where Nirvana left off artistically, turning the pain of dysfunctional relationships into heartfelt (if sometimes over-wrought) pop ballads, is the nu-metal band Staind, whose 2001 album *Break the Cycle* entered the *Billboard* charts at number one in May of that year. Band members betrayed no obvious self-loathing regarding their runaway success: the official band bio at www.staind.com, for instance, describes them as "both humbled and thrilled by their success and all the things that come with it," and guitarist Mike Mushok fairly gushes, "We love this record, and we can't wait to get out and play it for people."[31]

From another sector of the radio dial, Radiohead has again proved that selling doesn't have to mean selling out. Their three most recent studio albums, *Kid A, Amnesiac,* and *Hail to the Thief,* all went to number one in the album charts in the United Kingdom (number three in the United

States)—Top of the Pops!—while by consensus of both those who love and those who hate the records, they're among the most difficult commercial releases in years. Paradoxically, the commercial success of these albums may well be due to the exposure they received through online file-sharing programs: Radiohead ended up selling millions of copies in part because their music could first be heard for free, outside the distribution channels of Corporate Rock. In the age of Internet music, this may be the very definition of an underground hit.

But if any sector of the contemporary popular music scene has learned the lesson of *Nevermind,* it's hip-hop, which was negotiating the difficult passage from underground to mainstream at the same time alternative rock was trying to find its way. Perhaps because the politics of rap have always placed group and community concerns ahead of individual pain, hip-hop artists have by and large embraced commercial success (aka "bling") and the wider audience for their message it provides. Indeed, hip-hop now seems in danger of uncritically turning Calvinism on its head: if alternative rock sometimes suggests that a band's importance is inversely proportional to their popularity—a weird kind of populist elitism—hip-hop's in danger of just the opposite fallacy, suggesting that the more you sell, the better your flow. No less politically committed an artist than Chuck D. of Public Enemy came to the defense of the politically inert "sellout" MC Hammer: "You're supposed to sell out! If you got fifteen tapes on the shelf, your mission is to sell. You ain't giving it away."[32] Rap still struggles with the relationship between artistry and commercial success and still perhaps puts too much emphasis on the latter, or too simply equates it *with* artistry. Cobain, on the other hand, could not reconcile them; the title of a documentary-cum-concert film, released shortly after Cobain's death, punningly reinforced the paradox on which Cobain foundered and died: *Nirvana: Live! Tonight! Sold Out!*[33]

Of course Cobain's death, on April 4, 1994, suggested to many the end of—well, the end of something, something important. Gangsta rap killings, which claimed the genre's two most charismatic stars Tupac Shakur (aka 2Pac; d. September 13, 1996) and Biggie Smalls (aka the Notorious B.I.G., born Christopher Wallace; d. March 9, 1997), threatened to wipe out rock & roll's most vital stream; alternatively, claims were made that hip-hop's reliance on sampling meant that true creativity in rock & roll was over. On the technological front, the court decision handed down against the Napster file-sharing service in February 2001 marked the end of a certain kind of rock "freedom": the freedom to download and share digitally perfect, and perfectly reproducible, music. The announcement in October 2004, on the other hand, of a U2 special edition iPod, preloaded with compressed versions of U2's entire catalog, suggested to many the ultimate victory of corporate forces over rock & roll rebellion.

Funny thing, though: most of these important events, interpreted as signs of death by some, are seen precisely as signs of rock & roll's vitality by others. I was struck, having compiled this breezy sketch of how the death of rock & roll weaves in and out of rock's history, to come across a new book called *Turning Points in Rock and Roll*, which lists as milestones in rock & roll's development many of these same moments, as these selections from the table of contents suggest:

Chapter 7: 1954 [*sic*]: The Movie "Blackboard Jungle" Comes Out
Chapter 10: 1959: Buddy Holly Crashes
Chapter 12: 1965: Bob Dylan Goes Electric at the Newport Folk Festival
Chapter 15: 1967–69: From Monterey Pop to Woodstock to Altamont: Innocence Found and Lost
Chapter 16: 1977: The Sex Pistols Tour America
Chapter 17: 1981: MTV Launches
Chapter 19: 1991: Nirvana Hits #1 with "Nevermind"
Chapter 20: 1995: MP3, Napster, and the End of the World as We Know It[34]

Neil Young might easily be talking about rock & roll when, in "Barstool Blues," he sings about a friend who "died a thousand deaths."[35] Rumors of the death of rock & roll are very nearly as old as the music itself, a subject we'll pick up again at the close of this chapter, and in more detail again in the next.

The fact that rock & roll was "born dead"—stillborn, or perhaps murdered in its crib by jealous older siblings—suggests a number of intriguing things about the rhetoric of "the death of rock." *Is Rock Dead?* sets out to explore the varied and sometimes conflicting ways in which the "death of rock" trope has been deployed both within the discourse of popular music and in the larger arena of American culture, over nearly half a century, seeking insights into what Fredric Jameson would call the "cultural logic" of this rather perverse formulation. In the year 2003, for instance—a very bad year according to the music industry—rock & roll racked up more than $32 billion in worldwide sales, despite the supposed ravages of online file sharing. To judge by this one criterion alone—and clearly, it's a criterion that most rock (as opposed to "pop") artists are structurally constrained to eschew—rock & roll is quite vital indeed. What, then, does it mean to say that rock & roll is dead? If rock & roll is dead, when did it die? What does it accomplish, for various sectors of our culture, to be able to make this claim? Why, in other words, do some of us so eagerly hope for the death of rock & roll, to the point of mistaking signs of life for evidence of death?

Without going into a great deal of detail, most of which I'll postpone to later chapters, it might be useful here at the outset to suggest some of the recurrent themes in the rhetoric of the death of rock & roll. One, as I've suggested already, equates the death of a selected performer with the death of the music: *Time* magazine, for instance, the week of John Lennon's murder, carried his portrait on the cover with the headline, "When the Music Died." As we'll see in chapter 5, an entire subgenre of rock & roll, the rock elegy, has grown up around this conception.

A second common provocation for those who declare rock & roll dead is a belief that a once-pristine rock & roll, uncontaminated by the taint of the market, has now been polluted by commercial and technological forces. The notion of an old-time rock & roll made simply, and simply for its own sake, without larger cultural forces entering in, is of course painfully naive; there may well be self-taught folkie guitar heros out there somewhere, playing just for the love of it, refusing the blandishments of the industry—but you and I have never heard them. Mute, inglorious Robert Johnsons.

This is a variation on the theme of authenticity, and the eulogies for rock & roll are based on some perceived evidence of rock's flagging authenticity more often than any other cause. As we'll explore in more detail in chapter 3, these pronouncements occur most frequently, and in their rhetorically most extreme form, in journalistic or popular (as distinct from scholarly) writing. Consider, for a moment, this example from Joe Harrington's exhaustive, exhausting (556-page) chronicle of the death of rock, *Sonic Cool*, from the book's closing page:

> The fact that Rock n' Roll as we once knew it has become a mere demographic in a vast wasteland of mass-marketed swill shouldn't surprise anyone, seeing as, at its root, Rock n' Roll was never anything *but* that. Still, for a moment—probably in the '60s—it achieved the unique feat of being both commercially successful and artistically satisfying. That dream was squashed by a variety of cruel realities brought about in the post-Woodstock era when the big record labels realized they could formulate rebellion into a very effective marketing tool. Since that time, Rock has had little hope of escaping its inevitable servitude to corporate demands.[36]

It's an interesting, and symptomatic, example for a few different reasons. To begin with, it's clichéd; Harrington echoes FCC chairman Newton N. Minow's famous May 9, 1961, speech to the National Association of Broadcasters, in which he called television "a vast wasteland."[37] This seems to be an inherent problem in talking about the death of rock & roll: you're never the first, and you always seem to be quoting or plagiarizing a prior judgment. Once launched, the clichés seem to trigger one another in a kind of chain reaction: "vast wasteland" spawns "mass-marketed swill," for instance, and the notion, critiqued earlier, of Woodstock as rock & roll's Garden of Eden, seems to roll quite automatically from Harrington's keyboard.

While a bit of an eccentric, even an obsessive, Harrington does know his stuff, and his declaration is not without nuance; while falling into the rhetorical trap of equating commercial entanglements with the death of rock & roll, he does acknowledge the inescapable fact that rock was never uncommodified ("Rock n' Roll was never anything *but* that"). But the predominant tone is one of palpable nostalgia, which we might (as suggested earlier) take in its original, etymological sense: a longing, an aching, to return home ("we've got to get ourselves back to the garden"). No sooner has Harrington acknowledged that rock & roll was always a highly mediated form than he posits, without argument or evidence, a time when the music somehow transcended these tensions, "probably in the '60s"; and suggesting that such an accommodation of commercial to artistic agendas, forging a music that was "both commercially successful and artistically satisfying," was a "unique feat," ignores the considerable commercial and critical success of Cole Porter, Sammy Cahn, and the Gershwins, to go no further afield than these.

"When Rock became a cultural commodity," Harrington concludes, "an accepted part of the norm, it lost its reason to live.… The apocalypse is over. All that's left is eighty-eight billion mass-produced pieces of plastic encrypted with sounds that will be with us, in one form or another, until the end of time."[38] Harrington talks about rock "becom[ing] a cultural commodity," seemingly forgetting that he has already affirmed (on the same page) that it always has *been* a commodity; he suggests that "the apocalypse is over," in a reckless and heightened language that sounds strangely, suspiciously, apocalyptic. In the end, Harrington runs aground on a rhetorical and logical contradiction that dogs much of the hand-wringing writing about rock & roll: in attempting to celebrate the rise of a popular culture form, a form that proudly identifies itself as apart from elite art, Harrington wants to elevate some portion of it ("classic rock," say) to the status of art, leaving its embarrassing relations ("pop") behind. The rock critic who uses the broad brush of "commercialism" to tar the musics of which he does not approve—the critic who makes elitist arguments on behalf of popular forms—plays a very dangerous game.

A similar logic can be seen to work in Donald Clarke's impressively wide-ranging history *The Rise and Fall of Popular Music*, which at base is built on a very simple skeleton: the "rise" of popular music, in the twentieth century, culminates in the golden era of jazz and big band music, and the birth of rock & roll begins the steady decline he documents almost to the present day. Clarke's book, seemingly unwittingly, adopts a very strange rhythm, more pronounced the closer he gets to the time of the book's writing. Chapters, even those dealing with music he clearly does not esteem, remain more or less evenhanded, but each chapter closes with a kind of curtain-closer provocation, leading the reader breathlessly into the next chapter; in the book's last few chapters, these closers become undisguised in their disdain for rock & roll. We'll be considering Clarke's book again in chapter 3, but the following is representative of his strategy of demonizing the commercial success of rock & roll, without analysis or argument but simply by the force of his moral opprobrium:

> Technology and money have reigned supreme for so long that the manufacture, marketing and distribution of the product has long since become more important than its content, while an uncountable number of tiny record labels around the world who care about music cannot get their records into the shops or on the air. The confusion of values in the music business and the beginning of the complete abandonment of musical considerations are illustrated by the appearances of Elvis Presley on television variety shows in 1956.[39]

In Clarke's narrative, the beginning of the end of meaningful popular music is pegged quite explicitly to the commercial triumph of rock & roll; and perhaps echoing the logic of Harrington's assertion, the participation of popular music with the "vast wasteland" of network television is picked out as the precise moment of its demise. Again, this logic seems quite vulnerable: using a version of Theodor Adorno and Max Horkheimer's bogey, the "culture industry," Clarke seems to suggest that the medium that above all others might make popular music truly available to the widest audience, television, is precisely the agent of its banalization.[40] This, as I've already suggested, seems to me an incredibly risky, if not logically incoherent, theoretical position. It uses, whether explicitly or implicitly, the analytical tools and vocabulary fashioned by haters of popular culture to argue for the importance of popular culture.

In the work of Frankfurt School theorists like Adorno and Horkheimer, of course, a distinction is drawn between "popular" art and "mass" art; popular art, rising spontaneously from the people, can retain some kind of value and authenticity, while mass art, manufactured without regard for the experiences of the people by the "culture industry" and foisted on them, top-down, can be only a species of false consciousness. So, for instance, Clarke writes, "Lieber and Stoller had already been aware that they were making records rather than recording music, but they were smart enough and talented enough to keep that fact in perspective. Suddenly there was so much money in it that the trend became the manufacture of pop artefacts instead of the recording of musical events."[41] The past two decades, at least, of scholarship on "the popular" has worked to undo this kind of easy distinction, but it retains a pernicious power in the popular discourse about rock & roll.

Harrington again puts the point most artlessly:

> Right about that time [1960], Elvis was getting out of the army, but he didn't go back to Rock 'n' Roll. He—and mostly Colonel Tom—had a much shrewder agenda in mind, mainly to become a long-term commodity in the entertainment business, even if it meant staying in Hollywood for ten years making lousy movies. People didn't realize at the time, but this was to have a grim effect on the whole Rock 'n' Roll process. We were already seeing the pattern developing: Rock 'n' Roll had in a few short years already doomed itself to mass merchandising and crass commercialism. It would soon become the most popular music the world has ever known, but in its assimilation to the wills of the corporate devil, Rock would invent a system of control and dissemination that would

ultimately rob it of its intrinsic value: the ability to *rock*, free of pretense or ambition.[42]

This is a sentiment seemingly echoed by Michael Stipe of R.E.M., on "King of Comedy" from the *Monster* album (1994): "I'm not commodity," he repeats six times, as the song ends. But Stipe is singing in character, and the man who wrote this stingingly ironic album knows that the character who sings these words is deluded, in denial, protesting too much; every human relationship, the album carefully points out, is colored by commodity culture. Such is life under late capitalism; there's no use wringing one's hands about it or, worse, acting as if it weren't, or hadn't always, been true. If one believes, as many rock writers do, that "rebellion" is the essential spirit of rock & roll, this revelation is of course unnerving. "Welcome," as Pink Floyd sang, "to the machine."

One venue in which the distinction between "art" and "commerce," "content" and "marketing," has been successfully challenged is in postmodernism, and a good deal of the jeremiad culture surrounding rock & roll, on some level, is really a lament over the "death," the passing from primacy, of modernism.[43] Much of what some of these writers are complaining about is a perceived shift from a modernist-dominant to a postmodernist-dominant tenor in rock; a move away from the charismatic, sincere performer toward a more frankly self-reflexive, conflicted, less-confident model. For instance, only by privileging a modernist, even a Romantic, notion of "originality" could one come up with a charge like this one, leveled by Michael Cable in *The Pop Industry Inside Out* (and that title, of course, is telling):

> Most alarming of all is the fact that pop is fast running out of melodies. There are a limited number of notes and the various permutations are by no means endless. Songwriters will admit that it is increasingly difficult to come up with a basic melody that is totally original. And it shows.[44]

The idea that popular music is "running out of melodies" is—at one and the same time—as old as music itself and so preposterous as to defy refutation. Even if one were to grant that Western music's "limited number of notes" means that all is repetition, the (postmodern) hip-hop practice of sampling does suggest a way out of this seeming impasse—though hardly a solution seen as legitimate by all.

A final, important thread in the discourse of the death of rock & roll is a rhetorical strategy I'll call "Boomer Triumphalism": the tendency of baby-boom-era critics (like me) to assume, almost unthinkingly, that the best rock & roll was the music that they grew up with; everything created since has to be measured against that standard (and, more often than not, found wanting). Although not immune to this impulse—as I assume that *I'm* not immune—John Strausbaugh has done a good job, recently, of describing this phenomenon:

> We boomers make primary claim to all rock, and punk rock is definitely a genre of rock, created by tail-end boomers. In fact, boomers give punk rock a very honored place in rock history: To boomers, punk rock was the death of rock. As James Miller so handily outlined, 1977, the year Elvis died and the Sex Pistols rose internationally, is the terminus of the rock age. According to Miller, after 1977—after punk rock—rock is a fixed, "completed" art form, like jazz, and every supposedly new expression of it (hardcore, grunge, rap metal, etc.) has just been repetition and rehash of forms and idioms that were all originated and explored and established by the time punk came and went. That the supposed death of rock coincides so neatly with '60s boomers becoming too old to appreciate rock anymore is just a happy coincidence.[45]

James Miller's *Flowers in the Dustbin,* which we'll take up in some detail in chapter 3, is indeed the worst offender in this regard; it's an almost perfectly boomer-centric version of rock & roll history, beginning with the logic of its title. As *New York Times* rock critic John Pareles wrote in his review of Miller's book, "Mr. Miller is in his 50s, and *Flowers in the Dustbin* is a baby boomer's view of rock. It peaks around the time he turns 20, then settles into workaday routine, then sours; the loss of innocence is in the listener along with the music."[46] What is most worrisome about Boomer Triumphalism, from my perspective, is the way that it has been naturalized in the mainstream media; Miller worked for years as *Newsweek's* popular music critic. Just as our parents condemned Elvis Presley–era rock & roll as an abomination (something we'll consider in chapter 2), so the generation brought up on Elvis, the Beatles, and the Supremes now finds all music made in the wake of rock's first wave to be derivative, a pale imitation—dead. But as Pareles quips, "Rock isn't dead, Mr. Boomer. It's just dead *to you.*"[47]

Another, different kind of response to Boomer Triumphalism is articulated by, among others, Chuck Klosterman in *Fargo Rock City.* Klosterman is squarely Generation X, and among his generation's most incisive and opinionated rock critics. In a few short sentences, he reveals the incoherence of Boomer Triumphalism to anyone standing outside its assumptions:

> Elvis Costello has questioned whether or not '80s glam metal should even be considered rock 'n' roll, because he thinks it's a "facsimile" of what legitimate artists already did in the past. What he fails to realize is that no one born after 1970 can possibly appreciate any creative element in rock 'n' roll: By 1980, there was no creativity left. The freshest ideas in pop music's past twenty years have come out of rap, and that genre is totally based on recycled, bastardized riffs. Clever facsimiles are all we really expect.
>
> The problem with the current generation of rock academics is that they remember when rock music seemed new. It's impossible for them to relate to those of us who have never known a world where rock 'n' roll wasn't *everywhere,* all the time.[48]

About the only thing to quibble with in Klosterman's riposte is his identification of "rock academics" as the worst offenders. James Miller, while making his mark at *Newsweek,* does now teach at the New School in New York, and the University of North Carolina's Lawrence Grossberg is, as we'll discuss in chapter 4, another big offender; but most journalists are both far more extreme in their claims, and their opinions more widely disseminated and influential. We boomers, Strausbaugh writes, "think we invented popular music, and popular culture in general, and that everything kids today produce is an imitation of things we did first and better in the 1960s and '70s"; if this isn't prima facie a falsehood, its truth at least ought to be scrutinized.[49] It certainly serves quite suspiciously to uphold the values of one particular generation.

Where do the claims that rock & roll is dead rise from? The phrase is trotted out with some regularity by at least four distinct groups: rock journalists and critics, conservative cultural critics, rock fans—and rock musicians. To begin with, "rock is dead" is a bromide often intoned by rock critics and journalists, the rather flaccid hook to many a magazine and newspaper article. Scholarly narratives about rock & roll have been dominated by attempts to tell two pretty tired stories: one called "The Birth of Rock," the other, rather predictably, called "The Death of Rock."

When I e-mailed a friend who writes about American popular music to tell him I was working on a book about the putative "death of rock & roll," he wrote back, "I once lectured to a high school on the *birth* of rock; I guess you've got the other end covered."

Stories of birth and death, of course, are the very warp and woof of Western narrative tradition—from creation myths to apocalypse, Genesis to Revelation—and their ubiquity in histories of rock & roll should therefore come as no surprise. But our deep-seated need to tell these two stories about rock & roll is noteworthy in part because the "death of rock" doesn't stand at the other end from the "birth of rock," as one might logically assume: in fact, the two moments are practically coincident, and the two stories are most often told in tandem.[50] And their coincidence—and the fact that rock & roll's death certificate was signed almost before the birth announcements were mailed—is no coincidence. For the birth of rock and the death of rock are, I believe, two different metaphors for talking about the very same set phenomena, and rock & roll's death-rattle—or is it a newborn's cry?—has been sounding for half a century now.

Like many near-mythic births (those of Shakespeare and Samuel Beckett, for instance), the precise date of the birth of rock & roll is the subject of some debate, and one into which I'd prefer not to have to enter here. Dating precisely the birth of rock & roll is of little importance; what does need to be stressed, however, is that it did not receive adequate pre- and perinatal care: it was a high-risk birth. Rock & roll died, it seems, of a congenital condition. Something wasn't quite right from the start; it wasn't a healthy child. Or more precisely, rock & roll was born under terrible conditions—"born under a bad sign," as Booker T. Jones, and then Jack Bruce, were to sing years later—greatly diminishing the odds of its survival. "Born under a Bad Sign" is a blues tune, made blues rock by Cream; and fortunately, before the blues could "die," it had a baby, according to no lesser an authority than Muddy Waters, and "they named it rock & roll"—although it too passed away, apparently quite a long time ago.

In their book *What Was the First Rock 'n' Roll Record?* Jim Dawson and Steve Propes set as the boundaries for their investigation the recordings "Blues, Part 2" (1944) and Elvis Presley's "Heartbreak Hotel" (1956);[51] none but the most willfully perverse would argue for a birth date before the early 1950s, however, and by the time "Heartbreak Hotel" was released, rumors of the death of rock & roll were already circulating. Because my primary focus is the putative "death," rather than the birth, of rock & roll, I'm more interested in exploring the conditions into which rock & roll was born, rather than dating precisely its birth. What, in short, was responsible for its being born such a sickly child, "born astride a grave"? And why is the time of its birth, its death, "the same day, the same second"?

Of all the competing available histories of rock & roll, and possible birth dates and places, there is a logic to using the July 7, 1954, date: for all its specious authority, it is certainly the version of rock history best known outside of narrow music circles. In this most widely accepted version of the story, Elvis was the attending physician when something recognizable as "rock & roll" was born on that summer night in 1954, when Memphis disc jockey Dewey Phillips played Elvis's cover of Arthur "Big Boy" Crudup's "That's All Right" on his "Red Hot and Blue" show on radio station WHBQ. James Miller's dating rock & roll from 1947, while interesting and provocative, is something of a mandarin's trick: certainly no one playing popular music at the time, least of all Wynonie Harris, would have called his music "rock & roll" and, as we'll explore in chapter 3, Miller may have had his own reasons for picking 1947, Wynonie Harris notwithstanding.

If we accept that mid-1954 birthday for rock & roll, for argument's sake, we might well be surprised to learn that the death of rock & roll was first publicly announced in September 1956, scarcely two years later. For as best I can tell, the phrase "rock and roll is dead" was first used on a country & western single by the Maddox Brothers and Sister Rose ("The Most Colorful Hillbilly Band in America"), a track called "The Death of Rock and Roll"; and the song had been part of their stage act for some months before the side was cut, pushing the "death" and "birth" of rock & roll even closer together.[52] The single is more a novelty song than a serious shot across rock & roll's bow; its two minutes, nine seconds of frenetic hillbilly–rockabilly madness, and its simple lyric, have nothing explicitly to do with the death of rock & roll that the song claims to celebrate. Rather, the death of rock & roll was already seen, by 1956, as something fervently to be hoped for among purveyors of other, more established, traditional popular musics; as Jonny Whiteside, Rose Maddox's biographer, puts it, "rock & roll's dominance of the market in 1956 and 1957 had country music scrambling in profound confusion."[53] As we'll discover, however, there's something very "rock & roll" about the song's logic, and in a paradoxical way, the Maddoxes' "The Death of Rock and Roll" confirms rock's vitality in the very same breath with which it tries to extinguish it.

The Maddox Brothers and Rose are credited by some with "inventing" rockabilly in Modesto, California, back in 1937; according to Nick Tosches, they were a "West Coast Okie group" who "recorded stuff that not only rocked, but also contained many of the vocal fireworks—yelps, screams, howls—that became watermarks of rockabilly."[54] Mainstays of the Louisiana Hayride from 1951 until the group broke up in the summer of 1956, they toured Texas with Elvis Presley in 1956, giving them plenty of opportunity, up close, to see the hysteria building around rock & roll. Don Maddox, who sang lead on the record, recalls,

> We didn't really change anything; all the times were changin.' When Elvis first started, we just started doin' more rock & roll 'cause that's what the people wanted, but we just more or less kept the same style that we'd always had. "The Death of Rock and Roll," well, that was when Elvis was gettin' real hot, and I was just doin' a take off on him, just foolin' around and doin' it for laughs. I started doin' it onstage and it went over real big in person, so we decided to record it.[55]

"The Death of Rock and Roll" is the last side the group recorded before breaking up (although they reunited for a final session in 1957): the track then seems more accurately to have signaled the end of hillbilly music than of rock & roll, which was really just warming up.

The label of the Columbia 45 lists no songwriter, only crediting Fred Maddox with the arrangement; in this it is no different from many other items in the Maddoxes' catalog, which contained a fair bit of traditional material and gospel tunes. But the fuller listing in the Columbia catalog gives songwriting credit to someone archly called "Charles": not a given name, it turns out, but a surname. And here the gag begins to unravel; for while "The Death of Rock and Roll" sounds like nothing else you've ever heard before—"undoubtedly one of the goofiest songs they ever waxed," Whiteside writes, "it resembles nothing so much as the early sixties garage records done by groups like the Fendermen and Trashmen. It is all twisted vocals above a driving guitar and string-bass rhythm, with little rhyme or reason in either, save for sheer lunacy"[56]—there is also something very familiar about it. And the reason is simple: it's an especially manic cover of Ray Charles's 1955 hit "I Got a Woman."[57]

The group's decision to record the song, and to slap a death-sentence title on it, had everything to do with Elvis Presley and nearly nothing to do with Ray Charles. They would have had ample opportunity to hear Elvis perform Charles's hit, as he began to do during some of his Louisiana Hayride performances in late 1955 and into 1956; Elvis's biographer Peter Guralnick says that by May 1955, "I Got a Woman" was a "staple" of his live act, embellished with a "half-time, bluesy finish."[58] According to Whiteside, "The Death of Rock and Roll," one of the Maddox Brothers and Rose's "most notorious records," was "by no means an attack on the form [rock & roll]; it is instead a manic send up, and the 'death' referred to is how they murder 'I Got a Woman.'"[59] Like many other biographers, however, Whiteside is no critic; the Maddoxes' record is certainly playful but with an edge as well, which Whiteside acknowledges elsewhere: Charles's song is not the only thing they're trying to murder. Rock & roll and its putative death were, Whiteside writes, "not, as they soon discovered, a laughing matter," and his description of the end of their career—and the death of a certain kind of country music—is worth quoting at length:

> By 1956, country music's dance hall era was dead. Eclipsed by rock & roll, drive-in movies, and television, even Bob Wills could no longer pull in the thousands that were once routine for him. Beyond whatever internecine dissatisfactions the Maddox Brothers & Rose might have been troubled by, it was clear that their show-and-dance format couldn't survive the drift in public tastes.
>
> After the spectacular successes of first Roy Acuff and Eddy Arnold, then Hank, Lefty, and Elvis, the solo vocalist became the performer of choice in country music. As dance halls closed down, nightclub operators began insisting that headline artists perform with the house band. It became necessary for the Maddoxes to forego their hard earned title as "Kings of the Roadshow." ...
>
> For them, the signs were clear.... "The Death of Rock and Roll" only gathered dust. The band maintained a healthy following and certainly could have continued operating, playing at rural halls and rodeos. But they had become accustomed to the bright lights, brisk ticket sales, and prestige accorded Columbia recording artists. They considered themselves top of the line, just like their Cadillacs and clothing.
>
> Yet the Maddoxes saw the handwriting on the wall and agreed to end the family act.[60]

The Maddoxes' "The Death of Rock and Roll," then, was a kind of playful "bird" flipped at rock & roll in general, and Elvis in particular; and though they might ridicule the music in their parody version, Elvis was crying all the way to the bank.

The story does get weirder, though, as a student of R&B might already have recognized. In recording "The Death of Rock and Roll," the Maddoxes were covering Elvis covering Ray Charles; but Charles's hit was very controversial in its own right, as R&B began to "cross over" to white audiences, and listeners unaccustomed to blues conventions heard Charles sing, "I got a woman / Way over town / She's good to me." The particular kind of "need" about which Charles sings had largely been kept from white radio audiences up to this point; it was in turn precisely the kind of need that Elvis sought to exploit, and it's not hard to see why the song would have been attractive material for him.

But "I Got a Woman" wasn't just sensual, sexual; it was heard, in some quarters, as sacrilegious. In the Time-Life documentary history of rock & roll, Jerry Butler tells of his mother's reaction to the song:

> I remember the first time I heard Ray Charles sing. He was singing, "I got a woman / Way over town / She's good to me." And my momma said, "Now that's a shame. That man has taken that gospel song and turned it into the blues." Because the original lyric was, "There's a man / Goin' round / Takin' names." And then when she found out he was blind, then she really went off. Oh my God, this was sacrilegious.[61]

Even the Ray Charles "original," then, was a cover: a gospel tune smuggled into the disreputable neighborhood of R&B. When Charles set his salacious new lyrics to it, "There's a Man Goin' Round Takin' Names" was a gospel standard; it had been recorded by Josh White in 1932–33, and by Leadbelly in 1944; it also composed part of Paul Robeson's touring repertory. And its lyric, rather than carnal delights, speaks of the Day of Judgment:

> There's a man going 'round taking names,
> There's a man going 'round taking names,
> He's been taking my father's name,
> An' he left my heart in vain,
> There's a man going 'round taking names.

The more you look at it, the more it seems there are a couple of good reasons for locating the birth of rock & roll in 1954, for the trespassing of gospel–blues, sacred–secular boundaries that Charles performs in "I Got a Woman" is every bit as important in the formation of rock & roll as the black–white brinksmanship of Elvis. Peter Guralnick, in what is still

the definitive work on soul music, explains the impact of Charles's hit
this way:

> If you listen to the clunkety rhythms of "I Got a Woman" today, it's
> hard to imagine the impact that it had in 1954 and 1955 for blacks *and*
> whites, for a young Elvis and an only slightly older Sam Cooke, and for
> nearly every singer, writer, and producer that I have interviewed for this
> book. The very stratagem of adapting a traditional gospel song, putting
> secular lyrics to it, and then delivering it with all the attendant fanfare of
> a pentecostal service was, simply, staggering; it was like a blinding flash
> of light in which the millennium, all of a sudden and unannounced, had
> arrived. "I couldn't get over it," recalled Bumps Blackwell (not yet Sam
> Cooke's producer at the time of the record's release) to rock historian
> Charlie Gillett. "He'd taken a gospel song that Alex Bradford had
> recorded for Specialty and made it into an r&b number!"[62]

As Reebee Garofalo writes, "The impact of 'I Got a Woman' has been
remembered by popular music historians as nothing short of apocalyptic."[63]

Thus, "The Death of Rock and Roll" is a hillbilly cover of Elvis's cover
of Ray Charles's cover of a traditional gospel song. We find ourselves
again in the realm of Jean Baudrillard's "simulacrum," the copy with no
original, "the map that precedes the territory,"[64] quintessential artifact of
the postmodern era. Far from killing rock, the song perversely enacts
rock's own generative logic: "borrowing" so liberally that *borrow* is
hardly the word—did Charles, one wonders, receive licensing fees?—the
Maddox Brothers and Rose gleefully erased boundaries between gospel,
blues, R&B, country, hillbilly, and ended up making a rock & roll record
in spite of themselves (hence the uncanny aptness of Whiteside's compar-
ison to early-'60s garage bands like The Trashmen). Trying to kill rock &
roll, and extend their own careers, the Maddoxes threw shit at it and only
made it stronger.

Despite the insistence of those who proclaim rock & roll dead—
indeed, as is suggested precisely by the insistence and vehemence of those
who proclaim rock & roll is dead—rock's not quite dead yet. This struggle
bears some resemblance to a famous moment in the film *Monty Python
and the Holy Grail*. The scene: England during the Black Death; as the
Cart-master (Eric Idle) pushes a cart through the muddy road of a small
village, chanting wearily "Bring out your dead!," residents come forward
with their dead relatives, throw them unceremoniously on his cart,
and pay him. A man (John Cleese) steps up to the cart with an old man

(perhaps his father?) in a nightshirt slung over his shoulder, hoping to have him carted away, but the old man persistently, inconveniently, protests his vitality: "I'm not dead!" Tired ultimately of arguing about it, the younger man clouts him on the head, pays the cart-master, and has the old man hauled off. "Dead," this exchange suggests, isn't so much a *description* as a *decision:* you're dead when we decide you're dead, and there's nothing you can do to change our minds. And should you protest your death too vigorously—well, we'll simply have to have you killed.

Critics, fans, and performers have been eagerly proclaiming the death of rock music very nearly since the hour of its birth and have used a number of strategies over the years to try to bring about its demise; rock & roll, in response, has devised its own cunning repertory of survival strategies. *Is Rock Dead?* will explore some suggestive examples of these attempts at containment, and rock & roll's sometimes ingenious responses as it seeks to remain a vital imaginative resource for our culture. *Is Rock Dead?* charts an odyssey through post–World War II American musical culture, following the traces and elusive sources of the rumors of rock & roll's death, interested finally in what the persistence of this story tells us about ourselves, our brightest hopes, and our darkest fears. More than the secret history of a song (like Dave Marsh's wonderful *Louie Louie: The History and Mythology of the World's Most Famous Rock 'n' Roll Song*) or a paranoid history of a musical genre (Greil Marcus's baffling *Lipstick Traces: A Secret History of the Twentieth Century*), *Is Rock Dead?* seeks to understand the "structure of feeling" betrayed by the most common of all rock truisms: that it's dead, and you've already missed the best.

2

A Chip on His Shoulder and an H-Bomb in His Pants: American Nervousness about Rock & Roll

Our story begins in the 1950s. To represent (or even introduce) a decade as complex and self-contradictory as the '50s through one event or one figure is necessarily a distortion; the same era that gave us Sputnik also gave us *Peyton Place*. But Dwight D. Eisenhower did reign as president for the majority of the decade—from 1953 through the end of 1960—and thus was the president who was asleep at the wheel when rock & roll invaded these shores. It wasn't until the early 1960s, with Democrats in the White House, that what was later to be dubbed the "British Invasion" in rock & roll occurred. Yet despite the fact that 1950s rock & roll was entirely a domestic invention, its arrival was nevertheless most often experienced as an invasion: although where on Earth (or not on Earth) it had come from was a question of ongoing concern. To Eisenhower, in one of his few recorded remarks on the new music, rock & roll "represent[ed] some kind of change in our standards." "What has happened," he went on to ask, "to our concepts of beauty, and decency, and morality?"[1]

Tom Lutz has written about "American nervousness" at the turn of the twentieth century—an epidemic occurring in 1903, to be exact—and while my subject is a rather different phenomenon, and takes place almost exactly half a century later, Lutz's term is suggestive of the national state of wariness and uneasiness that characterizes at least some important features of the public life of the '50s.[2] Rock & roll was the cause, or at least the focus, of much of that '50s nervousness; but a complicated network of social forces and unarticulated fears, both domestic and foreign, conspired to create an especially tangled, and often internally contradictory, knot of generalized social anxiety. The complexity of the situation, however, did not always encourage complex analysis. The sources of domestic threats of communism, for instance, were frustratingly elusive, most often ruling out direct, decisive action. While the entire older generation seemed concerned about the presumed sexual promiscuity of the younger, any open articulation of these fears ran the risk of worsening the problem. Rock & roll, however, made a perfect target for middle-aged America's midcentury anxiety: the provenance almost exclusively of the young, African American in its genealogy, southern in pedigree, rock & roll became the lightning rod for all of middle-America's (and middle-class) fears. It seems amazing, in retrospect, that no one ever called their band The Scapegoats.

As Linda Martin and Kerry Segrave write in the preface to *Anti-Rock,* "Rock-bashing has remained constant since the mid-1950s both in content and style."[3] Their capsule summary of the indignities suffered by rock & roll since its birth provides a useful index, one for which we will, in the pages that follow, to some extent be filling in the details:

> With its black roots, its earthy, sexual or rebellious lyrics, and its exuberant acceptance by youth, rock and roll has long been under attack by the establishment world of adults. No other form of culture, and its artists, has met with such extensive hostility. The music has been damned as a corrupter of morals, as an instigator of juvenile delinquency and violence. Denounced as a communist plot, perceived as a symbol of Western decadence, it has been fulminated against by the left, the right, the center, the establishment, rock musicians themselves, doctors, clergy, journalists, politicians, and "good" musicians.[4]

In a decade that stigmatized the alien above everything else, it is not surprising that this new music, seemingly so alien and so threatening, was so thoroughly demonized in the popular mind and media. A form of expression important only to those with no solid power base in the culture—as one caustic commentator is at pains to remind the fans of rock & roll, for instance, most of them couldn't even vote—it was especially vulnerable to demonization and persecution.

Perhaps the most prominent target for the fears of the cold war establishment was a figure related by proximity with rock & roll, the newly minted figure of the American teenager. Teenagers, in the most obvious sense, were nothing new; but as a discrete developmental stage, distinct from children or young adults, the teenager is uniquely a product of the 1950s. The *Oxford English Dictionary* lists only one appearance of the term (in *Scientific American*) before W.H. Auden, in his long poem *The Age of Anxiety* (1947), wryly pointed out that teenagers had become both a demographic and a marketing reality. Auden describes a "modern product / Of nerve and know-how with a new thrill" which is "Exclusively used / By upper classmen and Uncle Sam. / Tops in tests by teen-agers. / Just ask for it always." American historian Glenn Altschuler explains,

> By the end of World War II, the term "teen-ager" was firmly established in the language. In the '50s, the *Dictionary of American Slang* subsequently pointed out, the United States was the only country "considering this age group as a separate entity whose influence, fads and fashions are worthy of discussion apart from the adult world."[5]

In any number of respects, postwar American teens were a force to be reckoned with. Older teens were able to drive, and the unprecedented prosperity of the postwar industrial economy meant that there was usually a car around to drive, even if it was Dad's. Teenagers in the '50s had at least some disposable income, whether derived from an after-school job or from another relatively new innovation, a teen's "allowance"; and the continued national migration from farm to city and suburb meant that, unless he worked an after-school job, the middle-class teenager had more time on his hands than ever before in history. Indeed, it has been suggested that the concept of "leisure time" is an invention of the 1950s,[6] and the simultaneous arrival on the scene of the American teenager and leisure time suggested a potentially volatile situation (one exploited in films like *Blackboard Jungle,* to which we'll turn our attention in chapter 5). The teenager was all dressed up—or probably, not dressed up at all but dressed down, even possibly wearing new fashions like "dungarees" and a T-shirt—with nowhere to go. The members of this newly coherent demographic made their parents nervous: what had been parent–child relationships before the war shifted, to some degree, to adult–teenager relationships—the same actors but rather different roles. Although he was twenty-four years old at his death, James Dean became the eternal icon of the American teenager, immortalized in the film *Rebel without a Cause* (which premiered in 1955, a few weeks *after* Dean's death). The fact that his initials were "JD" was just icing on the cake.

The juvenile delinquent, or JD, was the name for this frightening new figure—the teenager without firm moral anchor or proper parental supervision. By simply inverting these initials, we come up with the DJ, the "disk jockey"—a figure of 1940s vintage, but one that had been freighted with an entirely new cultural role and moral responsibility in the 1950s. From its earliest days, rock & roll had been associated with rebellion; and because it was the older generation who took the early lead in the public relations campaign against rock & roll, these teen rebels were consistently portrayed, as the James Dean movie title had it, as being "without a cause." Asked what he was rebelling against in *The Wild One* (1954), Marlon Brando had famously replied, "What have you got?" This notion of teens as aimless, unprincipled rebels predates the birth of rock & roll, but it was in place, powerfully, in the public consciousness when rock & roll appeared on the scene and was quickly attached to the Brando/Dean model.

The largely forgotten 1959 British film *Expresso Bongo*, starring heart-throb Cliff Richard as a transparent Elvis stand-in, makes this point in a wonderfully sharp, comic fashion. Johnny Jackson (played by actor Laurence Harvey), who serves as a kind of Colonel Parker to the new teen sensation "Bongo" Herbert, describes to his client the role he's destined to play: "For a few days you've become a sort of national anti-hero. You're every poor little fish in the country, only covered in gold chips. You've got a chip on your shoulder, and an H-bomb in your pants. A sneer, a twitch, a hell in your head. It's you against the world, baby, and the world loves you for hating it."[7] The film is, among other things, quite perceptive (quite early on) about the synergistic relationship between "bad" publicity and rock & roll's popularity.

The early association of rock & roll with juvenile delinquency, however, was more than just bad press: it was also something of an unavoidable historical fact. On March 25, 1955, Bridgeport, Connecticut banned rock & roll teenage dance parties. That November, 1940s middle-weight boxing champion Rocky Graziano told a Senate subcommittee hearing that juvenile delinquency was "a serious problem, a rock and roll thing." (His concerns did not, however, stand in the way of his accepting a supporting role in Alan Freed's 1957 film *Mister Rock and Roll.*) Another of Freed's films, *Rock Around the Clock,* his 1956 response to *Blackboard Jungle,* cashed in on the success of Bill Haley and provoked rioting across England similar to that which had greeted the earlier film: "All in all the film left an aftermath never matched by any movie shown in Britain. Over one hundred British youths had been arrested before the month of September was over. Curiously, the film had been shown in more than three hundred British cinemas before any disturbances broke out."[8] As a reporter for the *Los Angeles Times* remarked at the time, "No musical form since the waltz has caused as much controversy as the most recent addition to popular musical tastes, rock and roll. It's a violent, harsh type of music that, parents feel, incites teenagers to do all sorts of crazy things."[9]

As Altschuler points out, a rock & roll show that did *not* result in teen violence was, for a time, deemed newsworthy:

> For two years the [*New York*] *Times* printed dozens of articles linking destructive activities at, outside, or in the aftermath of concerts to "the beat and the booze" or the music alone. Public interest in rock 'n' roll was so great, *Times* editors even viewed the absence of a riot as newsworthy. "Rock 'n' Rollers Collect Calmly," readers learned, following a concert at the Paramount Theater in New York City.[10]

The *Times* article to which Altschuler refers actually manages to sound disappointed at the absence of teen violence; "Police Have Little to Do," the subhead reads, "as Times Square Show Crowd Fails to Repeat Uproar." Teens were "damned if they do, damned if they don't": somehow, one senses, the teenagers haven't met their responsibilities and have wasted the police's time.

Describing the fallout from the *Blackboard Jungle* and *Rock Around the Clock* riots, Altschuler writes,

> Many Americans believed that rock 'n' roll was an irritant that provoked conflict between parents and teenagers and increased antisocial behavior. Acknowledging that there was no simple, causal equation between enjoying Elvis and arranging a rumble, they remained convinced that rock 'n' roll reinforced the most worrisome aspects of youth culture: antagonism to adult authority and expectations; conformity to peer-group norms; and an ephemeral, erratic emotional intensity.[11]

In short, the newly evolving figure of the American teenager, and particularly that disturbing subgroup the juvenile delinquent (a group that was, as a movie like *Blackboard Jungle* shows with embarrassing frankness, imagined to be predominantly populated by immigrants, ethnic and racial minorities, and children of the working class), came over time (and with the willing cooperation of some parts of the entertainment industry) to be symbolized vividly in just one manifestation of youth culture: rock & roll. Rock & roll was, in the popular imagination, both symbol and fuel of post–World War II youth rebellion; and by controlling rock, it was thought—by silencing the sound track of the juvenile delinquents, this music that agitated, rather than soothed, the savage breast—society might once again gain control over its children.

As part of this effort, rock & roll was demonized, pathologized: treated not just metaphorically but also quite literally, as a form of contagion, a disease on the youthful body politic. Martin and Segrave note,

> One way some had of dealing with the threat was to pretend that it was just a fad and would soon run its course. One of the first such was bandleader Les Elgart who felt the music would have to run its course, like an "epidemic." He saw rhythm and blues as so limited that he felt kids would get over it in a hurry. Elgart used the term rhythm and blues because he made his pronouncement in March of 1955, before rock and roll had even established itself fully. He was thus writing the obituary almost before the birth.[12]

Newspapers of the day were full of stories equating a liking for rock & roll with a kind of illness; one representative story in the *New York Times*, for instance, opens with a statement of exemplary clarity: "A noted psychiatrist [Francis J. Braceland, psychiatrist in chief of the Institute of Living] described 'rock-and-roll' music today as a 'communicable disease' and 'another sign of adolescent rebellion.'"[13] Turning to psychiatrists as expert witnesses on rock & roll quickly became almost reflexive in mainstream media reporting; it is more accurate, then, to say that rock & roll wasn't so much medicalized as *psychopathologized*. Once again, the film *Expresso Bongo* parodied this trend brilliantly; on a televised talk show organized to discuss Bongo Herbert's meteoric success, a composite caricature of all these psychologist pundits and talking heads says, "Adolescents in our time demand outlets for their frustrations. The drums Bongo beats may stand for someone he doesn't like, or they may be a simple means of evacuating tension. The whole mass of whirling conflict surge up to a pounding climax. Afterwards, in its relaxation of tension, the face is almost beautiful." The language of building sexual excitation and release, of course, points to another of the psychologists' predictable analyses of rock & roll.

One fascinating small-scale case study in the way that the rhetoric of mental illness was used in the press to stigmatize rock & roll—and, further, the way that this rhetoric was later picked up and applied quite literally to rock & roll's teenaged consumers—concerns the loose analogy constructed between the somatic response of rock & roll audience members to the music, and the neurological condition Sydenham's chorea, popularly known as "St. Vitus dance." St. Vitus is the patron saint of dancers, young people, and dogs; St. Vitus dance is characterized by violent, involuntary jerking, which, apparently, is how the dancing of rock & roll audiences appeared to the members of an older generation. Before the rumors of the "death of rock & roll" had really gotten started, it turns out, a myth was afoot that equated rock spectatorship (especially the specter of the dancing concertgoer) with a kind of psychic or spiritual death: in the discourse of the popular media, the rock fan lost him- or herself to the alien influence of the music, and his or her body was taken over in a kind of St. Vitus dance. This image—which comes up with quite surprising frequency in newspaper reports of the time and, though sometimes used metaphorically, is just as often suggested as a real diagnosis—recurs with predictable regularity in descriptions of rock & roll concerts.

The first reference I have found likening a rock & roll audience to the frenzied movements of religious fanatics (on pilgrimage to the shrine of St. Vitus, where they hoped to be cured) dates from April 1955. Rock & roll, yet to be definitively christened, is referred to in this piece as "bop": "Bop is everywhere: it's the biggest teen-age epidemic since Frank Sinatra. It's the St. Vitus dance set to loud, bouncy brass. Some youngsters—and parents—swear by it; some at it. It has its fans and its foes, but you can't ignore it. It's bop!"[14] This phrase, or image, or metaphor—rock & roll is a contagious disease, a contemporary version of St. Vitus dance—spread early in the rock & roll era with a momentum and logic of its own. Thus in January 1956, a short item published in, of all places, the *Wall Street Journal*, resurrects the figure that the *Los Angeles Times* had put in circulation: "Candid Comment: The patron saint of the modern high school dance is probably St. Vitus."[15] Sneeringly dismissive, this short jibe doesn't really amount to much; parents have been making fun of their children's dancing, it seems, since at least the turn of the twentieth century. But this anonymous witticism "had legs," as they say; it began turning up with increasing frequency in the press: in news items, editorials, and editorial cartoons. A few months later, for instance, it is invoked again in the *Los Angeles Times,* the flagship newspaper of the West coast: "The male rock 'n' roller, like the male bird, is much more dazzling in plumage than the female. He wears a coat that reaches almost to his knees, a sports shirt that flaunts a dozen different colors, and he cavorts like a candidate for the Olympic St. Vitus team."[16]

Predictably, the *enfant terrible* of early rock & roll was tarred with this same brush: "I suppose," sniffed the *Washington Post's* John Crosby,

> it's a sign of advancing age but some of the enthusiasms of the younger set do leave me open-mouthed. One in particular is a singer—or shouter—named Elvis Presley who yells a song called "Heart Break Hotel" [*sic*] with great vigor and seems to have some sort of St. Vitus dance. He's the latest of a rash of entertainers—not all of them singers either—who appear to be candidates for a spastic hospital. In place of talent or voices, they twitch, they jerk, they convulse.[17]

By the following year—to truncate radically what is in fact a complex and quite fascinating history—"St. Vitus dance" was no longer just a condescending way for parents to ridicule their children's dancing and music; it had become, instead, the subject of serious medical study:

> Psychologists suggested yesterday that while the rock 'n' roll craze seemed to be related to "rhythmic behavior patterns" as old as the Middle Ages, it required full study as a current phenomenon.
>
> One educational psychologist asserted that what happened in and around the Paramount Theatre yesterday struck him as "very much like the medieval type of spontaneous lunacy where one person goes off and lots of other persons go off with him."
>
> Meanwhile, a parallel between rock 'n' roll and St. Vitus Dance has been drawn by Dr. Joost A.M. Meerlo, associate in psychiatry at Columbia University, in a study just completed for publication.
>
> Dr. Meerlo described his first view of rock 'n' roll this way: Young people were moved by a juke box to dance themselves "more and more into a prehistoric rhythmic trance until it had gone far beyond all the accepted versions of human dancing."
>
> "Why are rhythmical sounds and motions so especially contagious? A rhythmical call to the crowd easily foments mass ecstasy: 'Duce! Duce! Duce!' The call repeats itself into the infinite and liberates the mind of all reasonable inhibitions ... as in drug addiction, a thousand years of civilization fall away in a moment."

"Rock 'n' roll is a sign of depersonalization of the individual, of ecstatic veneration of mental decline and passivity."

"If we cannot stem the tide with its waves of rhythmic narcosis and of future waves of vicarious craze, we are preparing our own downfall in the midst of pandemic funeral dances."[18]

There's a lot for a cultural critic to chew on in this rich story, and we'll return to some of its metaphors later in the chapter; but the striking way in which rock & roll, at first metaphorically pathologized, medicalized, and psychopathologized, suddenly becomes subject to actual medical and psychological interrogation is quite striking. As *Rebel without a Cause* (again) dramatizes quite memorably, the post–World War II institution of psychology and psychiatry was one of the primary mechanisms through which nervous parents attempted to police and discipline their newly unruly sons and daughters. And as the Nicholas Ray film also makes plain, it wasn't on balance a successful campaign.

As with the analogy (which in time became much more than just an analogy) to St. Vitus dance, much of the onus of the psychological commentary on rock & roll in the popular press was to condemn the music as a "primitive" form of expression, seemingly one out of step with the ideology of American progress so powerful in postwar discourse. A June 1956 story in the *Washington Post*, for instance, quoted Dr. Jules Masserman, "psychology and neurology professor at Northwestern University," who describes rock & roll as "primitive quasi-music that can be traced back to prehistoric cultures"; in the same article, he compares it to "dionysian revels in Greece, where the god of sex (Priapus) and the god of drink (Bacchus) were feted in the same two-beat rhythms."[19] The discussion of the "primitivism" of rock & roll seems quite clearly, in retrospect, to have been a not-so-subtle way of addressing fears of violence, sex, and what was still known in some circles as "race mixing."

Indeed, the racism of some of these commentaries is, by contemporary standards, quite extraordinary:

What, precisely, is this rock-'n'-roll business, which so far from soothing the adolescent breast is said to agitate it and to incite the impressionable, like a kind of musical marajuana [*sic*], to rhythmic—or possibly duthyrambic [*sic*]—exploits of mayhem? ... The general musical pattern of rock-'n'-roll, they say, is about the way the familiar hillbilly music would be if it were recast into the rhythms of a Mau Mau war dance or the festive chorus of a tribe of Amazonian cannibals. Our consultants

also agreed that to confuse a naive and primitive form of music like rock-
'n'-roll is confused [*sic*] with such sophisticated and intricate noises as
those of Dixieland jazz is to betray a most shameful and lamentable
esthetic ignorance.[20]

These writers take the connection between the "primitive" rhythms of
rock & roll and the behavior of teenagers as axiomatic. According to an
editorial in *Music Journal* in February 1958, adolescents are "definitely
influenced in their lawlessness by this throwback to jungle rhythms.
Either it actually stirs them to orgies of sex and violence (as its model did
for the savages themselves), or they use it as an excuse for the removal of
all inhibitions and the complete disregard of the conventions of
decency."[21] That same year journalist Vance Packard—whose pop-sociology
book *The Hidden Persuaders* had been a surprise bestseller in 1957, teaching a popular audience to be hypervigilant for the manipulations and
predations of an increasingly secretive media network—appeared at a
Senate subcommittee hearing as a paid witness, explaining that rock &
roll "was inspired by what had been called race music modified to stir the
animal instincts in modern teenagers."[22]

First and foremost among those "animal instincts" were, of course, the
sexual instincts. Much cultural and musical history has been written about
the sexual panic occasioned in the establishment by rock & roll, such that
we probably do not need to rehearse that history in detail here. It is worth
reiterating, though, that in the 1950s American nervousness about rock &
roll, and anxieties about sexuality and race are never very far separated.
The first appearances of rock & roll in the early '50s provoked fears that
the earthy sexuality of the blues and R&B would escape from the African
American ghetto and cross over to win the hearts of white teenagers
(a fear that Alan Freed's movies like *Mister Rock and Roll* and *Don't Knock
the Rock*, featuring largely African American musical talent playing to
largely white audiences, did nothing to assuage). Hank Ballard and the
Midnighters' "Work with Me, Annie" (1954), for instance, is hardly the
raciest of race music records, yet it was rewritten and sanitized as "Dance
with Me, Henry" and covered by Georgia Gibbs in 1955 for mainstream
(white) America.

Martin and Segrave write about the way these sexual and racial anxieties
were articulated in various kinds of bans and boycotts against the music:

> By 1955 rock and roll had become firmly established in the national
> psyche. Its popularity grew exponentially. While 1954 had seen a surge

of complaints against the off-color music, 1955 produced a tidal wave of opposition, led by the trade papers, but then quickly picked up by various segments of the general population. For the trades it was a continuation of the attempts by the white, pop music ASCAP to remove its growing competitor, the black, rock and roll BMI.

Variety ran a three-part series in February and March on what they called "leer-ics," their term for alleged obscene lyrics.[23]

Those obscene lyrics—and really, Martin and Segrave's qualifier *alleged* isn't fair, because the lyrics to a large number of early rock & roll and R&B songs that were brought over from the blues tradition were unquestionably salacious—were the more troublesome because, in the vocal style that rock & roll was to make popular, they were often all but incomprehensible; as Dave Marsh has wonderfully documented in his book-length study of the 1963 Kingsmen's hit "Louie Louie," there's finally nothing smuttier that a song whose words your parents can't quite make out.[24] In February 1954, before the "Big Bang" of rock & roll had even sounded, Representative Ruth Thompson introduced legislation into Congress "to ban the mailing of certain records through the U.S. mail," to have "certain rock records ... added to the list of 'pornographic' materials that are illegal to send through the postal service."[25]

The teenager, then, was a figure representing the seemingly infinite potential of postwar America. The teen *could* be a force for good: study hard; date only the "right" kind of girls or boys; put a high premium on personal grooming—in short, keep both mind and body firmly in check. To promote this choice, a new, particularly didactic, art form came of age in the 1950s: the "social guidance" film, screened in high school classrooms across the country, with titles like *Last Date, Keep off the Grass, The Bottle and the Throttle,* and *Are You Popular?* As the feature-length *Reefer Madness* had for the previous generation, these ten-minute, 16mm morality tales probably served more effectively to reassure parents than to shape teenagers; they have by now traced the same trajectory as *Reefer Madness* as well, collected and viewed today largely as camp entertainment rather than moral tales. Marx was right: the first time, tragedy; the second time, farce.[26]

So too, guardians of the status quo, both musical and more broadly cultural, treated rock & roll sometimes as tragedy, but very often as farce. Their critiques follow a regular and somewhat predictable alternation between vilification of and condescension toward popular culture in general, and rock & roll in particular. Martin and Segrave tidily sum up this journalistic line, pointing out,

Articles appeared sporadically announcing the imminent demise of rock and roll music, pointing out that the fad was dying, musical tastes were changing, good music was making a comeback, and so on. One such story in *Variety* was headed "Onward 'n' Downward with R 'n' R." Most of these reports were exaggerated and represented wishful thinking on the part of the writers more than they mirrored reality. Others took a more active part in trying to hurry rock into the grave.[27]

William Coleman, writing in 1956 in the *Washington Post,* provides a representative example of this genre: "The tidal wave of Rock 'n' Roll rhythm that has engulfed teenagers for the past three years is on the ebb," he confidently announces. "The crest of the craze is past. Melody is back and, much to the relief of parents, the high school kids are sticking their heads above water to ask for sweet songs and danceable tunes."[28] Indeed one remarkable example of this kind of early death certificate comes from a most unlikely source—the venerable *Encyclopedia Britannica,* which wrote, using a hopeful past tense, in its *Book of the Year* for 1955: "The rock n' roll school in general concentrated on a minimum of melodic line and a maximum of rhythmic noise, deliberately competing with the artistic ideals of the jungle itself."[29]

Sometimes these attacks can seem quite harmless, especially taken out of context: the skill and talent of rock musicians are called into question in a lighthearted way, or the odd behaviors of teenaged rock & roll fans are described in a mock-anthropological style. Rock historian Charlie Gillett, for instance, describes a novelty record by Stan Freberg that attempted to throw a wet blanket on rock & roll—or, perhaps, just to throw in the towel and acknowledge defeat:

> "The Old Payola Roll Blues" came near the bone in 1960, presenting a cynical producer who stopped a kid out in the street, congratulated him on having such a marketable name ("Clyde Ankle"), and provoked a satisfactory vocal performance out of him by judicious use of a sharp stick. The record is probably the best available document of how badly the industry establishment felt about rock 'n' roll and the men who made money from it.[30]

Payola, of course, was no laughing matter, especially for New York disk jockey Alan Freed. The scandal over "pay for play" in the recording and radio industries, which was investigated by the FTC and a Senate sub-committee in 1960, resulted in a prison term for Freed and destroyed his career; he died five years later.[31] But for the older musical establishment, the scandal provided a relatively high moral ground from which the new music might be attacked, if only by association.

Columbia Records, which released Freberg's "The Old Payola Blues," was one of the most persistent of the established labels in attacking the upstart rock & roll. Columbia's Mitch Miller was among the first to start the rumor that rock was dead: both an accomplished musician (an oboist) and an arranger of "MOR" (middle-of-the road) music for groups like the Percy Faith Singers, Miller was made head of A&R at Columbia in 1950. Members of the older popular musical establishment, Miller repeatedly suggested, need not worry, because rock & roll would turn out to be only a "fad." In a story from the *Washington Post* in 1956, for instance, Miller is already claiming that the music is played out: "'Rock 'n' Roll is to music what comic books are to literature,' says Mitch Miller of Columbia Records. 'It's a fad, dictated by kids under 16 and played on the air away [*sic*] out of proportion to its musical importance. Quality show tunes are pushing Rock 'n' Roll back into its proper place.'"[32] Show tunes are still with us, of course, but so is rock & roll, and surely Columbia's head of A&R was wrong to suggest that show tunes were in the process of strangling rock in the popular music marketplace. Then again, Miller's prediction about a future for comic books was equally myopic.

But Miller's hopeful stumping for show tunes and "quality songs" was in fact a popular line of argument made against rock in the daily press during the '50s and early '60s. A handful of news items approached the topic by asking professional songwriters—hardly a dispassionate group!—their opinion of rock & roll:

> The term "rock 'n' roll" may soon once again be applied only to rowboats. Because the "good solid old-fashioned song" is coming back into its own again.
>
> So say an enormously successful pair of Tin Pan Alley creators of the "good solid old-fashioned song"—Al Hoffmann and Dick Manning.
>
> They dismiss the type of popular music called rock 'n' roll with "We can't write that bad." Furthermore, they say the public, even teen-agers, is beginning to weary of this current craze.[33]

Anyone suggesting in July 1956 that American teenagers were tiring of rock & roll either wasn't paying any attention or refused to believe the evidence; and surely the scare quotes that persist in the story around "good solid old-fashioned song" betray a kind of anxiety, a false bravado.

The riots accompanying the premieres of *Blackboard Jungle* in 1955, and Alan Freed's *Rock Around the Clock* the following year, provide at least one very crude indicator that rock & roll was still producing a reaction from America's (and Britain's) youth. Hoffmann and Manning's "Allegheny Moon" was a big hit for Patti Page in 1956, the number-two *Billboard* hit for the year; but Elvis's "Heartbreak Hotel" was number one. The rest, as they say, is history—and Elvis, not Hoffmann and Manning, wrote it (or rather, sang it).

In May 1957, the *Chicago Tribune* ran its version of this same story, talking with local songwriters Jack Fulton and Lois Steele, described in the article as "composers of such hits as 'Ivory Tower' and 'Wanted.'" ("Ivory Tower" was a big hit in 1956, peaking at number two; Perry Como had taken "Wanted" to number one back in 1954.) They join Mitch Miller in predicting the early death of rock & roll:

> The craze for rock 'n' roll is beginning to show signs of waning, Jack Fulton and Lois Steele, Chicago's best known song writers, asserted the other day. Over the luncheon table the composers … said the popular music pendulum is beginning to swing away from the sexy beat of rock 'n' roll and is moving again in the direction of sentiment, love, and romance.[34]

Using the time-honored propaganda principle (sometimes attributed to Josef Goebbels) that if you say something often enough it becomes true, the fading away of rock & roll was reported time and again, as if it could become a self-fulfilling prophecy by dint of sheer repetition.

The *Los Angeles Times* even went so far as to query Russell Arms, an actor who landed a regular gig performing on the 1950s edition of *Your Hit Parade*. Though not yet dead when the story was written in early 1958, certainly the show was on the ropes, yet Arms's opinion of rock's future was deemed worthy of consideration, his obvious conflict of interest notwithstanding:

> Is rock 'n' roll beginning to skid? Russell Arms thinks it is and he's one young singer who isn't sorry, although he has sung lots of it.
>
> For five years a regular on the weekly Hit Parade TV show, he was one of four interpreters of the nation's tastes in music and during that time these tastes leaned heavily to rock 'n' roll.
>
> Now he feels that this music form will not dominate the field as it has in the last few years and he thinks it is a healthy trend.[35]

In a variation of the famous joke about God and Nietzsche, it's *Your Hit Parade,* and not rock & roll, that's dead, and rock killed it. *Your Hit Parade,* which aired on Saturday nights for twenty-four years, finally signed off in April 1959. A relic of a musical era in which songs were more important to audiences than particular performers or arrangements, *Your Hit Parade* could not survive the paradigm shift ushered in by rock & roll—a shift bolstered by the availability of inexpensive recordings—that rendered generic "covers" of songs (like those performed by Arms and his colleagues) of no real commercial interest.

In a 2005 interview, Arms acknowledged the reasons that *Your Hit Parade,* and not rock & roll, died in 1959—reasons that he suggests were clear to anyone who was paying attention at the time:

> Rock & roll was the demise of the *Hit Parade,* because how many weeks in a row can you do—well, "Blue Suede Shoes," or any of the three-chord guitar songs that were on? Because some of them were really—were really pretty bad. We knew it right away; the performers knew it, and the production people knew it. Toward the end of the program, of the *Hit Parade* being on the air, it was kind of a tug of war between rock and good songs, Broadway show songs, just good songs that came along.[36]

Without necessarily assenting to the strict dichotomy Arms sets up between rock & roll and "good songs" (a dichotomy he inherits from pundits like Mitch Miller), it does seem clear that Arms, along with many others whose affective (and often financial) investments remained in the older model of popular music, was eager to accomplish the death of rock & roll.

In the most preposterous example that I've come across, a popular columnist for the *Washington Post,* John Crosby, quite literally mistakes the burgeoning of rock & roll for its demise:

> One thing about Elvis Presley, the convulsive shouter of rock 'n roll songs—if that's what they are: This may be the end of rock 'n' roll and just conceivably a return to musical sanity. I mean where do we go from Elvis Presley? ... Popular music has been in a tailspin for years now and I have hopes that with Presley it has touched bottom and will just have to start getting better.[37]

As we'll explore in chapter 3, a number of baby boomers are eager to suggest, for sometimes transparently personal reasons, that the death of Elvis Presley in 1977 marked as well the death of rock & roll, but Crosby is perhaps the only critic ever to suggest that the ascent of Elvis spelled "the end of rock 'n' roll." This confusion of growth with death suggests that a complex set of cultural contradictions is at work.

By the same token, the angriest, ugliest contribution to the genre belongs to William Leonard, writing in 1957 for the *Chicago Tribune*. His disdain fairly (or unfairly) oozes from the passage:

> Maybe you don't care when an ex-teenager like me tells you your rock 'n' roll music sounds like two firemen chopping down a door. That's your privilege. Just don't try to tell us grown folks, complete with the right to vote, that it's important, and history-making.
>
> You and your rock 'n' roll music and your "revolt against authority" are embarked on a children's crusade. For the great majority of you who don't know anything about history—the children's crusade ended nowhere, with all the kiddies dead.
>
> That's where your "revolt" is going. Relax for a few years, and, first thing you know, you'll be grown up.[38]

This short passage has the advantage of functioning as an anthology of nearly all the dismissive put-downs hurled at rock & roll in its early days. It manages, by turn, to deny any songwriting or instrumental expertise to rock & roll; to imply that teens have no regard for the opinions of adults (when in fact, rhetorically, it's the opposite that's graphically demonstrated here); to mock teens for not yet having the rights and privileges of adults (a fact for which it seems downright perverse to blame the teens); to suggest that no action or commitment on the part of a teen is of consequence; to belittle, through its scare quotes, the notion that rock & roll might represent a gesture of resistance to authority; to infantilize the newly coherent demographic group, teenagers, by referring to them as "children"; and to insult teens' intelligence by assuming they'd have no historical frame of reference for his oh-so-clever insult grounded in the children's crusade. And finally, perhaps most offensive of all, Leonard suggests, in his closing sentence, that if teens will just bide their time and ignore this rock & roll nonsense, one day they'll arrive at a complacent and self-satisfied middle age, like that of the author—that these "children" who play at revolting against authority will, one day (if they're lucky), become that very authority. "Hope I die before I get old," indeed.

When the suggestion that rock was already dead didn't carry the day, newspaper writers often moved on to argue that rock & roll was so devoid of redeeming artistic or social value that it ought anyway to be left for dead—although, as in the Leonard piece just cited, these two rhetorical strategies were hardly mutually exclusive. One argument that surfaces with great frequency in popular newspaper reporting during the '50s was to suggest, as a generation of popular critics had done regarding abstract expressionist painters like the recently deceased Jackson Pollock, that in effect "my child could have done this." Or worse, a machine could have done this, as in this dystopian vision from 1957:

> The coming of the machine age has been accompanied by considerable apprehension, some of it quite justified. One of the most apprehensive [*sic*] things we've heard lately concerns a machine that was exhibited at a conference of 100 scientists and mathematicians in Seattle.
>
> This machine, in addition to solving all kinds of complicated mathematical problems in a split second, has written a song. The scientists say that numbers of these machines can turn out popular songs far superior to those presently on the market, including rock 'n' roll numbers.
>
> It chills one's flesh to imagine hundreds of machines grinding out millions of rock 'n' roll selections. Even human producers have overloaded the market.
>
> And think of what it will do to the song-writing business. A lot of the glamour and romance will be lost; no one is going to work up much sympathy for a starving, lonely machine, or care whether it produces a hit or a miss.[39]

Rock & roll is a music *so* crude, *so* repetitive and predictable, *so* devoid of genius, that a machine could make it—a charge that, mutatis mutandis, we've heard again with great frequency in the eras of disco, electronica, and, now, rap.

A music requiring no talent or dedication to produce, rock & roll is also figured, with great frequency, as making very few demands on its listeners: it's a music for the intellectually challenged (or those who simply refuse to challenge themselves intellectually). The writer of the this piece, published in the *Christian Science Monitor* in February 1960, takes obvious glee in reporting a story titled "Gorilla Digs Rock 'n' Roll."

> The hulking creature [Bamboo, a gorilla in the Philadelphia zoo] has fallen in love with radio voices belting out tunes of far greater volume than meaning. What used to be a terrible-tempered 300 pounds of menace, every hair bristling misanthropically, is now a mere moony, gooey gorilla with ears cocked for hot numbers.... Bamboo showed up when the radio was on, and almost always when it was blaring rock 'n' roll.[40]

Here rock is not just primitive, but primate.

Thus was rock & roll systematically caricatured during its early years. To deal directly with the music's strengths, its appeal—even with its supposed aesthetic limitations—is most often thought to be infra dig; instead, it's lampooned. With (as yet) no real defenders with any cultural authority, the debate over rock & roll remained, at least until the British Invasion, on the level of ad hominem attack on both producers and consumers of the new music.

Another tactic employed with some regularity in the press was to interview a "respectable" musician about the current crop of rock & roll; these scenarios largely played out with quite predictable results, although the style of invective, the "individual color," could sometimes delight. A reporter for the *Los Angeles Times,* for instance, thought it would be instructive to query the then 80-year-old cellist Pablo Casals regarding his opinion of rock & roll. Casals's opinion is not surprising, but his vehemence is, suggesting that gorillas are perhaps the only appropriate audience for this antimusical music:

> You know the French have a word, *abrutissant,* for anything that brutal-izes man and tends to turn him into a beast. That's the word for this terrible, convulsive sound. It is against art, against life. It leads away from that exaltation and elevation of spirit that should spring naturally from all good music. A half century ago a phonograph, with a few scratchy records, automatically became the cultural center of the home. Today you have 500,000 splashy-colored juke-boxes wherever you look, and what are they? They're coin-catching meat-grinders which butcher melody and hack out sick rhythms and rancid lyrics.[41]

This same line of attack, though pursued with a great deal more erudition, energizes Martha Bayles's argument in *Hole in Our Soul* (which I discuss in chapter 4).

Although I'll later make clear my fundamental disagreement with Bayles, she provides a useful corrective to the sometimes over-the-top rhetoric of those who discern a conspiracy against rock & roll lurking in the 1950s. An otherwise extraordinary scholar of American popular music, Russell Sanjek, has written of the music industry joining forces with the government to wage the "War on Rock";[42] and while it's clear even from the little evidence we've examined thus far that various power-ful cultural figures opposed the mainstream success of rock sometimes with fury, sometimes with comedy, to imagine these isolated voices coordinating their efforts is perhaps to fall prey to the same paranoid mind-set that, during the '50s, saw rock & roll as a conspiracy, a plot. "They're compelling, these tales of gimlet-eyed rednecks and greedy-eyed capitalists plotting against rock 'n' roll," Bayles writes,

> not resting until they have precipitated not only the McCarthyesque payola hearings, but also the lonesome death of Alan Freed, the music's brave champion.... Not surprisingly, these images reinforce a second myth—that of a counterrevolution deliberately set in motion by a "system" terrified at the powerful social and political forces being unleashed by rock 'n' roll.[43]

While Bayles is certainly correct to point out the often overheated rhetoric of these pro-rock narratives, however, she does too simply dismiss the fact that many, and sometimes very powerful, voices tried to boo rock off the stage. Furthermore, Bayles's own rhetoric becomes more than a bit overheated: while Alan Freed did shamelessly portray himself as a martyr to the vulgar tastes of the censors, in movies like *Mister Rock 'n' Roll*, I can't recall ever seeing someone in print calling Freed anything like a "brave champion" of rock & roll—although one must admit he had instincts like no one else (if only he'd had Dick Clark's talent for self-preservation). Nonetheless, Bayles is right that conspiracy theorists err in suggesting there was an organized, orchestrated effort to kill rock & roll; the real opposition was much more incoherent than that.

Not everyone who believes that rock & roll met real, and serious, opposition during the '50s and '60s, however, is what Bayles calls a "mythologizer"; surely one can recognize the historical fact that rock & roll encountered huge resistance in the culture without descending into paranoid conspiracy theories. Bayles insists, however, on caricaturing this position:

> To most mythologizers, such as this *Rolling Stone* writer, the music didn't die, it was killed: "It is a measure of Fifties rock's genuine revolutionary potential (as opposed to the revolution-as-corporate-marketing-ploy so characteristic of the Sixties) that while Sixties rock eventually calmed down, was co-opted or snuffed itself out in heedless excess, Fifties rock & roll was *stopped*. Cold."[44]

It's worth remarking that Bayles has either overread or misread this passage by the *Rolling Stone* writer. As she quotes it, the passage doesn't say anything about who or what might have been *responsible* for stopping rock & roll cold in the '50s: it could have been those plane and car crashes, after all. Rock & roll *was* stopped cold—by fate, perhaps. The *Rolling Stone* writer certainly doesn't suggest that rock & roll was being persecuted, that it was "killed"; there's no conspiracy suggested here, although Bayles seems to see one. A fondness for conspiracy theories plagues much analysis of American popular culture, and rock critics are certainly not immune;[45] but hearing the suggestion of a conspiracy when in fact no such suggestion has been made—what shall we call that? Paranoid?

The attacks on rock & roll were no less real for their lack of central oversight: indeed, some of the most dramatic attacks were quite violent, if symbolic. The LP bonfires set across southern states after John Lennon had declared the Beatles "more popular than Jesus" in March 1966 are well known; less well remembered, perhaps, is a whole series of prohibitions of rock & records on radio stations during the late '50s and early '60s. In January 1958, for instance, the *New York Times* ran a story about a St. Louis radio station that was not simply pulling rock & roll records out of circulation but also destroying them, as if to purge the evil:

> Beginning tomorrow, Station KWK will play each such record in its library once—then break it with a sharp snap clearly audible to the listeners. The supply is expected to be exhausted in a week.
>
> Robert T. Convey, KWK president, who gave the order after conferring with his disk jockeys, said they were in agreement that rock 'n' roll "has dominated the music field long enough."
>
> Mr. Convey said he thought what had started as a novelty has "grown to such proportions as to alienate many adult listeners." "The majority of listeners will be surprised and pleased at how pleasant radio listening can be" (without rock 'n' roll), Mr. Convey said.[46]

Glenn Altschuler has written of the wave of U.S. cities banning rock & roll shows in the wake of *Blackboard Jungle*, observing wryly that "cities across the United States joined the 'ban wagon'";[47] such bans quickly moved from the ground to the air, as it were. Eric Nuzum notes that in October 1954,

> WDIA [Memphis] and several other large popular-music radio stations ban[ned] several songs for their sexually suggestive lyrics.... The station

periodically [ran] an on-air announcement saying, "WDIA, your goodwill station, in the interest of good citizenship, for the protection of morals and our American way of life, does not consider this record, [name of song], fit for broadcast on WDIA. We are sure all you listeners will agree with us."[48]

And listeners who did not agree with WDIA's ban of rock & roll were, presumably, un-American; the movement to suppress rock & roll was very quickly allied with issues of patriotism, a strategic move to which we'll return shortly.

Nuzum writes that in 1958,

The Mutual Broadcasting System drop[ped] all rock and roll records from its network music programs, calling it "distorted, monotonous, noisy music." To coincide with the ban, the network changes the title of its twenty-one hours of music programming from "Top 50" to "Pop 50." Songs removed from play include "Splish Splash" by Bobby Darin and Elvis Presley's "Hard Headed Woman."[49]

As part of this nationwide movement, WGN radio in Chicago banned "the big beat." "Rock 'n' roll has been grossly overexposed on radio," program manager Bruce Dennis explained. "The quality of the so-called 'hit' tunes seems to be growing progressively worse. On one current 'popular' record list eight out of ten numbers are trash not acceptable for radio presentation."[50] Out in Los Angeles, vigilante DJ Dick Whittinghill took a personal stand in late 1957, refusing to play any more rock & roll on his show. "Good music was coming back," Whittinghill explained in a familiar refrain, "and I was going to make sure my listeners heard it. I had to make a stand. I was tired of charts, surveys and talk of 'formula' radio approaching."[51]

At first, rock & roll was seen by the musical establishment as an inferior brand of music, a "fad"—what the Frankfurt School theorists would have called "kitsch." Because no product this inferior can long survive under market capitalism, the initial reaction of the establishment was simply to leave it alone, allow it to play itself out. Four or five years later, the arbiters of taste (in particular, radio programmers) are no longer sanguine about the fad passing quickly; the operative principle here might be, to paraphrase the economics maxim, "bad music drives out good." In the event, some market intervention was deemed necessary, and the next phase in the battle against rock & roll was a series of supply-side interventions, a perilous flirtation with the managed economy so despised in our communist enemies.

One interesting, long-term attempt to kill rock has been carried out by the preeminent new post–World War II medium: television. We've already looked a bit at how radio attempted, in some cases, to bring about the death of rock & roll by banning it from the airwaves; on the other hand, TV nearly killed rock & roll by using exactly the opposite strategy: welcoming it with open arms. In the mid-1950s, Pat Boone was the "spoonful of sugar" that helped the bitter "medicine" of rock 'n' roll go down "in a most delightful way." If Boone was a rock star, it was against his better judgment—his handlers made him a rock star almost against his will. As Charlie Gillett writes in his landmark study *The Sound of the City*,

> With the rest of middle-class America, Boone regarded rhythm and blues material as being rather crude, musically and lyrically ... he did not seem to be involved with the spirit of the musicians behind him, and he was important to rock 'n' roll only in the role he played bringing a little conservative respectability to the music's image.[52]

His attitude problem notwithstanding, Boone scored an astonishing string of thirty-eight top-forty hits during the '50s and early '60s; most of those, especially early in his career, were what used to be called "hijacked" hits—inoffensive cover versions of more volatile African American recordings by artists like Fats Domino, Ivory Joe Hunter, and Little Richard.[53]

In addition to putting a photogenic white face (or perhaps "whiteface") on a burgeoning African American popular music, Pat Boone is important to the story I want to tell for another, intimately related, reason. From 1957 to 1960 he hosted *The Pat Boone–Chevy Showroom* on ABC, the first television variety show to be hosted by a "rock star"; almost by default he became, for a rapidly expanding American TV audience, the human face of the inhuman music that was beginning to be called rock & roll. As Gillett writes, "Both large segments of the general public and the music industry establishment looked upon the growing popularity of rock 'n' roll with uneasiness. There were three main grounds for mistrust and complaint: the rock 'n' roll songs had too much sexuality (or, if not that, vulgarity), that the attitudes in them seemed to defy authority, and that the singers either were Negroes or sounded like Negroes."[54] Pat Boone, sporting a big smile and white bucks, was television's calming answer to all this menace.

Boone was the acceptable, polite, white version of a whole lotta unacceptable African American music, but he was also a more palatable alternative for "Elvis the Pelvis," the young man from Tupelo with "a chip on [his] shoulder and an H-bomb in [his] pants." Elvis's early television appearances are of course legendary, setting off a crisis of representation that still plagues televised rock & roll performances; but even Elvis wasn't able to withstand television's domestication. On July 1, 1956, Elvis was scheduled to appear on the Steve Allen show; Allen was nervous, however, about the growing criticism of Elvis's stage gyrations, and he sought a way to neutralize him. "We want to do a show the whole family can watch and enjoy," Allen said, by way of introducing his guest star, "and we always do, and tonight we're presenting Elvis Presley in his, heh heh, what you might call his first comeback—and at this time it gives me extreme pleasure to introduce the new Elvis Presley."[55] On the program, Elvis was dressed in a tuxedo and made to sing "Hound Dog," with faux-romantic devotion, to a female basset hound. In another segment of the show, Elvis played the part of the yokel Tumbleweed in a Western skit, "Range Roundup," with Steve Allen carrying a child's toy guitar as a prop. Six months later, for his second appearance on the Ed Sullivan show on January 6, 1957, Elvis was famously filmed exclusively from the waist up—though the shrieks of the live studio audience left little doubt about what was going on beneath the television frame. This, then, is the Faustian bargain: rock & roll is allowed onto prime-time TV only by mugging for the camera; when within the television frame, television makes the rules, and they're rules that favor television at the expense of rock & roll. In Elvis's appearances on both Ed Sullivan and, much more dramatically, Steve Allen, rock & roll was tamed, even humiliated.

Television has, from the very start, managed to present a sanitized, domesticated, disinfected vision of rock & roll—rock with all the fight gone out of it. It started with *The Pat Boone–Chevy Showroom;* Pat Boone on TV, like Pat Boone on the radio and onstage, is explicable only as a frightened response to the unruly spirit of African American rock & roll. It is for that reason perhaps an unfortunate coincidence that Pat Boone was name-checked in the first episode of *The Chris Isaak Show* back in 2001, because the specter of "Tutti Frutti" is probably not something contemporary pop-rock star Isaak wants consciously to invoke. Leaving a conciliatory message on the answering machine of his girlfriend, Isaak seeks to remind her of all they share, including the fact "We both really like Pat Boone—you like the metal Boone, I like the early Boone." "The metal Boone" is the somewhat preposterous Pat Boone who in 1997 recorded *In a Metal Mood,* a bizarre album of heavy-metal standards with big-band arrangements; the album has in some circles become a cheesy cult item (and Boone's rendition of Metallica's "Enter Sandman" is perhaps the most effective strategy ever devised by a parent to turn kids off heavy metal forever). And "the early Boone" is the barely effaced prototype of Isaak's stage persona.

TV's first "rock show" is entirely typical of the way rock has been presented on prime time—up to and including *The Chris Isaak Show.* What did rock look like on television in the '60s? First and foremost it looked like the Monkees, the first band formed precisely to star on prime-time TV (the show, and the band, were the brainchild of television producers Bert Schneider and Bob Rafelson); legend has it that Stephen Stills, later of the supergroup Crosby, Stills, and Nash (and sometimes Young), failed his screen test owing to the gap in his front teeth. The Monkees TV show ran from September 12, 1966, until March 18, 1968; starting a year earlier, and running a year later, the Beatles were produced for TV as a Saturday-morning cartoon series on ABC, with voice actors filling in for the Fab Four. Together, these shows served to suggest that rock & roll music (both the British Invasion and its domestic Doppelgänger), while sometimes unfamiliar and frightening, was actually made by a bunch of loveable mop tops, whose madcap high jinks posed no real threat to anyone. Thus nervous parents could watch and agree (unwittingly) with the verdict of the Who: "The kids are alright."

Something passing itself off as rock & roll was even more visible on TV during the '70s: viewers had their choice among Sonny & Cher, the Captain & Tennille, Marilyn McCoo & Billy Davis, Tony Orlando & Dawn, Donny & Marie—and those are only the ampersand shows. Wholesome, easy-listening acts like Glen Campbell, Mac Davis, Jim Stafford, Bobby Goldsboro, Helen Reddy, the Carpenters, and the Starland Vocal Band hosted musical variety shows that used lush orchestral arrangements to take the edge off of popular rock songs—not to mention the zany psychedelic rock & roll ethos of *Rowan & Martin's Laugh-In.* Again, in a weird manifestation of its televisual unconscious, *The Chris Isaak Show* seemed compelled to name-check Glen Campbell, the Osmonds, and the Carpenters in its earliest episodes: Isaak worries, for instance, that the only way he'll get on the bill at an upcoming Johnny Cash tribute is if Glen Campbell drops out, and he declares in a backstage conversation with the band, with no apparent trace of irony, "I dig the Carpenters." His phrasing can't help but evoke, for those of us old enough to remember it, Peter, Paul, and Mary's hokey folk (faux?) tribute to rock, "I Dig Rock and Roll Music."

In many ways the most interesting of the '70s TV rock confections— and one altogether atypical in its premise, a sitcom like the Monkees rather than a variety show—was the popular *The Partridge Family,* which aired for four seasons and was succeeded by a cartoon version, which ran a further year. *The Partridge Family* took TV's domestication of rock & roll to altogether new places, featuring as it did a band that was also a single-parent household, everything kept together by that most rockin' of all moms, Shirley Partridge (aka Shirley Jones). *The Partridge Family* began its run in the fall of 1970; by the fall of the next year J. Edgar Hoover and his FBI, under instruction from Richard Nixon, were compiling a file on John Lennon as part of a campaign to "neutralize" him—by deportation, if possible. If TV was busy making rock look harmless—literally domesticating rock, making it a comfortable part of the home (Latin, *domus,* house)—in other quarters, rock was still feared as a popular art form with genuinely revolutionary potential. Until TV can get past its fear—or is it envy?—of rock's raw vitality and vision, video will—with due respect to the Buggles—never kill the radio star.

Like television, rock & roll was thought by conservative cultural commentators of the 1950s to turn its consumers into mindless zombies—a metaphor to which we will now turn our attention. If the birth of rock was attended with even more anxiety than most, it was a nervousness related to a larger cultural anxiety manifest in such disparate phenomena as the McCarthy hearings and the boom in science fiction films during the 1950s, including the subgenre of the zombie film. As American studies scholars of the '50s have argued, the sci-fi films of the era betray, in more or less disguised form, a general cultural anxiety about "invasion," "infiltration," and the taking over of the nation (especially the nation's vulnerable youth) by "alien" forces, thus figuring in various forms the sinister culture of suspicion promoted by the red scare.

Invasion of the Body Snatchers (1955) is the locus classicus here, though I would argue as well for the importance of otherwise rather unimportant films like *The Zombies of Mora Tau* (1957), *Zombies of the Stratosphere* (1958), *Plan 9 from Outer Space* (1958), *Invisible Invaders* (1959), *Carnival of Souls* (1962), *Horror of Party Beach* (1963), and *The Incredibly Strange Creatures Who Stopped Living and Became Mixed-Up Zombies* (1963). Those "strange creatures" who inexplicably "stopped living and became mixed-up zombies" are on one level a symbolic representation of the '50s teen in thrall to rock & roll; and in an interesting variation of the "rock is dead" motif, these texts together suggest that rock is *undead*, which, for all practical purposes, amounts to the same thing. But there's a staggering thicket of other cultural concerns to work through before we can turn our attention fully to the rock zombies.

It is difficult to deal with these individual threads in an orderly, sequential manner. Fears of immanent nuclear holocaust combine and overlap with concerns about the encroachment of communism, the threat to America's youth posed by narcotics, and a culture of passivity and mindless conformity, summed up in William H. Whyte's 1956 bestseller *The Organization Man*—a passivity that seemed to some to be encouraged by contemporary mass culture. What ties all these concerns together is a real fear of infiltration and influence by an outside agent: whether the radioactive fallout from an atomic blast, the godless ideology of communism (which was believed to be communicated to American minds through a variety of media, including fluoridated drinking water), communism's powerful opponent the American corporation, or the psychoactive powers of illegal drugs. This fear of infiltration and infection is captured nicely in one of the last voice-overs from Dr. Miles Bennell in *Invasion of the Body Snatchers:*

> I've been afraid a lot of times in my life. But I didn't know the real meaning of fear until … until I kissed Becky. A moment's sleep and the girl I loved was an inhuman enemy, bent on my destruction. That moment's sleep was death to Becky's soul, just as it had been for Jack and Teddy and Dan Kaufmann, and all the rest. Their bodies were now hosts, harboring an alien form of life. A podden form, which to survive must take over every human man. So I ran, I ran, I ran as little Jimmy

Grimaldi had run the other day. My only hope was to get away from Santa Mira, to get to the highway, to warn the others of what was happening.[56]

It is a commonplace of current criticism to suggest that this film is a thinly veiled allegory of communism and McCarthyism in 1950s America. As Michael Rogin writes in *Ronald Reagan, The Movie,* 1950s popular film is "an unintentional register of anxiety," and, further, "the aliens of cold war science fiction are deliberate stand-ins for Communists."[57] This analysis applies not just to *Invasion of the Body Snatchers,* even if the cold war communist allegory reaches its zenith with that film; the 1953 film *Invaders from Mars,* for instance, similarly explores the quality of fear generated by aliens who take over the bodies and minds of good people, making it finally impossible to distinguish between "us" and "them." The "enemy within" had burrowed even further inside than we had previously imagined.

Aliens, in the form of both B-movie "space aliens" and the "illegal aliens" (undocumented workers) troubling U.S. borders, threatened to infiltrate Fortress America; so did communists and communism. J. Howard McGrath, Harry Truman's attorney general, declared in 1949, "Communists are everywhere—in factories, offices, butcher shops, on street corners, in private business, and each carries in himself the germs of death for society."[58] Even film was seen as an invasionary force, as Rogin cleverly discerns: "Film, as the HUAC investigators understood, was an intruder. It entered the unconscious of those who watched movies in darkened theaters throughout the land."[59]

For a time in the '50s, it seems that every perceived problem with the functioning of American culture was attributed by someone in public discourse to the nefarious influence of communism—an influence that was, in turn, allegorized through the figure of the zombie. The zombie was one of the preferred stand-ins for the soul of humankind under communism, in the reportage of the day. For instance, a conservative reader, writing in to Barry Goldwater's syndicated column to bemoan the influence of organized labor in the United States, asks rhetorically whether "we who believe in freedom and the right to choose for ourselves" must "become zombies and robots just so we can eat and have a roof over our heads?"[60] Labor unions practically turn the American worker into a communist; and communists, as we all know, are a mindless, faceless, undifferentiated mass of zombies.

Several nonfiction books appeared underscoring this menace. James Cameron's *Mandarin Red*, for instance, in the words of the *Los Angeles Times* reviewer, highlights the sacrifice of the individual in the name of the state:

> A trained observer like Cameron was equipped to see beyond that which was laid out in the mandarin red carpet style. New China is a drab, even terrifying, place and the enthusiasm recited like rote by those selected to talk to him has a curious, zombie-like quality.... "Why had they to produce me for [*sic*] who talked like Samuel Smiles? I think this deadening moral process is possibly necessary to the Communist development, but it brings out some sad features in the human personality."[61]

Likewise a review of Richard Condon's novel *The Manchurian Candidate*, reissued to coincide with the release of the 1962 Frank Sinatra film, notes that "Raymond Shaw, stepson of a U.S. Senator ... is transformed into a walking zombie by the Communists."[62]

Again and again, the communist enemy in the cold war is likened to a vast zombie army, and their influence, should it be allowed to extend to these shores through a relaxation of American vigilance, threatens to make zombies of freedom-loving American citizens everywhere. "Do You Want to Be a Zombie?" was the title of a talk delivered by Reverend Leslie F. Brandt to the Westminster Republican Federated Women in the summer of 1961, its title "referring to those who submit to Communist influence."[63] So too an incensed Ida Turner Siemers, writing in the *Chicago Tribune*, asserted,

> Our state department and our President do not even acknowledge our pleas for peace. The Kremlin has confused us and intimidated us and made Zombies out of us so that we do their bidding, wasting our strength in sporadic Koreas, bankrupting ourselves while we help Europeans who do business as usual with the Communists and letting Communists here at home confuse us so we do not know the difference between good and evil.[64]

Even at the outset of the 1960s—in words that would be incomprehensible had they been written just five years later—college students are praised in the *Washington Post* for their willingness to stand up and protest American government policy, because it demonstrates that they're responsible and thinking citizens, and not mindless proles:

Riots are always ugly; and the riot that took place last Friday in San Francisco's City Hall against the House Committee on Un-American Activities was no exception.... Students ought to protest against a Committee of Congress which has long since ceased to serve any purpose but punishment by publicity. It is heartening, despite the excesses, to see American students behaving once more like American students—and not like robots or zombies.[65]

This praise is repeated, even more improbably, almost two years later in the same newspaper, when students are praised for coming to Washington to protest U.S. foreign policy: "In coming to the Capital to express their views they are behaving responsibly in precisely the way that the founders of the American Republic intended citizens to behave. These are no automatons, robots or zombies. These are live students. And wherever there is life, there is hope."[66] Like the figure of St. Vitus dance when applied to rock & roll dancing, the figure of the zombie as a symbol of communist mind control took on a life of its own and, as befits its revenant status as the living dead, once awakened, it refused to die.

The 1956 date of *Invasion of the Body Snatchers* suggests the possibility, to a popular music scholar, that more than just the fear of communism is being figured in these '50s sci-fi films because all of the characteristics of the "body-snatched" automatons of Siegel's film were attributed as well, in public discourse, to rock & roll fans. Like the denizens of the film, America's youth were apparently in danger of being infiltrated by a malignant, alien force, which would rob them of all volition and individuality, turning them into passive receptors for the messages of their masters. Even phenomena seeming as far afield as the recently rediscovered classroom "mental hygiene" films from the period, and advertising for sanitation products like Lysterine and Lysol, betray a generalized anxiety regarding infection by the Other, which, while displaced onto space aliens, racial aliens, ethnic aliens, national aliens, communism, germs, and disease—or even the plague just beginning to be called "rock & roll"—was larger and much harder to locate and pin down than any of these other contagions.

In one familiar and oft-repeated scenario, the use of illegal drugs by the youth culture mimicked many of the features of communist "mind control" and was, as well, a favorite mechanism by which communists seized control of free, democratic American minds. At the close of a 1951 antidrug instructional film, *The Terrible Truth,* for instance, Judge William B. McKesson makes this appeal to his teen audience:

> Some say the Reds are promoting dope traffic in the United States to undermine national morale. They did it in China a few years back. It's certainly true that the increased use of narcotics plays right into their hands. But why not show everybody, including ourselves, that young American men and women have too much intelligence to make such a stupid, ghastly, tragic mistake.[67]

A mind on drugs has lost possession of itself and in this weakened state is vulnerable to communist propaganda; in McKesson's free-associative string of adjectives in the closing sentence, the word *ghastly,* etymologically related to *ghost,* again suggests that the drug user has been alienated from himself. In *Invasion of the Body Snatchers,* even letting one's guard down to sleep can prove fatal. The ingestion of narcotics, in this scheme, is simply inconceivable for a nation ever vigilant to the predations of communism.

When classical musician Pablo Casals wanted to impress on his interviewer the dread effects of rock & roll, he resorted, almost naturally, to a metaphorical description colored by the language of drug addiction (with an allusion to nuclear fallout serving as a kind of grace note at the end):

> You want to know what I think of that ... that ... abomination? ... Well, I think it is a disgrace. Poison put to sound. When I hear it I feel very sad not only for music but for the people who are addicted to it. I am also very sorry for America—that such a great country should have nothing better to pour into the expectant ear of mankind than this raucous distillation of the ugliness of our times—performed by juveniles for juveniles. It is a terrible and sardonic trick of fate that the children of the present century should have to grow up with their bodies under continual bombardment from atomic fallout and their souls exposed to rock 'n' roll.[68]

Here, in one paragraph, we have an entire litany of '50s neuroses: nuclear war, poisoning (literal, political, and spiritual), addiction, and juvenile delinquency. Rock & roll is an addiction, apparently, and like a narcotic it saps its "users" of the drive, imagination, and ingenuity that are the raw materials of American prosperity. Hence rock & roll, like marijuana or heroin, is ultimately un-American. No less careful a writer than

Gay Talese, in a 1957 article on wrestling in the *New York Times,* refers without apology or qualification to fans of rock & roll as "addicts."[69]

By the 1960s the association of rock & roll with communism had become a commonplace of the cultural right. According to a story in the *Washington Post,* Asa Carter, a leader in the Birmingham, Alabama, White Citizens Councils, "declared that Communist-infiltrated groups were waging a 'psychological warfare' for the minds of the children and teenagers of the United States by attempting to integrate the white with the Negro. He cited 'rock 'n roll' music as one of the most effective means of achieving this aim."[70] The idea that music made the populace more vulnerable to the siren song of authoritarian rule was not a new one; Frankfurt School cultural theorist Theodor Adorno, in his 1936 essay "On Jazz," had remarked on the ready adaptability of jazz, the youth music of an earlier generation, to the ends of totalitarianism.[71] Though a complex essay not easily excerpted, this passage is representative of this thread of Adorno's argument:

> The more deeply jazz penetrates society, the more reactionary elements it takes on, the more completely it is beholden to banality, and the less it will be able to tolerate freedom and the eruption of phantasy, until it finally glorifies repression itself as the incidental music to accompany the collective. The more democratic jazz is, the worse it becomes.

We have already seen this charge made against rock & roll in the 1957 *New York Times* story reporting on the psychological study likening rock & roll to St. Vitus dance, in which, in the fantasia of the writer, the ventriloquized bodies of American teens respond "Duce! Duce! Duce!" to the music's implicit demands; in a similar vein, a 1956 article in *Time* magazine suggested that rock & roll fans were like totalitarian subjects in their devotion to a powerful leader, with rock & roll shows "bear[ing] passing resemblance to Hitler's mass meetings."[72]

These associative arguments about rock & roll and repressive, totalitarian governments, generalized to suggest a link between rock & roll and communism, persisted into the '60s and even the '70s. "Spawned by the McCarthy-Era Communist hearings," Eric Nuzum reports,

> fear of Communism spread into criticism of music in the mid to late 1960s. In 1965, the Reverend David Noebel wrote a pamphlet titled *Communism, Hypnotism and The Beatles: An Analysis of the Communist*

Use of Music. Noebel claimed that the Beatles' music is part of a Communist plot to jam the nervous systems of young people.[73]

As late as 1970, Nuzum reports, "A group known as the Movement to Restore Democracy call[ed] for the banning of rock music to end the spread of socialism in America. Joseph R. Crow, speaking at a rally in Minneapolis, sa[id] that rock musicians are 'part of a Communist movement to incite revolution throughout the world.'"[74]

The image of the rock & roll fan as a mindless consumer, stripped of all active intelligence and volition in thrall to the music, is a familiar, indeed a persistent one; it enjoyed a powerful resurgence, for instance, during the heyday of trance and house music, and rave culture more generally, in the 1980s and '90s and has a perdurable icon in the image of the Grateful Dead fan, the "Deadhead." But as we pursue this image through the '50s, we quickly run into a contradiction, and one not easily resolved. For if one looks carefully at the various ways in which rock fans are portrayed in the popular media they seem, on the one hand, to be the most violent, willful, and rebellious of beings, while on the other they appear entirely passive, manipulable, and compliant. What happened to the riotous mobs of juvenile delinquents portrayed in early press coverage, their rage fueled by the insistent rhythms of rock & roll? Where did these pliant and mindless fans come from?

Dr. Joost A.M. Meerio, the associate in psychiatry at Columbia from whom we heard earlier in the chapter, opined that "rock 'n' roll is a sign of depersonalization of the individual, of ecstatic veneration of mental decline and passivity."[75] Evidence of this mass surrender of personhood comes from this report on rock & roll dancing moving uptown:

> Cafe society, having ignored rock 'n' roll for years, has suddenly, apparently by a process of mass hypnosis, embraced the teen-age craze.
>
> The elite of the social set and celebrities of show business have discovered a sensuous dance called the Twist, performed to rock 'n' roll, and are wallowing in it like converts to a new brand of voodoo....
>
> On the dance floor, couples gyrated in a joyless frenzy. They scrupulously confined themselves to a few inches of space apiece, but everyone was being jostled nonetheless....
>
> Several psychiatrists, questioned informally, seemed to agree that the rite approximated certain primitive, ritual dances.[76]

While early commentators saw in rock & roll a martial music that whipped impressionable young fans into a frenzy of violence and unbridled sexuality, news stories toward the end of the decade favored a different caricature: that of a passive, lifeless fan for whom any "frenzy" whatever would be impossible. The larger culture, then, shifted in its depiction from the association of rock & roll with the juvenile delinquent (like those running riot in *Blackboard Jungle* or represented by James Dean in *Rebel without a Cause*) to a new symbol of the rock fan: the teenage zombie. This changeover, however, is by no means neat or complete; like marijuana as depicted in *Reefer Madness,* rock & roll seems capable of provoking both profound passivity and extreme agitation and violence, by turns—sometimes in the same person.

It's a paradox that is touched on in the 1957 Jerry Warren film *Teenage Zombies.* The plot is comically broad in its allegorical designs, as summarized by this bemused contemporary reviewer:

> Four late adolescents … stumble onto a mysterious island where a female Mad Scientist … is preparing a new nerve gas designed to convert Americans into Zombies. (Why go to the extra trouble? Has she seen Hollywood Blvd. on a Saturday night?)
>
> The carelessly done script—also cleverly uncredited—mixes all this up with the Pentagon, an unnamed Cold War enemy (guess who?) and a traitorous American. Also to be noted are a large gorilla and the head Zombie who looks like Fidel Castro under heavy sedation.[77]

The nefarious Dr. Myra, having lured these teens onto her island, plans to use them as experimental subjects as she tests her latest serum for creating zombies (and thereby extending communist control over the free world). She locks up two of the teens in the test booth—a soundproof, glassed-in affair that looks exactly like a recording booth. However, when the zombie gas is introduced into the room, the drug has entirely opposite results on the two subjects:

> Dr. Myra: I worked out this highly concentrated buffer and tested it on four separate subjects.
> Agent #1: And the results?
> Dr. Myra: About zero consistency. Have a look. [*She reveals two experimental subjects in glass booth.*] One has no spark, nor desire for anything. The other teems with rage.[78]

Agitation or calm, either seems an equally likely outcome; but a cultural agent that produces such diverse results might with equal justification be said to have no real effect. Although hardly the first or most interesting of zombie films, *Teenage Zombies* provides a treasure trove for the cultural critic attempting to understand the complex intersection of cold war culture and youth culture in the 1950s.

The sheer volume of zombie movies produced during the period is noteworthy. Eighteen zombie films were released by the time of Elvis's first Sun Sessions, starting with Bela Lugosi's *White Zombie* in 1932; more than forty had been released by the start of the British Invasion. Indeed 1964, the year of the Beatles's first U.S. tour, was also the annus mirabilis of the zombie movie, with six feature films brought to the big screen.

The only film to date that explicitly links rock & roll and zombies is the schlocky 1985 film *Hard Rock Zombies,* a strange farce about a rock band playing a concert in a small hicktown populated by sex maniacs, various other freaks, and Hitler. In that film, heavy metal both raises the (un)dead and makes zombies of the band members. But these two taboos—zombies and rock & roll—did come within kissing distance in a 1963 B movie, *Horror of Party Beach,* with two other hot genres, the beach movie and surf music, thrown in for good measure. *Horror of Party Beach* is a truly awful movie, with bad writing, bad production, bad costumes, and a fantastic plot. This film is, above all else, about the need to keep teens in control; in one of the opening scenes, the "wild" girl Tina, hell-bent on having some fun, pays for it (as the genre demands) with her life. As a cop artlessly puts it, "Some kids were havin' a party. She wandered off; ten minutes later she was dead."

At that party, though, the kids are dancing on the beach to the rockin' surf sounds of the Del Aires as they play "The Zombie Stomp": "Oh, everybody do the zombie stomp / … / It's the livin' end." Ozzy Osbourne was later to do a song by the same name, but accept no substitutes: on the sands of *Party Beach,* rock & roll and the zombie forged an enduring alliance.

"The Zombie Stomp" is a dance-instruction song, along the lines of "The Loco-motion" or "The Twist." To perform it, partners move stiff-legged toward one another, arms extended like somnambulists, until their lithe young torsos crash into one another. "It's the livin' end"; it's also a pretty good send-up of the establishment stereotypes about rock & roll fans and their dancing, for no one could be more self-conscious, less passively controlled from without, than these dancers, taking their zombie instructions from the swingin' Del Aires.

During the cold war, rock & roll sometimes became the symbolic ground on which U.S. and Soviet partisans debated the relative merits of the two different economic systems and forms of government. One particularly interesting set of skirmishes began with the comments of Igor Moiseyev, the leader of a famous Moscow dance troupe that was making a tour of the United States. "The leading Soviet master of folk dancing," reported the *New York Times*,

> deplored today the attraction of the youth of his country to "the disgusting dynamism of rock 'n' role [*sic*] and the twist." While condemning the "poverty of thought and spirit" of Western dances, Mr. Moiseyev conceded that they were "attractive because they allow people to forget themselves, which is required apparently by those people who are leading joyless lives."[79]

This is cold war cultural diplomacy of a very familiar variety. Representing his nation, which boasts perhaps the most distinguished dance tradition in the world, Moiseyev cannot resist suggesting that it is American influences, rather than godless communism, that threatened to ruin his country's dance heritage. In Moiseyev's narrative, it is the free capitalists, rather than the "enslaved" communists, who lead "joyless lives" and require the diversions of rock & roll.

The reason that Moiseyev was asked for his opinion of rock & roll in the first place was that his Moiseyev Dancers were touring the United States with a program that culminated in—or descended into—a closing number known at first as "Back to the Monkeys" but that was later dubbed, simply, "Rock 'n' Roll." The *New York Times* reporter described the dance this way: "The closing number, which Warsaw audiences thought was wonderful, was a frantic, fifteen-minute parody of American rock 'n' roll. At the end, the dancers throw themselves into a human pyramid. A male dancer who mimes a dazed drug addict springs to the top of the pile. He is wearing a gorilla mask."[80] This piece would seem to have it all: frenzy, lethargy, addiction, even savagery. When the tour made its way to the West Coast six months later, the *Los Angeles Times* reported that the company had

> worked out a good natured parody on the American rock 'n' roll as an amusing encore.... At the first performance in New York's Metropolitan Opera House, the Associated Press reported that the "dancers made the standard American version of the rock 'n' roll seem like a minuet of zombies."[81]

In the United States, we say that the communists are zombies; the communists, on the other hand, say that U.S. rock & roll makes zombies out of American teenagers.

This closing routine and Moiseyev's comments were much discussed. Finally, a leading international figure arose to defend rock dancing—but not an American cultural ambassador. After all, how could any official representative of the United States go on record as defending a music so regularly and systematically stigmatized by America's cultural guardians? No, the rebuttal, or at least qualification, came from one of Moiseyev's comrades, the celebrated Russian poet Yevgeny Yevtushenko. "I have heard many terrible words about this dance [the Twist]," Yevtushenko wrote in *Literaturnaya Gazeta* (*Literary Gazette*):

> Someone has even said about it that it is a typical product of capitalist society. I personally do not understand how dances can be divided into capitalist and socialist.... I have seen how they dance the rock 'n' roll hysterically, as a parody—this is repulsive. But at the same time, in American workers' clubs they dance it simply and beautifully.[82]

We have seen that before the cries of "rock is dead" began in earnest, a substantial body of cultural material had evolved suggesting that, despite the vigorous assertion of liveliness embodied in the rock dancer, rock audiences were composed entirely of the living dead, the rock zombies. During the cold war, the zombie was the symbol of passive submission to centralized authority par excellence. The 1950s, of course, also saw the invention of the cocktail called the Zombie; with its 3 ounces of rum and 1 ounce of brandy, it was potent enough to render its consumer a mindless automaton.

As rock matured as a musical and cultural form, it increasingly took the criticisms of its opponents as the raw material for its own artistic expression. Naming a band the Kinks, for instance, or even more to the point the Zombies, was the equivalent of flipping the bird at those conservative critics who thought rock & roll musicians incapable of real thought—who thought them, in fact, to *be* zombies. One of rock & roll's early camp lunatics, Dave "Screaming Lord" Sutch, recorded a novelty track in 1961, a horror-rock platter called "My Big Black Coffin." In it, tongue firmly in cheek, he appropriates all the demonology rock had to that point called down on itself and turned it to profit: while "the zombies are a-dancin' / And the skeleton's prancin' / I get back into my big black coffin." Sutch wasn't much, and "My Big Black Coffin" looks, in retrospect, like a pretty harmless step along the way to Alice Cooper, Ozzy Osbourne, and Marilyn Manson; indeed, while the stakes have been raised to a significant degree, Sutch's strategy is precisely that of a Marilyn Manson title like *Antichrist Superstar*.

Perhaps the strangest artifact of the era of the teenage rock zombie, however, is one that is also terribly ambiguous. There was of course a popular British Invasion band called the Zombies, and their first big hit, which reached number two in the U.S. charts in 1964, was a brooding, minor-key composition called "She's Not There." When asked about the source of the band's name, founder Rod Argent has always said that it was simply the most off-the-wall thing they could think of: "I think in the end the reason we liked the Zombies was just that it sounded so unlike anything that people were using at that time."[82] I'd prefer to think, of course, that they were in some perhaps unconscious manner channeling the Zeitgeist, drawing unselfconsciously on all those clumsy zombie movies monopolizing drive-in screens during the '50s and early '60s. About the song "She's Not There," Argent has explained, quite plausibly, that it's about a failed romantic relationship.

But might there be a kind of late-'50s, early-'60s cultural unconscious at work in the song as well? The famous refrain concludes, "Her eyes were clear and bright / But she's not there." "She's not there": her voice and face familiar, she is to all outward appearances the same girl, but something essential has changed, has died. The song's protagonist finds himself in precisely the position of Dr. Miles Bennell in *Invasion of the Body Snatchers*, as he gradually realizes that Becky has been turned into a zombie.

Although all of the zombie films of the '50s and early '60s caution that they're not easy to kill, perhaps the Zombies singing farewell to a white zombie in the form of a pop song was enough to break the spell. For while we've seemingly never tired of declaring rock dead, the fad for suggesting that it's undead seems now to belong to rock & roll's history.

3

DEATH IN THE FOURTH ESTATE

If rock weren't widely believed to be dead, it's possible we'd be completely at a loss as to how to talk about it. Or rather, not how to *talk* about it but, specifically, how to *write* about it: as in painting, still lifes are easier for most of us than capturing a live subject, and rock & roll would be a lot easier to write about if it would just hold still. For rather different reasons, as we'll explore, both popular rock writers and journalists, on the one hand, and scholars writing about rock, on the other, share the same proclivity to declare rock dead as a doornail. In both outlets, the popular and the scholarly, the death of rock is the story of rock: it's rock writing's enabling, foundational myth.

It's probably important to admit, from the outset, that while these two different tendencies, in general terms, are easily recognizable, there is finally no rigorous way to differentiate "popular" writing from "scholarly" (or "academic") writing about rock & roll: the borders are porous. Popular rock & roll writing appears in mass-circulation magazines and newspapers like *Rolling Stone, Spin, Newsweek,* even the *New Yorker* and the *New York Times;* book-length popular treatments are published by trade presses, like Simon & Schuster or Henry Holt. Scholarly writing on rock, on the other hand, tends to appear in specialist academic journals devoted to music and musicology, cultural studies, or sometimes literary studies, broadly construed; the scholarly books on rock & roll are published by university and other scholarly presses, like Harvard University Press and Routledge. At the one extreme, then, we have popular books like Fred Goodman's *The Mansion on the Hill,* published by Vintage, or *The Vibe History of Hip-Hop* (Three Rivers Press/Crown Books), and at the other, Greil Marcus's *Lipstick Traces* (Harvard University Press) and Theodore Gracyk's *Rhythm and Noise* (Duke University Press).

But there's an awful lot of wiggle room within and between these categories, and some of the most vital voices in rock writing move, seemingly effortlessly, between the two. Greil Marcus is something like a test case, demonstrating the futility of trying to maintain any absolute distinction between the popular and the scholarly. Although not a member of the academy, Marcus wears his learning lightly; he has published both with tony academic presses like Harvard and in all the highest-profile periodical venues, from *Rolling Stone* to the *New York Times,* and even had a long gig as a regular columnist for the highbrow *Artforum.* Marcus's writing glibly crosses over, and crosses right back; to call him either a popular or a scholarly rock writer would be to deny at least half of what has made his voice one of the most important in the still burgeoning discourse of rock & roll writing. So although these two poles, popular and scholarly, are easy to identify in their pure forms, the most vital writing about rock & roll regularly partakes of both streams.

While there's finally no shining line separating popular from academic writing about rock & roll, the two modes do deploy the "rock is dead" rhetoric for rather different purposes. In popular writing, the announcement that "rock is dead" is always presented as if it were a scoop: "EXTRA, EXTRA! ROCK IS DEAD!" Although the support for this claim often takes the form of a thinly historicized narrative of decline and fall ("The Who, 1970, Leeds—now that was rock & roll!"), in fact journalistic claims of the death of rock & roll tend to be strangely ahistorical: the declaration of the death of rock will be made in 2006 with no idea that it was first uttered in 1956, long before the contemporary epigone thought to prove the bankruptcy of the music was even born. In popular writing, the death of rock is treated something like a hoary rumor for which definitive evidence is lacking (the Loch Ness monster, Area 51), and the newcomer to the debate gets his scoop by being the guy finally to produce evidence of the death ("Ashlee Simpson caught lip-synching on *Saturday Night Live!*"). Rock journalists and popular music writers tend to produce the most unnuanced, unembarrassed declarations of the death of rock, because they work under a different set of discursive expectations than do academic writers. They're also far more interested in making claims that will reach out and grab a reader—a trick that some of us academic writers are trying to learn, but without which a popular writer simply cannot survive.

When rock is declared dead in scholarly writing, on the other hand, we can ordinarily see some other agendas at work. Scholarly writers aren't so much interested in a scoop as in marking out turf, establishing an area of expertise: the intellectual version of what one Nirvana song dubs "Territorial Pissing." While a popular writer hopes to break a scoop and then move on to find another, the scholar tends to try to make a scoop the basis for an entire career. Scholarly rock writers are of course interested in what's new, interesting, challenging, but given the very different time frame of academic work (deadlines months and years off, rather than hours or days), what counts as urgent news in scholarly writing has already withstood at least a minor test of time in the very process of production. For instance, an essay that I had commissioned for a scholarly collection on rock & roll dealing with the public reputations of Courtney Love and Madonna had to be rewritten between its acceptance and publication of the collection, because both women had, in the interim, become mothers: this fact rather changed their images as feminist icons. Furthermore, almost all scholarly writers are essentially "moonlighters," writing at night, on the weekends, over the summer months—in and around their duties as teachers and members of the university community. The modes of scholarly production—both the intellectual work of researching and writing and the production schedules of academic presses—are ill suited to the mercurial nature of rock & roll.

Scholarly rock writers are inclined to historicize their observations, almost to a fault: humanities scholars especially are, by training and perhaps by disposition, inclined to favor phenomena that have already run their course. We write about dead authors, dead presidents, dead languages: it's perhaps not surprising, then, that when a generation of scholars first began to turn its attention to the music of its youth, it found it convenient to treat it as dead rather than living, as a corpse rather than as a still-vital body. I'll have more to say about this disturbing trend in the next chapter, when we turn our attention more fully to scholarly rock writers.

Keeping in mind the relative porosity of these categories, we'll examine some symptomatic popular and scholarly writing that maintains that rock is dead. What this exercise will ultimately confirm, I believe, is not how differently these two different discourses approach their subject but how, uncannily, they often seem to be singing from the same score. When it comes to declaring rock dead, no writing, it seems, is altogether scholarly. For now, we'll look at those writers whose insistence on the death of rock & roll garners far more attention: those who publish in the popular media.

One group of popular writers who declare rock to be dead seems to do so from a selfish, if predictable, motivation: the writers are partisans of an earlier genre of popular music, so that if R&B or jazz for them represents the pinnacle of American popular music, what follows must, perforce, represent a falling off. The first popular rock writer whose writing made this claim is also one whose best-known book is acknowledged a master-piece by everyone in the field: Charlie Gillett. In his 1970 study *The Sound of the City*, the notion of a "day the music died" (although not yet formu-lated in this memorable way by Don McLean) is quite literal: by February 1959, in Gillett's story, the only music with a right to the name "rock 'n' roll" (an orthography to which, as we've seen, Gillett attributes some importance) was for all intents and purposes dead:

> The mostly slow and unsympathetic response of the major companies to rock 'n' roll enabled independent companies to dictate the fate of the music. They brought it to life in 1953, force-fed it for five years, and left it for dead in 1958. Yet if they thought they could outlive the music which put them shoulder-to-shoulder with the majors, they were to dis-cover that nothing was so easy; within five years, most of the indies had themselves followed rock 'n' roll to an early grave.[1]

Given the contemporary public debates about the ethics of life support and forced feeding, Gillett's description of rock in a persistent vegetative state (or is it a minimally conscious state?) takes on an especially chilling edge: rock & roll is imagined as a kind of Frankenstein's monster that, having been brought to life and kept alive on artificial support, somehow lives on despite the plug being pulled.

Rock is dead—long live rock; in Gillett's somewhat idiosyncratic narra-tive, "rock 'n' roll" is replaced by "rock and roll," a pale and bloodless imi-tation, for the most part, and certainly no longer the vital "sound of the city." This is a story haunted, it seems, by the trope of the "rock zombie" (see chapter 2). Gillett continues,

Rock 'n' roll ran its course—inexplicably long to some, and disappoint-ingly brief to others. To those young people in its audience who did not know its source, rock 'n' roll seemed like a necessary, and surely eternal, part of urban life. The industry with typical sleight of hand, killed off the music but kept the name, so that virtually all popular music (with the exception of what came to be called "easy listening") was branded rock and roll. The abolition of the apostrophes was significant—the term looked more respectable, but sounded the same. Perfect.

Upon a younger generation than that which had discovered and insisted on the original rock 'n' roll was palmed off a sober substitute which carried nearly the same name. And, fittingly, a section of this new music was stuff that still went by the name "rhythm and blues," although much of it had slight connection with the pre-rock 'n' roll styles of the same name.[2]

Zombies, pod people, vampires: the entire dramatis personae of the 1950s B movie animates Gillett's sensationalistic story of rock's unnoticed demise.

Although he would doubtless be distressed by the rather blunt way in which this line of argument is carried on into the present day, we can also see quite clearly in Gillett's critique the seeds of the "blame the industry" argument so often encountered in contemporary rock writing. The inde-pendent record companies, Gillett suggests, cared about the music above and beyond any thought of profit, nurtured artists, took creative chances, and allowed the music to grow and thrive; scenting a good thing, the major labels assumed the job in a sort of hostile takeover, deployed a heartless marketplace logic, took profits where they could, and allowed the music to die. Rock & roll, in short, stopped being art and was reduced to the status of a mere commodity:

Almost all of the white singers—now called rock 'n' roll singers— stopped trying to represent personal experience in their records and dutifully sang the material that their producers handed to them, while the studio orchestra played the beat that enabled the company to pro-mote the product as rock 'n' roll. And rock 'n' roll, which had seemed to be a significant expression of the adolescent culture, was revealed to be as transitory as any other pop style, a fashion with no genuine cultural roots. Or that was how it appeared at the time, 1959 to 1963. Events after 1964 suggested that rock 'n' roll had cultural roots after all—that although the music industry lost interest in it, the audience who had bought the records did not, and kept listening to them.[3]

"No genuine cultural roots": the "invention" in the 1990s of the marketing category known as "roots music" responded quite cunningly to the hunger for authenticity among rock fans first articulated by Gillett more than a quarter century earlier.[4] If Gillett seems to a critical contemporary reader to draw somewhat arbitrary lines between rock & roll as art and rock & roll as commerce, he was clearly responding to a change in the "rock formation" that troubled him; the music he loved—the love of which clearly moved him to write *The Sound of the City*—was a form that had been one of rock & roll's vital sources. If Gillett mourned the death of rock & roll in *The Sound of the City*, it was because he thought it had lost its way, and he was genuinely concerned about it.

This is manifestly not the case with Donald Clarke's 1995 book *The Rise and Fall of Popular Music*. In Clarke's narrative, the "rise" of popular music culminates in American jazz, and the fall is what follows in its wake (in both senses of that word)—which is to say, rock & roll. Clarke is what once would have been called in jazz circles a "moldy fig"—the term was first applied to those critics who championed early forms of the music in the face of the bebop revolution of the late '40s, and now more generally to any conservative listener who resists change in music—and rock & roll never has a fighting chance in his chronicle. Described on the front jacket as "a narrative history from the Renaissance to rock 'n' roll," the book loses considerable energy and interest along the way, peaking with mid-twentieth-century jazz and evidencing little enthusiasm whatever for rock. As time marches on through the twentieth century, and especially as it passes midcentury, Clarke's tone becomes increasingly dour, his rhetoric increasingly reckless.

A chapter on jazz of the 1950s, with the pointed titled "Music for Grown-Ups," for instance, ends with these ominous lines:

> A few jazz records were selling tens of thousands, at a time when six thousand was a good average sale. But demographic and other changes were about to turn the whole business upside down: millions of kids who had never heard any jazz were about to wreak revenge on a business that had fed them pap ever since they could sit up and listen. The tragedy of rock 'n' roll is that it was forced to become more than music.[5]

Clarke's condescension is so thick you can cut it with a knife; commenting on the tragic accidents and misadventures that cut short or interrupted the careers of early rockers like Buddy Holly, Little Richard, Chuck Berry, Gene Vincent, and others, he writes, "None of these careers ever recovered its momentum. The music appeared to have been strangled in its cradle, yet it was too late: the rock generation had already been born." The tragedy, apparently, is not that the infant rock & roll was "strangled in its cradle"—here again, we see the practical coincidence of the birth and death of rock & roll reflected in Clarke's prose—but that (and here the metaphor breaks down entirely) the infant rock was able to reproduce *before* its death.

With the conclusion of each succeeding chapter, Clarke's predictions of immanent doom become increasingly dire. Given his overheated (and flatly illogical) rhetoric, we're not surprised to come across a chapter called "The Heat Death of Pop Music," in which Clarke pronounces: "Today's pop-rock is a paradigm of a society that has no values; it is ubiquitous even though the record companies admit that most of it loses money."[6] Rock & roll has somehow, in Clarke's free-floating invective, gone from detritus to absolute paradigm, and while elsewhere it is precisely rock's profitability that renders it suspect in Clarke's judgment, here its uneven sales suggest to Clarke that it ought no longer to exist. Rock & roll can't win for losing: for popular music to succeed or (with the exception of jazz) to fail as a commercial venture is equally evidence of its artistic bankruptcy. Closing the chapter subtly called "The Abdication of a Generation," Clarke writes, "What we now call pop music (defined as what we hear on the radio, and including a large amount of 'rock') was invented in the late 1950s in an artistic and commercial vacuum. Layers of this lucrative, faddish rubbish have been accumulating for over thirty years."[7]

Clarke's fulminations quickly degenerate into self-parody; it makes for an interesting rhetorical exercise simply to read the last paragraph or two of the last handful of chapters, where he is clearly just going through the motions, "covering" music that he is obliged to consider but for which he has no sympathy. The chapter on the 1960s, for instance, ends this way:

> Rock'n'roll had seemed to be over in 1960. A decade or so later rock should have been mercifully allowed to retire to the roadhouses of Austin and Lubbock. But by then there was far too much invested in it; the younger generations knew nothing else, and neither did the greedy music business. The pop charts of the last two decades have been dominated by the toys of technology and the sound of money talking.[8]

Picking on the rock music of the early 1970s, as Clarke proceeds to do, is rather like shooting fish in a barrel. In recent writing growing out of a more honest intellectual engagement with the music, however, the greater challenge has been to recover what was genuinely innovative and compelling about the music made, say, between the breakup of the Beatles and the first Sex Pistols 45.

Clarke, however, is content to recycle clichés about a body of music with which he betrays no real familiarity, never mind sympathy, while proceeding to contextualize it in a bizarre and idiosyncratic manner:

> In 1970 all we heard on the radio was the style of Glenn Miller and Tommy Dorsey, but played absurdly loud by synthesizers. That is what we have got now: rock'n'roll, the urban folk music of the working class, has been around for over forty years (if you count its hillbilly and rhythm and blues antecedents), and it is as inflated and worn out as minstrelsy was a century ago. The economic machine unwittingly created by the counterculture sees to it that pop-rock is aimed at each generation of new customers, yet each year not only is it of less musical value, but the market gets smaller, so it is not selling very well these days.[9]

The targets of Clarke's attack seem to be, based on external evidence (since he makes no mention of specific popular music artists), primarily progressive rock (Emerson, Lake, and Palmer; Genesis; Yes; Pink Floyd) and disco; which one of these genres is thought to be cannibalizing "the style of Glenn Miller and Tommy Dorsey" I can't even guess, unless the reference be to the one-off 1982 novelty song by Taco, a slick electronic cover of Irving Berlin's "Puttin' on the Ritz."

In a line of criticism that seems to be peculiarly Clarke's own, rock & roll is condemned for having moved beyond a narrow working-class audience and reached the middle class. However, this success cannot easily be dismissed as the death of the music, unless one accedes uncritically to some pretty counterintuitive notions about the popular music marketplace. "During the 1970s," Clarke writes, "it was already obvious that the original thrill that was rock'n'roll had become a middle-class marketplace, as many of the heroes of the 1960s became tax exiles and Elvis Presley killed himself with pills.... The answer to the problem of the death of rock'n'roll, since the younger generations knew nothing else, was more of it. Rock split into the rock generation's answer to Montovani on the one hand and punk rock on the other."[10]

Some of the most rewarding popular music scholarship of the past two decades has challenged the visceral dismissal of heavy metal by rock fans and critics anxious to police the borders of pop. I grew up with the same unthinking disdain for metal common to most middle-class suburban kids; and although he must certainly have come by it differently, Clarke, without ever condescending to consider an actual metal song, album, or band, issues one of his trademark offhand dismissals of this music: "Heavy metal is the ultimate in phoney rebellion, the logical and boring exaggeration of rock'n'roll as the music to make our parents angry, just as a logical and boring heat death of the universe may be the ultimate result of the original Big Bang."[11] A good editor, it seems to me, would have saved Clarke from himself here: nowhere in this very cranky book does he seem more like an aging hipster, pissed off that he just doesn't get it; furthermore, he seems not to understand that it's not about him. In a telling slip of the pen, he suggests that the function of metal is to make "our" parents angry when, if anyone, Clarke is himself the judgmental parent whom the music hopes to provoke. It has, it seems, succeeded admirably.

To cite just one more dismissive passage in a book rife with them, we can close our consideration of *The Rise and Fall of Popular Music* with the text's last three sentences: "We cultists who have money in our pockets can celebrate six centuries of music on records, but our own best musicians and composers live on hand-outs. Our republic has failed; our Caesars have feet of clay; the barbarians are inside the gates. We have seen the enemy; he is in the mirror."[12] The precise enumeration is somewhat captious, perhaps, but Clarke manages to pack, by my counting, fully six clichés into these three breathless last sentences; they function somewhat like the last thirty seconds of the Beatles' "A Day in the Life" without any of that song's style or artistry, both announcing and self-importantly enacting the death to which they bear witness.

Furthermore, it's not hard to hear in Clarke's fulminations the earlier, and far more influential, jeremiad of Allan Bloom in *The Closing of the American Mind*. Including Bloom in my discussion of popular writers is somewhat tendentious, given the fact that he was a professor of the humanities at the University of Chicago. But *The Closing of the American Mind* was a sensation in American publishing, a huge bestseller, and so a certain logic does support its inclusion here. This one book, although not primarily concerned with popular music, far outsold any other considered in this chapter and arguably had a far more profound effect on the cultural conversation about rock & roll.

Bloom writes (paradoxically) of rock as being both dead and deadly (again, the very paradox that animates the figure of the zombie) in his notorious chapter on music. Here, for instance, is his hysterical description of "a thirteen-year-old boy sitting in the living room of his family home doing his math assignment while wearing his Walkman headphones or watching MTV." Bloom calls him

> a pubescent child whose body throbs with orgasmic rhythms; whose feelings are made articulate in hymns to the joys of onanism or the kill-ing of parents; whose ambition is to win fame and wealth in imitating the drag-queen who makes the music. In short, [his] life is made into a nonstop, commercially prepackaged masturbational fantasy.[13]

It's hard to believe, although it's a difficult charge to prove, that either Bloom or Clarke has actually listened to any real representative sampling of the music they take it upon themselves to excoriate. As Michael Bérubé writes in another context (discussed in more detail below),

> The complaint that popular culture lacks quality is itself an indiscrimi-nate complaint, usually made by people who know little about popular culture and are unequipped to distinguish among its many textually dense and intellectually rewarding artifacts, on the one hand, and its innumerable, interchangeable Backstreet Boys and Spice Girls, on the other.[14]

In the pattern among conservative cultural critics that Gerald Graff elegantly demonstrated in *Beyond the Culture Wars* (a book meant, in part, to correct the myopic dyspepsia of conservative cultural commentators), Clarke's and Bloom's points of "reference" appear to be rumors about songs rather than actual songs. Bloom's attack on songs celebrating "the joys of onanism," for instance, seems to be an uncited reference to Tipper Gore's infamous attack on Prince's "Darling Nikki." And to give credit where credit is due, unlike Bloom, Gore did actually listen to *Purple Rain* before launching her crusade against it.[15]

There are many other critics in this category, many of whom, like Bloom, aren't primarily music writers. Contemporary popular music seems to provide irresistible fodder for those of the "Bloom and Gloom" school, who bemoan in general the licentious character of post–World War II American culture. For these, I briefly suggest, the declaration of the death of rock serves the function of killing off that which they wish dead. For while "rock is dead" is uttered with remorse by rock journalists and critics, who had (at some point in their lives, at least) made passionate affective investments in the music, the phrase has a tinny, triumphalist sound in the mouths of rock's conservative critics. As deployed by these critics, the phrase "rock is dead" is what speech-act theory would call a "performative": an utterance that seeks to bring about the state of affairs that it putatively describes. Thus *dead* in this usage isn't so much a *description* as a *decision:* rock is dead when we decide it's dead, and there's nothing it can do to change our minds. And should rock protest its death too vigorously—well, in that case, we'll simply have to have rock killed. Although it will come baaaack ....

The Dean of "Rock Is Dead" among popular writers—the journalist who, largely because of his depiction by Phillip Seymour Hoffman in Cameron Crowe's 2000 film *Almost Famous,* is perhaps currently more closely associated with the phrase than anyone else—is a cult favorite of the underground press, Lester Bangs. Bangs today enjoys an outsize reputation, out of proportion to what he actually wrote. He has had famous champions, including Greil Marcus and Jim DeRogatis, both accomplished rock writers. And the fact that Bangs's star faded so early (he died in 1982, at the age of thirty-three) has only helped to burnish his reputation among rock fans who are, as has been pointed out, like the Romantic poet John Keats, "half in love with easeful death." Following his short, wild life and tragic death, Bangs has been canonized by writers like Marcus and DeRogatis, as well as Crowe, and has assumed the role of patron saint of underground rock writing: St. Lester.[16]

In *Almost Famous,* which, for better or for worse, seems destined to define Bangs's image for a generation, the young would-be journalist William Miller has the chance to meet his role model, and Bangs attempts to throw cold water on William's dreams of being a rock writer: "You know, your writing is damned good. It's just a shame you missed out on rock & roll. It's over.... I mean, you got here just in time for the death rattle—last gasp—last grope." William replies, with a poise remarkable in a young teenager, "At least I'm here for that," but Bangs goes on, in the following scene, to describe both the death of rock and the modus operandi of its undoing. The killers of rock, in a conspiracy theory that is by now altogether too familiar, are the forces of corporatization—an ill-defined, shadowy "they":

> They're going to buy you drinks; you're going to meet girls; they're going to try to fly you places for free, offer you drugs. I know, it sounds great. These people are not your friends. You know, these are people who want you to write sanctimonious stories about the genius of rock stars; and they will ruin rock & roll, and strangle everything we love about it. You know, because they're trying to buy respectability for a form that is gloriously and righteously dumb. You know, you're smart enough to

know that. And the day it ceases to be dumb is the day it ceases to be real. Right? And then it just becomes an industry of cool. I'm telling you, you're coming along at a very dangerous time for rock & roll. The war is over. They won. And 99% of what passes for rock and roll these days—*silence* is more compelling.[17]

The Bangs character in *Almost Famous* singles out ambitious progressive-rock bands like Jethro Tull and Yes as the harbingers of a new, utterly bland form of rock & roll, being forced down the throats of passive fans by the corporate machinery. For Bangs, the commercial superstructure of rock is the enemy; artists must devote themselves to fighting off its advances, just as the critic must (while the industry, symbolized perhaps by Eric Carmen of the Raspberries, sings, in a representative corporate-homogenous song of the early '70s, "Please, baby, go all the way..."). In Bangs's Manichean view of the music business, the critic and the rock star are homologous (which makes Bangs's punk-rock birth name all the more fortuitous): both must be outlaws, fighting off the taint of commercial influence; the Bangs character reassures William, for instance, that he'll "never make any money," which is made to seem both a blessing and a curse. Bangs, in the film, argues that commercial forces will "ruin rock & roll." One might make an equally compelling argument that, to the contrary, it is the willful (and "dumb") disdain for the industry that most threatens to kill rock & roll; the very logic Bangs articulates perversely influenced both the suicide of Kurt Cobain and the wholesale piracy of music through illegal file sharing. Only through intelligent cooperation can both sides of the commercial equation get what they want.

What might be Bangs's more troubling legacy, for those of us interested in rock & roll as a cultural form, is his insistence that rock remain "dumb"—"gloriously and righteously dumb." His championship of garage-rock and American proto-punk is well known; but to suggest that the Count Five, the MC5, and the Guess Who are "authentic" rock acts, and bands like the Doors and Cream mere impostors—well, that seems to me cutting off rock's nose to spite its face. "Rock is basically an adolescent music," Bangs wrote in 1970,

> reflecting the rhythms, concerns and aspirations of a very specialized age group. It *can't* grow up—when it does, it turns into something else which may be just as valid but is still very different from the original. Personally I believe that real rock 'n' roll may be on the way out, just like adolescence as a relatively innocent transitional period is on the way out.

What we will have instead is a small island of new free music surrounded by some good reworkings of past idioms and a vast sargasso sea of absolute garbage.[18]

For Bangs, the day the music grew up is the day it died ("Hope I die before I get old"), and that seems to have occurred sometime in the late 1960s. He pinpoints the moment differently in different essays:

About 1970 … everything began to curdle into a bunch of wandering minstrels and balladic bards and other such shit which was already obsolete even then. Man, I used to get up in the morning in '65 and '66 and just *love* to turn on the radio, there was so much good jive wailing out. (1971)[19]

I don't know about you, but as far as I was concerned things started going downhill for rock around 1968; I'd date it from the ascendance of Cream, who were the first fake superstar band, the first sign of strain in what had crested in 1967. Ever since then things have just gotten worse, through Grand Funk and James Taylor and wonderful years like 1974, when the only thing interesting going on was Roxy Music, finally culminating last year in the ascendance of things like disco and jazz-rock, which are dead enough to suggest the end of popular music as anything more than room spray. (1977)[20]

In one version of the story, Bangs twits his readers by declaring, "Everybody should relax. Rock 'n' roll died when Elvis went down for his physical."[21]

In his gonzo style of rock journalism, Bangs was an important force early in the genre's history; his attempt to forge a writing voice as willful and dumb as that of Guess Who singer Burton Cummings was freeing to an entire generation of rock writers coming in his wake, paralleling in important ways the explorations of a fellow contributor to *Rolling Stone*, Hunter S. Thompson. But Bangs's essentialist definition of rock & roll as the music of retarded intelligence and arrested development hasn't always been salutary.

One of the popular rock writers to have carried on Bangs's argument about the corrosive influence of the rock-industrial complex is Fred Goodman, whose book *The Mansion on the Hill* is a diatribe not just against the industry but more specifically against one of the captains of the industry, David Geffen. In Goodman's narrative, Geffen is the serpent lurking in the tree of the knowledge of good and evil.[22] Goodman's study of, as his subtitle has it, "Dylan, Young, Geffen, Springsteen, and the head-on collision of rock and commerce" is bookended with laments for the death of rock & roll. He begins complaining about the deleterious influence of money on the music in his preface, before the book properly begins:

> [David] Geffen is a visionary businessman and a generous philanthropist, but I never sat around the shack behind the kitchen when I was sixteen trying to divine the secret language of business, and I don't know anyone else who did. I wasn't looking for the mansion on the hill, and I didn't think rock and roll was, either.
>
> Perhaps it is my own professional cynicism, but after years of covering the music business as a reporter, it is hard for me to believe that many of the performers who stake a claim to that old folk ethos—making music with conscience and meaning—are as interested in that message as they are in what it does for their careers as messengers.[23]

Goodman's nostalgic standard for authenticity in rock & roll is as smug as it is callow. It's also an essentially modernist position about the possible relations of art and commerce: to wit, none. To suggest that this is a fundamental misreading of the history of American popular music is just to scratch the surface; although it's another argument for another day, the long-term synergistic relationship of rock & roll and commodity culture is easily enough demonstrated. To take just one obvious example: what arrangement was more businesslike than that of the Brill Building composers who, while looking out for their careers and making their rent, somehow managed to write "Save the Last Dance for Me," "You've Lost That Lovin' Feeling," and "Walking in the Rain"?

Goodman, however, hews to the cartoonish vision of the rock industry as a vampire that sucks the creative juices from all who suffer its embrace. Thus he ends his book more or less where he had started:

> [Bruce Springsteen's] accepting rock as a business was an admission that its goals were no longer to question the assumptions of the mainstream entertainment industry but to reap its rewards. If rock was still as capable as any other commercial entertainment of expressing the most noble sentiments, the buyer had better beware that it was just that—entertainment—and not life and death.
>
> The passion and naiveté of the next generation remained rock's best hope. But those born of the underground had found the massive financial rewards of their commercial success overwhelming and misspent the

better part of the music's artistic currency. That failure of nerve had simply and tragically reduced rock's practical power to the power of the business.[24]

The "either–or" logic of this passage is representative of a larger weakness in Goodman's book, and it is a rhetoric that has become almost reflexive in rock writing: that a band or artist may be artistically successful or commercially successful—or neither—but never both. Hence, commercial success proves, ipso facto, artistic bankruptcy; whereas one might have thought, in a conversation not contaminated with the rhetoric of art versus commodification, that wide distribution of one's music was a desirable outcome in and of itself. So where Bangs had said that rock must remain stupid to remain real, Goodman adds "poor" (without taking away "stupid" or, as here, "naive"); neither formula provides a satisfactory space, however, for artistic creation within a capitalist economy.

In James Miller's 1999 *Flowers in the Dustbin,* we learn that hell hath no fury like an ex-rock critic—one who has moved on to a tenured position, although clearly Miller's is a popular, not a scholarly, book. Miller's book, ironically enough, takes its title from the Sex Pistols' song "God Save the Queen" (and more immediately from Neil Nehring's smart 1993 book of the same title on music and British youth culture—a book that treats youth culture with a respect and critical sophistication that Miller cannot seem to muster).[25] Miller's subtitle is, tellingly, "The Rise of Rock and Roll, 1947–1977." A little bit of digging reveals to the industrious reader that Miller was born in 1947—the very year that rock was born!—and, thus, turned thirty (and according to the hippie motto, officially too old to be trusted) in 1977—the very year that rock died! Ostensibly Miller's bookend dates refer to the release of Wynonie Harris's single "Good Rockin' Tonight" at the one end (the "birth of rock") and the death of Elvis at the other. But the suspicious convenience of Miller's arbitrarily declared death-of-rock is suggested by one customer at the Amazon.com website, who writes, "Rock died when Elvis did.... I didn't know!"[26] (And if Miller's right about the time and place of its death, one shudders to think what rock's last words were.) Miller, seemingly anticipating this criticism, acknowledges on the book's penultimate page, "Of course, the history of rock and roll did not stop when I stopped writing about it, any more than it stopped after Elvis Presley died."[27] That he senses the need for that last-minute apology suggests that the book tells a very different story.

One might as easily locate evidence of a major sea change in the rock formation, if not its demise, in the short unhappy life of the Sex Pistols (who played their first public set on November 6, 1975, and disbanded on January 14, 1978); to do so would be to suggest a source of ongoing vitality and intelligence in rock (despite the brute stupidity of some of its players), what Gina Arnold has called "punk in the present tense."[28] But Miller's having none of that. Having written about popular music for a period spanning four decades, and most recently having served a ten-year stint as *Newsweek*'s rock critic, Miller now finds the time ripe for his own postmortem of rock. Looking back on his work as "a professional journalist in the Seventies and Eighties," he writes,

> In many ways, it was an exhilarating time to be listening to popular music, and to be writing about rock and roll. Yet despite a steady stream of new artists and a relentless flood of publicity for every passing fad—and despite the fact that for many years I made my living by contributing to the flood of publicity—the rock world as I came to know it professionally seemed to me ever more stale, ever more predictable, ever more boring.[29]

This angst directly led to his decision to leave *Newsweek* in 1991, "in part because I no longer felt able to feign enthusiasm."[30] "Most of *my* friends," he goes on to write, "(discounting those who have continued to make their living by writing about, or recording, popular music) long ago stopped listening to rock."[31] There's a terminal confusion here of cause and effect, one that it will be more profitable to analyze in detail when talking about scholarly rock writing (see chapter 4). But the summary version of Miller's logic here is as follows: we've stopped listening, therefore it's dead. He feels free to announce, as early as page 19, that "rock now belongs to the past as much as to the future." Miller's eulogy for rock & roll is throughout, and transparently, a requiem for his own youth.

Miller's tone resembles that of Donald Clarke more closely than the other rock critics that we've considered here, and the resemblance is disappointing, because Miller has extraordinary credentials as both a rock & roll writer and as a scholar (a professor at the New School for Social Research in New York, he is the author of an award-winning critical biography of French philosopher Michel Foucault). But the argument in *Flowers in the Dustbin* is both tendentious and embarrassingly self-serving; because the music's fallen out of favor with *him,* all things serve to suggest its moribund state. For example, he makes an interesting observation about a Hollywood film that rock writers almost never take seriously: George Lucas's *American Graffiti*, which Miller describes as "a revealing exercise in nostalgia, suggesting that in the minds of many listeners no longer young, rock's golden age was already over."[32] This is a fair point, as far as it goes; Miller invokes the opening of *American Graffiti*, to the strains of Bill Haley's "Rock Around the Clock," to suggest its thin echo of the film that started America's rock & roll nervousness, *Blackboard Jungle,* and one thinks of Marx's maxim: the first time as tragedy, the second time as farce. But Miller is too quick to accept as evidence of rock's death the fact that a proto-baby boomer like Lucas (b. 1944) was willing, in 1973, to write rock off as the exclusive property of his youth.

Like Clarke, as his chronicle progresses, and the apogee of the music he loves recedes into the distance, Miller's writing becomes more and more nostalgic, more and more bitter, more and more reckless. In another potentially interesting reading, Miller suggests that the use of "oldies" on movie sound tracks is

> not an unmixed blessing. To anyone raised on the old songs on these soundtracks ... it sometimes seemed that a handful of recordings had achieved a new, and terrible, sort of immortality: and that these musical traces of youthful inspiration, products of whimsy preserved on tape, were fated to be repeated over and over again, in film after film, in ad after ad, aimed at the young, and at those who wished they still were, until nobody, young or old, could any longer experience the core feelings—of wonder and surprise—that rock and roll had really excited, once upon a time.[33]

The "once upon a time" at the end almost seems almost tongue in cheek, but only almost; it's as if Miller recognizes the rhetoric of nostalgia into which he's descending, but he can't stop himself. The music of his youth has ceased to be his exclusive property, and that of his peers, and is now broadly, crassly, commercially democratized. He seems, strangely enough, to wish that this broadly popular (and populist) form could be retained for an elite audience. Miller's horror at his music being made available to those who weren't around to witness its creation reminds me of my own peers who are distraught that their children, or students, are familiar only with cover versions of songs whose sacred originals belong to our generation—kids who think of "Behind Blue Eyes" as a Limp Bizkit song, for instance. The consumption of a secondhand artifact in lieu of the "real thing," according to this thinking, can be only a derivative kind of joy.

What this mind-set cannot fathom is that both the modes of production and the modes of consumption have shifted in a rock audience that has its iTunes delivered by means of an iPod, leaving unreconstructed baby boomers behind. I grew up believing, as a big brother like James Miller would have taught me, that albums are the minimal unit of rock art, not songs, and that compilations, "greatest hits," and (a later innovation) soundtrack albums are abominations, because they violate this minimal unit of artistic integrity. For boomers like Miller and me, rock & roll is intimately tied to its producers; one cruel joke my friends and I would sometimes spring on one another was to play an anonymous snippet of music, unidentified, and force the anxious listener to say whether it was "good" or not. (How can I know whether it's good if I don't know who it is? It was under such sadistic conditions that I first discovered my liking for Bruce Springsteen, a performer whom kids in my clique in high school "didn't like").

This torture holds no terror for my children. For them, the music makes its own argument in its own way; contemporary radio stations often play long sets of songs without identifying artists, and both my kids and I can sing entire songs, note perfect, without knowing who recorded them, sometimes without even knowing their titles. My own children and their generation devour soundtracks, compile and burn their own greatest hits, use the "shuffle" play on their CD players—a feature that I have always disdained. Indeed, as I write this, Apple's new iPod shuffle seems poised to make a killing—a musical listening device that forbids the user from choosing which of its tracks she'll hear. ("Meet iPod shuffle," the website welcomes, "the unpredictable new iPod. What will it play next?") This was not how I, or Miller, was taught to listen to music: but my kids have taught me otherwise, to respect, if not always to imitate, their modes of musical consumption. Miller refuses to learn—refuses to listen.[34]

The logic that undergirds Miller's argument in *Flowers in the Dustbin*— and that has infected others already discussed, and much more saliently ventriloquizes the writing of some others we've yet to consider—is what I'll call Boomer Triumphalism, a kind of generational ethnocentrism: "boomercentrism," an inability to take any but its own interests, values, and tastes as central, even "natural" and right. To the Boomer Triumphalist critic, *Sgt. Pepper's* isn't just one model for a satisfying rock album: it is the prototype, the quintessence.[35] It is what nineteenth-century literary and cultural critic Matthew Arnold would have called a critical "touchstone": a standard whose excellence cannot, need not, be proved (only accepted, as if by faith) but that then becomes the test of quality for all those texts that follow in the tradition. Open to a fault in so many areas, rock & roll is the great blind spot of the baby boom generation—the one area in which, for many of us, there is no room for debate or difference of opinion. We take the greatness of the music of the '60s as a fact—calling it "classic rock"—and move out from there.

In Miller's argument, this Boomer Triumphalism in part manifests itself as a kind of reverse populism: we know that the music has become degraded, he suggests, because so many now enjoy it. Regarding the spring of 1974—the same fateful year that Bangs in one essay identified as the most fallow in rock & roll history—Miller writes, "More people than ever before were listening to the music—on radio, on television, on film, and not least on recordings, which were selling in larger quantities than ever. But the more pervasive rock and roll became, the less it seemed to matter."[36] This isn't just the argument of indie versus industry that we've seen play out in Bangs, Goodman, and others, although certainly it reeks of that; indeed, the syntax of this sentence is telling, because it suggests that rock mattered *less* not in spite of being pervasive but precisely *because* it was so pervasive. For Miller, this relationship seems not paradoxical but logical: big sales mean little artistic import, and vice versa.

But there's something else going on here, something quite interesting: almost Lester Bangs in reverse. Bangs, remember, suggests that rock dies when it stops being stupid; Miller, here, argues instead that rock dies when it stops being smart, "difficult," and becomes, instead, accessible.[37] That in and of itself is a troubling, too-narrow definition of the power of rock & roll; but it also seems to be in direct contradiction of the elegiac ending to his book, in which he writes nostalgically of the populist roots of rock & roll:

> For years, I had celebrated rock in print as a vibrant, triumphant hybrid of everything interesting about America's older vernacular musical traditions. But as I watched the sun set and thought about Louis Armstrong and what had come after, I was assailed with a doubt. What if rock and roll, as it had evolved from Presley to U2, had destroyed the very musical sources of its own original vitality?[38]

It's finally impossible to determine whose side Miller's on: the rock elitists or the populists. And the reason, probably, is that his allegiances are to neither; rather, this is a boomer critic frustrated that the "music of today" has passed him by. The disdainful tone of the book's close is hard to miss: "Because people around the world want to hear this sound, and share in the fantasies it still excites, rock and roll is here to stay—for better; for worse; and for a long time to come."[39]

But to my mind the most disappointing recent baby-boomer defection is that of Nick Hornby, who has written the most significant book to date on the life of the rock fan, the 1996 novel (and 2000 film) *High Fidelity*. Hornby's novel celebrates the music made directly in the wake of (one is tempted to say, *during* the wake of) the death of rock & roll in 1977, as announced by James Miller, and the film adaptation does an intelligent job of updating the musical references from punk-era London to late '90s Chicago. In *High Fidelity*, novel and film, the protagonist Rob learns, by the story's end, how to embrace the music that his girl-friend Laura loves and to stop forcing his own music on her; he learns that—contrary to the creed he and his coworker at Championship Vinyl, Barry, embrace—it's not *what* you like but what you *are* like that finally matters. Rock & roll is at its most powerful, Hornby suggests in the novel's closing tableau on a club dance floor, when it's bridging cultural divides rather than creating them: bringing people together rather than being used to draw artificial divisions. "Come together right now over me," a wise man once sang; and we did, for a short while, but only after he'd been shot dead.

It's a lesson that Hornby seems not to have learned as well as his protagonist. Riding high on the success of the film released that spring, in October 2000 Hornby wrote a review essay of Radiohead's *Kid A* for the *New Yorker;* the album was the band's eagerly awaited follow-up to their huge 1997 critical success *OK Computer* (voted, rather preposterously, the greatest rock & roll album of all time by the readers of the British rock magazine *Q*). In terms that eerily echo the antimodernist stance of Philip Larkin in his writing on modern jazz, Hornby attacked *Kid A* for being—gulp!—*too challenging:*

> You have to work at albums like "Kid A." You have to sit at home night after night and give yourself over to the paranoid millennial atmosphere as you try to decipher elliptical snatches of lyrics and puzzle out how the titles ("Treefingers," "The National Anthem," and so on) might refer to the songs. In other words, you have to be sixteen. Anyone old enough to vote may find that he has competing demands for his time—a relation-ship, say, or a job, or buying food, or listening to another CD he picked up on the same day. He may also find himself shouting at the CD player, "Shut up! You're supposed to be a pop group!" (The music critics

who love "Kid A," one suspects, love it because their job forces them to consume music as a sixteen-year-old would. Don't trust any of them). I suspect that people who have been listening to rock music for decades will have exhausted the fund of trust they once might have had for "challenging" albums. "Kid A" demands the patience of the devoted; both patience and devotion become scarcer commodities once you start picking up a paycheck.[40]

Hornby's agenda here is so transparent as almost to beggar comment. Difficult music is ruled out of court; for us fortysomethings, Hornby argues, life's difficult enough without art challenging us as well. This is the man who wrote *High Fidelity*? Does he no longer listen to Elvis Costello, the performer who provided his novel's title and who, though he turned fifty last year, continues to make challenging music—to challenge himself and his audience?

There is a familiar ring to Hornby's argument. In his insistence that the music stay stupid, or at least not get too challenging, Hornby sounds like a genteel, self-satisfied Lester Bangs; in his suggestion that any critic pretending to like *Kid A* has been co-opted and infantilized—that any "adult" who pretends to like *Kid A* is guilty of a kind of aesthetic bad faith—he sounds like James Miller claiming that his only friends who still listen to rock & roll do so because it's their job. I'm only about eighteen months younger than Hornby—not much as these things go, between middle-aged men—but I think that *Kid A* is a staggering accomplishment. Even though I've "been listening to rock music for decades," I've somehow made time in my busy life to listen to it, over and over again.[41]

Unlike his character Dick in *High Fidelity*, who from the start is always looking for ways to use his music to make people happy—and unlike Rob and even, miraculously, the "snob obscurantist" Barry, both of whom see the light by the end of the novel—Hornby decided to use the status he'd achieved by the success of *High Fidelity* to set himself up as a dictator of pop taste. And the taste that's dictated is best described as "easy listening": nothing too challenging, nothing too grating, nothing that requires any focused attention. "Everything," as Radiohead's front man Thom Yorke sings on *Kid A*'s opening track, "in its right place." Indeed, Hornby seems to be calling for precisely what Moby supplied on his 2002 album *18*—"music for soccer moms," Moby once playfully called it (an especially apt sound track for Hornby; his most recent book to be made into a Hollywood movie is *Fever Pitch,* originally a nonfiction work about the English passion for football). Hornby seems to have become what the Kinks derisively called (in a track from their 1965 U.S. album *Kinkdom*) a "well respected man about town."

Now, each of us makes decisions every day—and seemingly more of them, as we reach middle age and have the kind of crowded quality to our lives that Hornby well describes—about what we have space and time for, and what we don't. Adult responsibilities squeeze out some of our youthful pleasures; William Wordsworth was exploring that calculus two hundred years ago in "Tintern Abbey." What's offensive about Hornby's posture in this first of his rock-pundit pieces, however, and has been perpetuated in everything that has followed, is the false universality he accords his own taste: "I don't find I have time for challenging music" becomes, imperceptibly, "challenging music isn't worth any adult's time."

Perhaps it's only because we're about the same age, but I would have liked to believe that Hornby was too young to be a curmudgeon. It was therefore tempting to chalk up this snide attack on some of the most intelligent music being made today to the fact that Hornby was writing for the *New Yorker* and had succumbed to the temptation to suck up to his older and more conservative readers; one can hardly avoid the sense that, in his *New Yorker* pieces and the other popular music writing that followed, Hornby is transformed somewhat by the knowledge that he's writing for an audience even more self-satisfied and curmudgeonly than he is.

But his first essay for the *New Yorker* proved to be just the beginning in a vein that Hornby's apparently still mining. Hornby is perfectly positioned to be a pop pundit: he's exactly young enough to seem hip to the establishment, while old enough now to be grumpy about the "young people" and the awful noise they listen to. Having written so insightfully and lovingly about the transformative power of rock & roll in *High Fidelity*, he has been promoted to the role of interpreter of the music for those outside the fold, a kind of impostor native informant. He's used that bully pulpit almost entirely to bully those who continue to stretch the boundaries of rock & roll, to explore the expressive limits of the music: those performers, one suspects, who make him feel bad because he's growing old, and not altogether gracefully. In short, Hornby seems to be suffering from an acute case of what Michael Bérubé has called the "Elvis Costello problem": "Popular culture is designed, after all," Bérubé writes, "to move products quickly, and that means short shelf lives for the vast majority of cultural artifacts in any genre, from good-quality paperbacks to eight-track tapes."[42] It's difficult for anyone to keep up with the mercurial trends of contemporary popular music, and we old guys look more ridiculous

trying to stay hip now than we did when we were in high school. This is
no easy game for middle-aged men.

After his trashing of *Kid A,* Hornby wrote a few more pieces for
the *New Yorker,* sometimes employing a brand of pseudoethnography
("listening to what the kids are listening to"), which culminated in a group
of personal appreciations (and depreciations) of roughly contemporary
"pop songs," published as *Songbook.*[43] In one sense, this collection is what
Radiohead, on another track of theirs, describe as "bulletproof": published
in a deluxe edition (with an accompanying CD) first by überhip Bay Area
publisher McSweeney's, and with all its proceeds benefiting two charities,
it's a tough book to criticize. Indeed, it was a finalist for the National
Book Critics Circle award in criticism for 2002.

There's much that's tender and lovely about *Songbook,* and its popular
and critical success is not difficult to understand. We need models of how
to talk about the emotional impact of the songs we love, without recourse
to a musicologist's technical vocabulary, and Hornby does this wonderfully. There's a winning simplicity and naïveté about the best of the
writing in *Songbook;* Hornby begins, in fact, by explaining that the appeal
of the best songs is sort of ineffable:

> When people ask me what music I like, I find it very difficult to reply,
> because they usually want names of people, and I can only give them song
> titles. And mostly all I have to say about these songs is that I love them,
> and want to sing along to them, and force other people to listen to them,
> and get cross when these other people don't like them as much as I do.[44]

But the sweetness of his appreciations is more than balanced by a
pervasive midlife dyspepsia: this book of appreciations turns out, on examination, to bear a closer resemblance to Guillaume Apollinaire's awarding of
"merde" (actually, "mer de") and *"rose"* in his 1913 manifesto *L'antitradition
futuriste,* or Wyndham Lewis and Ezra Pound's impulse to "Blast" and
"Bless" in the "Vorticist Manifesto" of the following year. For every song
that's given a *rose* by Hornby, there's another that's dismissed as pure *merde.*

Hornby's short entry on Led Zeppelin's "Heartbreaker," for example,
makes one of the ideological foundations of these reviews painfully clear:

> The thing I like most about rediscovering Led Zeppelin—and listening
> to the Chemical Brothers, and [Radiohead's] *The Bends*—is that they
> can no longer be comfortably accommodated into my life. So much of
> what you consume when you get older is about accommodation: I have

kids, and neighbours, and a partner who could quite happily never hear another blues-metal riff or a block-rockin' beat in her life; I have less time, less tolerance for bullshit, more interest in good taste, more confidence in my own judgement. The culture with which I surround myself is a reflection of my personality and the circumstances of my life, which is in part how it should be. In learning to do that, however, things get lost too, and one of the things that got lost—along with a taste for, I don't know, hospital dramas involving sick children, and experimental films—was Jimmy Page. The noise he makes is not who I am any more, but it's still a noise worth listening to; it's also a reminder that the attempt to grow up smart comes at a cost.[45]

Hornby is a pop critic masked with Matthew Arnold's face. The objections here, obviously, aren't aesthetic but have to do with "quality of life"; Led Zepplin's just not who Hornby *is* anymore, and after a certain point, apparently, one no longer has time to listen to music that doesn't unambiguously affirm one's place in the world. Hornby used to like Led Zepplin—then he grew up; the clear implication, of course, is that we will too, or should. I'll admit to being somewhat puzzled by his last sentence, however: the first half seems to acknowledge the importance of music that's "other" than ourselves, while the second half describes an adolescent infatuation with Jimmy Page as a kind of mistake to be learned from. It's hard to see how you can have it both ways.

Throughout *Songbook,* the songs Hornby considers are evaluated for their use value. No longer interested in picking up girls, or even, it seems, in growing as a person, Hornby can be quite ruthless with music that doesn't fit comfortably into his comfortable life:

Suicide's "Frankie Teardrop" is ten-and-a-half minutes of genuinely terrifying industrial noise, a sort of aural equivalent of *Eraserhead*.... "Frankie Teardrop" is in all sorts of ways an extraordinary piece of work, but I have no use for it now; I listened to it once upon a time, when I was in my twenties and my life was different, but I probably haven't played it for a good fifteen years, and I doubt whether I'll ever play it again.... I don't want to be terrified by art anymore.

It's a strange critical phenomenon that only works of art that are "edgy," or "scary," or "dangerous," are regarded as in any way noteworthy.[46]

"I have no use for it now": here, as throughout Hornby's nonfiction music writing, the egotism is just stunning. Mike Doughty, the lead singer of the now-defunct 1990s band Soul Coughing, attacks John

Strausbaugh (in an exchange that, to his credit, Strausbaugh quotes in his book) for betraying this quintessentially boomer attitude. Strausbaugh has just suggested that Mick Jagger and the Rolling Stones are too old for rock & roll and ought to quit, and Doughty replies, "There's *nothing* to tell this guy [Jagger] he should stop. Yours is a quintessentially baby-boomer argument: *I don't like this. This displeases me. Take it away. This is no good anymore.*"[47]

As for Hornby's other claim here—that only "dangerous" music warrants serious attention—I would briefly suggest that empirical support for it seems lacking. Look, for instance, at *Rolling Stone* magazine's top-fifty album list for 2004: it includes albums by Jimmy Buffett, Ray Charles, Franz Ferdinand, Jimmy Eat World, Loretta Lynn, Modest Mouse, Gwen Stefani—even the sound track for the remake of *Alfie*. A scary list, it's not. Serious music will always garner serious critical attention; a Beck album, say, will invite more engaged commentary than a Celine Dion album, whether it's an artistically successful record or not, if only because it's so much more ambitious. To that extent, Hornby's right. One thread running through Hornby's music journalism is the attempt to resurrect and revalue the degraded category of "pop"; it's an interesting project, and at times he makes it sound like a worthwhile one as well. But belittling music simply because it's edgy—because it refuses to be slight, trite—sounds like pop's rock envy breaking through. Toward the end of the essay on "Frankie Teardrop," Hornby breaks down and begs,

> It is important that we are occasionally, perhaps even frequently, depressed by books, challenged by films, shocked by paintings, maybe even disturbed by music. But do they have to do all these things all the time? Can't we let them console, uplift, inspire, move, cheer? Please? Just every now and then, when we've had a really shitty day?[48]

Everyone has experienced this need, of course, and certainly it's a need that pop is far better suited to meet than rock. But to pretend as Hornby does that there isn't loads of music out there, now as ever, to soothe the savage breast—well it's simply dishonest, isn't it?

Songbook is full of this kind of thing, and it's probably not productive to root through it all. At one point he enthuses, tongue perhaps in cheek, "Rubbishing our children's tastes is one of the few pleasures remaining to us as we become old, redundant and culturally marginalized";[49] rubbishing the majority of Gen X's music has been Hornby's MO for a few years now, but for him to claim to be any of these things—besides, perhaps, old—is disingenuous. In another of the essays, Hornby complains about all the free music he receives by post in his role as music writer (poor dear!) and brags that he does, in fact, judge these albums by their covers (and a number of other equally superficial criteria):

> Usual response to these unwanted CDs is as follows: a) I look at the cover. If it has a parental advisory sticker, and the artist is called something like Thuggy Breakskull, or PusShit, I don't play it.... Sometimes—although admittedly not often—I turn the CD over, to check the song titles, song lengths, occasionally the name of a producer, hoping something will lead me to conclude that this album is Not For Me—that it's for teens, or squares, or ravers, or headbangers, or conservatives, or anarchists, or just about anyone other than a forty-four-year-old who lives in North London and likes Nelly Furtado and Bruce Springsteen.[50]

So much for the community-building power of rock & roll. Many of us have areas in which we're disappointingly close-minded; few of us brag about it quite so publicly as this, creating cartoonish caricatures to stand in for the objects of our disdain (I got rid of my Thuggy Breakskull CDs *years* ago). Hornby's writing here is either untethered crankiness or pure pandering. In American consumer culture, many of us are concerned about being reduced to a set of demographic data and buying habits stored on a Wal-Mart computer; Hornby seems to long for it. Record company executives, please, stop sending this man music he already knows he won't like. It's just so, well … *exhausting*.

The most recent of Hornby's popular music essays (as of this writing) also descends to an embarrassing level of self-absorption. In a May 2004 op-ed essay for the *New York Times*, Hornby, seemingly attempting to temper some of his earlier remarks from the *New Yorker* and *Songbook*, writes,

> In truth, I don't care whether the music sounds new or old: I just want it to have ambition and exuberance, a lack of self-consciousness, a recognition of the redemptive power of noise, an acknowledgment that emotional intelligence is sometimes best articulated through a great chord change, rather than a furrowed brow.[51]

A number of desiderata are thrown out here—some of them familiar from Hornby's earlier writing, some of them in direct contradiction to those earlier essays. "Ambition"—isn't this precisely the petard on which Hornby hoisted *Kid A*? "Exuberance," check—though I'd hate to lose the lassitude of Cat Power (Chan Marshall) or Dizzee Rascal; "the redemptive power of noise"—well, amen to that. And yes, a great chord change does often trump carefully wrought lyrics, although Elvis Costello and Aimee Mann certainly have more of the latter than the former. Hornby has professed, at various times, to being fond of both.

Perhaps the most surprising requirement in Hornby's personal ad seeking new music, however, is his insistence on music that isn't "self-conscious." Though Hornby would no doubt resist the characterization—indeed, I resist making it—but the stigmatization of self-consciousness, in aesthetic discussion, is typically the bugaboo of the political right.[52] Self-consciousness in art is the side effect of a certain kind of critical intelligence, an awareness of the tradition within which one works; it is to acknowledge, in the famous formulation of Roland Barthes, that every text is but a tissue of quotations. It might even drive one—who knows?—to name one's novels self-consciously after the titles of pop songs (Elvis Costello's "High Fidelity," for instance, or maybe Patti Smith's "About a Boy").

The withering charge of self-consciousness is nothing new; Thomas Carlyle complained that it was the hallmark of his age in his 1831 review "Characteristics":

> Never since the beginning of Time was there, that we hear or read of, so intensely self-conscious a Society. Our whole relations to the Universe and to our fellow-man have become an Inquiry, a Doubt; nothing will go on of its own accord, and do its function quietly; but all things must be probed into, the whole working of man's world be anatomically studied.[53]

Self-conscious art isn't something that was swept in with postmodernism, say, or that demarcates a bright dividing line between the "classic rock" of Hornby's (and my) youth and the rock & roll that's being made today. Indeed, I have argued that the best rock & roll has always been blessed with a healthy, rather than a disabling, dose of self-consciousness.[54] Anyone who fervently wishes for a return to unself-conscious rock & roll is either wishing for a music that has never existed, *can* never exist, or ushering in an era of all Dave Matthews Band, all the time. Either way, we've got a problem.

Hornby seems to recognize the first of these dangers, at least, because he makes this disarming admission:

> I understand that I run the risk of being seen as yet another nostalgic old codger complaining about the state of contemporary music. And though it's true that I'm an old codger, and that I'm complaining about the state of contemporary music, I hope that I can wriggle out of the hole I'm digging for myself by moaning that, to me, contemporary rock music no longer sounds young—or at least, not young in that kind of joyous, uninhibited way. In some ways, it became way too grown-up and full of itself.[55]

Here we see the paradox of Boomer Triumphalism displayed, naked. Hornby is, by his own admission, getting old; a forty-four-year-old rock fan is like a forty-four-year-old baseball player, and there just aren't that many Nolan Ryans out there. But Hornby here manages to say that he's old but *not as old as the youngsters:* not only did his generation, my g-g-g-generation, when young, define for all time what "real" rock & roll would be but now that we're old, we'll even define what young is, what youth sounds like. To Hornby, it sounds like Marah and Nelly Furtado (remember her?); to me, it sounds like Radiohead, and Lucinda Williams, and Eminem, and even Led Zeppelin, old as they are—bands and performers who are precisely—like Nick Hornby—gloriously full of themselves.

I'll close this chapter by giving the last word to a contemporary rock performer, one whom, I suspect, Hornby would have little time for; certainly, she has little time for him. Three days after Hornby's essay appeared, the *Times* ran some letters of response, including this one from a fixture of the Olympia, Washington, music scene:

> It can't possibly have passed Nick Hornby's notice that rock 'n' roll doesn't go by rules. It's not especially fond of wistful old people, either. I'm not that psyched to stand at the rear of the show, trying to act dignified when some 19-year-old says, "That lady there must be here to pick up her kid." But I'd rather suffer that chagrin than wish the musical tastes of my youth on kids who want their own sound.
>
> Yeah, it's tough to be old and still love what's new and good about music, but we're not the arbiters of what's going on.
>
> It may be Mr. Hornby's version of excitement and exhilaration to hear a set end with the Righteous Brothers' "Little Latin Lupe Lu," but guess what? Rock 'n' roll doesn't care.
>
> **—Lois Maffeo**[56]

If our kids are embarrassed when we adopt "their" bands, attend "their" concerts—well, we embarrass ourselves when we dismiss them out of hand, according to criteria designed (though often not well) to ensure the dominance of the music we grew up with. As we'll see in chapter 4, this is hardly the prerogative of popular writers; indeed, I've started by looking at some representative popular writers in large part because in their work, these ideological machinations are relatively transparent. The scholars, I'll argue, far too often do the same thing—the difference being, we're far less honest about it.

4

THE DEATH OF ROCK IS
THE STORY OF ROCK, OR,
THE PEN IS MIGHTIER
THAN THE POWER CHORD

At the conference "Re•pre•sent•ing Rock," held at Duke University in the spring of 1997, Lawrence Grossberg, the Morris Davis Distinguished Professor of Communication Studies and Cultural Studies at the University of North Carolina, made in person the claim that he had been making more and more forcefully in print since 1984: that "rock's conditions of possibility have been transformed so radically as to suggest that rock's operating logic might no longer be either effective or possible"—that is, in vernacular terms, "rock & roll is dead."[1] To say that this verdict surprised his audience would be a gross understatement; various attendees of the conference had come by plane, train, and automobile to discuss their research on Stereolab, U2, Fugazi, Polly Jean Harvey, Radiohead—artists and bands generally thought not to be quite dead yet. Indeed, the first night of the conference featured a gig by the Chapel Hill band and indie sweethearts Superchunk, and the closing night featured a performance by a clearly undead Jon Langford, founding member of the British punk band the Mekons. (Sandwiched in between these was a reading by late-'70s New York punk figure Richard Hell; now, he *might* actually have been dead.)

Grossberg's evidence for rock & roll's morbidity was entirely anecdotal, which he passed off as "ethnographic." His "study" consisted of spending a good deal of time "hanging out" with high-school students during the summer two years earlier, and he could find no commonality in their listening habits or their tastes. And worse: he couldn't find anything to listen to in their music. In the published version of these remarks, Grossberg writes,

> The apparatus that is "becoming dominant" is a new mainstream that actually looks a lot like and is committed to much of the logic of the Top 40.... The fans within this formation may like some classic rock, some country, some punk, some disco, some rap, and so on. And because these fans happily switch among these genres from song to song, spending an evening with them can be a strange experience for someone who still lives within the becoming-residual formation.[2]

What Grossberg did, in effect, was to suggest (without stating it quite explicitly) that rock & roll was dead because he had stopped listening to it. Surely it's a rather remarkable—as well as imperial and imperious—gesture to suggest that something has died because one has lost interest in it, stopped paying careful attention. It's different in degree, perhaps, but not in kind from what Nick Hornby has been doing ever since *High Fidelity* hit the big screen.

Although it may seem like a stretch, Grossberg's offhand dismissal reminded me of the famous deathbed scene of Colonel Kurtz in Joseph Conrad's *Heart of Darkness* (1899/1902). Charlie Marlow's narration of Colonel Kurtz's "last words" is, I believe, a much misunderstood scene, although one nevertheless central to the modern imagination. Kurtz's words that close this tableau—"The horror! The horror!"—are among the most famous in modern literature and have been seen by subsequent commentators as a proleptic capsule summary of twentieth-century history. In Conrad's tale, Kurtz's words are brimming with implicit, potential meaning, but dramatically—in the context in which it's uttered—the phrase refers to nothing in particular: a tale told by an idiot, full of sound and fury, signifying nothing. What, precisely, the "horror" might be that haunts Kurtz we never hear from Kurtz's own lips.

But if we look at Conrad's text closely, we discover that "The horror! The horror!" aren't necessarily Kurtz's last words; rather, they're the last words that Marlow, our protagonist and narrator, the high-handed guardian of Kurtz's story, sticks around to hear. "The horror! The horror!" are

Kurtz's last words only because after they were uttered Marlow blew out his candle and left Kurtz's cabin; that is to say, they are the last words spoken by Kurtz that are heard by a white man. It is some time later, while eating his supper, that Marlow hears a native cabin boy announce, "Mistah Kurtz—he dead." When Kurtz actually died—and what, in fact, his last words were—neither Marlow nor we readers will ever know. What is clear, however, is that Marlow's claim to have been the sole audience for Kurtz's death and last words gives him an extraordinary amount of authority and power. Kurtz was dead *because* Marlow had stopped listening, and Marlow proceeds to spin out pages of interpretation of that oh-so-pregnant phrase, without Kurtz around to contradict him.

According to a similar (il)logic, rock & roll is often declared dead these days because scholars like Grossberg—and a disturbing number of other recent scholars—have stopped listening to anything new. The decision to stop listening to new music, for a music critic—or to stop watching new films, for a film critic, or to stop reading new texts, for a literary critic—is on one level a perfectly legitimate one. To delimit however arbitrarily the boundaries of one's expertise and interests creates a subject of manageable size within which one might hope to make a significant contribution: it's a fundamental scholarly move, the articulation of a scholarly "field." But surely there's a world of difference between admitting, for instance, "I don't find time to read a lot of contemporary poetry," on the one hand, and pronouncing, "No significant American poetry has been written since Robert Lowell," on the other. One is a candid admission of the (human, all too human) limitations of the critic; the other is an embarrassingly defensive parry from one who, finding himself out of sympathy with the art now being made, can find fault only with the new artists, seeing no fault in himself.

As I noted in chapter 3 in my discussion of popular writers on rock & roll, we're starting to see, I think, the rise of a new class of music writers. I've already called this group of writers Boomer Triumphalists; we might equally call them Rock Curmudgeons. When rock & roll first erupted in America's heartland with performers like Chuck Berry, Bill Haley, and Elvis Presley, there were plenty of critics hostile to it, as we've explored in chapter 2; one need hardly rehearse in great detail the avalanche of criticism that greeted this rough beast, seeing in rock an overturning of all the traditional values that had made this country great (and which made of Pat Boone such a sanitized retro-icon). These reactions are pretty predictable and can be seen throughout the history of art criticism; they are largely generational in character, the Fathers and Mothers calling for discipline among anarchic Sons and Daughters. Reviewing T.S. Eliot's early poem "The Love Song of J. Alfred Prufrock," for instance, literary curmudgeon par excellence Arthur Waugh charged that the generation of younger poets, "beginning with the declaration 'I knew my father well and he was a fool,' naturally proceeds to the convenient assumption that everything which seemed wise and true to the father must inevitably be false and foolish to the son."[3] Some of the late British poet Philip Larkin's most energetic prose was devoted to jazz criticism—but exclusively post–World War II jazz that was, to Larkin's taste, formless, chaotic, undisciplined: precisely the epithets applied by earlier critics to the first generation of jazz artists who comprise Larkin's pantheon.[4] So too, early criticism of Elvis seems to have held out at least the putative hope that he might be shamed back into the kind of polite white pap that Pat Boone was busy turning into a cottage industry. No less an authority than Frank Sinatra, never one to mince words, said of the King, "his kind of music is deplorable, a rancid-smelling aphrodisiac"[5]—in stark contrast, one assumes, to the sweet-smelling aphrodisiac the Chairman of the Board sent floating off phonographs all over the world in the wee small hours.

But for the Rock Curmudgeons, the rock & roll that gave my parents nightmares wasn't some monstrous perversion, a sudden, unprovoked disruption of the musical landscape they'd always known: it's the music of their youth, the musical paradigm through which all subsequent records would, perforce, be heard. For a kid born in the 1940s, the music of his "wonder years" would likely have included not only Elvis but also Ike Turner and his Kings of Rhythm, Bill Haley and his Comets, Little Richard, Chuck Berry, Jerry Lee Lewis, and Buddy Holly—plenty to get your folks upset. The rock & roll revolution had already been fought and won by the time the Rock Curmudgeons came of age as music consumers; and in this case, Gil Scott-Heron notwithstanding, the revolution *was* televised, with Elvis making his first appearance on the Dorsey Brothers' *Stage Show* on January 8, 1956.

A large cohort of rock critics who were born after World War II but before rock & roll see rock as something like an inheritance, a legacy—their birthright. Many of these critics, I suggest, are now suffering collectively from a kind of midlife crisis; declaring rock & roll dead means that they don't have to deal with the fact that it will go on, even thrive, without them.[6] Nearly all of the biggest names in rock criticism's first generation—Charlie Gillet, Greil Marcus, Simon Frith, Fred Goodman, James Miller, Lawrence Grossberg, and, most famously, as depicted in Cameron Crowe's film *Almost Famous,* Lester Bangs—have under various circumstances jumped on the bandwagon to declare rock dead; Robert Christgau must be nearly alone in having kept faith with the music he grew up with, demonstrating an admirable willingness to change as the music changed, rather than equating change with death. "Narrow-mindedness camouflaged as specialization is one reason journalists aver themselves weary of pop," Christgau has recently written—"or, more often, bitch that it's played out. Critically, my experience tells me this is a lie. Spending fourteen hours a day listening to it is my definition of nice work if you can get it, and it wouldn't be such a great job if there weren't always more avenues opening up, more small geniuses and cultural byways revealing themselves."[7]

It would, unfortunately, be rather easy to go through quite a long list of recent scholarly books and articles that trade on the putative death of rock (and relish in a kind of survivor's glee); one writer has described this phenomenon as "a certain unexamined 'death drive' at work in cultural/popular music studies."[8] Martha Bayles's 1994 *Hole in Our Soul: The Loss of Beauty and Meaning in American Popular Music* was an early harbinger of this recent resurgence; her tone is by turns wistful, elegiac, and indignant, as she proffers a by-now predictable narrative of decline and fall, "offering," as she describes it, "a cogent survey of the major strains [of American "popular music"] from spirituals and ragtime to blues, jazz, country, and gospel; from 1950s rock 'n' roll to 1960s rock; and from 1970s heavy metal, disco, and punk to MTV and rap today." Bayles's nostalgia is palpable: her analysis is undertheorized and only superficially historicized, and ultimately, as she admits from time to time, the book is simply a plea for "the music I admire most." "The central argument of *Hole in Our Soul,*" as she sums it up in the book's early pages, "is that the anarchistic, nihilistic impulses of perverse modernism have been grafted onto popular music, where they have not only undermined the Afro-American tradition, but also encouraged today's cult of obscenity, brutality, and sonic abuse."[9] Bayles's narrative arc is one that, as we have seen, is quite common in writing about the death of rock: of all its cultural versions, perhaps the most famous are found in the third chapter of Genesis and its greatest literary reimagining, John Milton's *Paradise Lost.* For Bayles, the heyday of Brill Building pop and early Motown are the Garden to which we strive to return.

I regret that in an earlier version of this argument, I represented *Hole in Our Soul* as much more simplistic than it in fact is.[10] In her letter to the editor responding to that essay, Bayles suggested that James Miller, Fred Goodman, and Nick Hornby would all be offended by being grouped with her as rock curmudgeons, because they all object to contemporary rock & roll for reasons different from hers. "I'm not offended, mind you," she wrote, "I'm used to being cast as the Church Lady of popular music by people who haven't read so much as the blurbs on my books." She closed by posing the question, "How does Dettmar know that I've stopped listening? He's never met me, never spoken to me, and offers no evidence from anything I've ever written."

In one sense, Bayles is right; while I have read and studied her book, and do think I've understood her argument, I have no firsthand knowledge of her listening habits. Nor, would I have thought, is that really the issue. It's perfectly possible for someone to listen with "ears closed," as Hornby seems to do with the newer Radiohead—or better, to listen while lashed to the mast, like Odysseus before the Sirens. When reading Allan Bloom's *The Closing of the American Mind* or Donald Clarke's *The Rise and Fall of Popular Music*, one can't help but wonder whether they've really listened to the music they excoriate. With Hornby and Bayles, there can be no question that they've listened, but I'm personally not convinced that they've actually *heard*. Indeed, in that same letter, Bayles "admits to being bored by Radiohead": "I've listened to a lot of 'paranoid millennial' music in my day, and the only 'work' I'd compare it to is dental work." This is the eternal complaint of parents about their children's music, and a timeless excuse, too, for not really listening; Lou Reed's infamous *Metal Machine Music* does in fact sound at times like a dentist's drill, but that curiosity aside, this analogy is the stuff of borscht-belt stand-up, not cultural criticism.

The first half of Bayles's book, as much as I disagree with her argument and her aesthetic judgments, is carefully researched and argued: a work of admirable scholarship. But the second half devolves very quickly into simple caricatures of the music for which she has neither patience nor sympathy—that is to say most post-1967 pop-rock; in this she resembles no one so much as Clarke. In lieu of the nuanced critique of her early chapters, her later chapter heads and subheads suggest the blunt critical instrument she wields: "Hard Rock Becomes a Hard Place"; "Bludgeoning the Blues"; "Soul Loses Its Soul"; "Loveless Love Men"; "Deliverance to Decadence: James Brown to P-Funk"; "Disco: Invasion of the Sex Robots"; "The Triumph of Perversity"; "Punk: The Great Avant-Garde

Swindle." Again, the parallel with Clarke is perhaps instructive (although Clarke's study was, in fact, published a year after Bayles's).

For all her sympathies for early-'60s African American music, Bayles (again, like Hornby) has none to spare for the most vital African American music of the past two decades: rap. Instead, as she writes on the book's first page,

> I argue that something has gone seriously wrong, both with the sound of popular music and with the sensibility it expresses. It is still possible to find the tough, affirmative spirit of the blues in contemporary forms. But increasingly, that spirit is rejected in favor of antimusical, antisocial antics that would be laughable if they weren't so offensive.[11]

Bayles is all for African American music—and for American popular music, more generally—when it dedicates itself to what would have been called, early in the last century, "uplifting the race"; this music, she writes in the book's closing sentence, "does not forget that its original purpose was to affirm the humanity of a people whose humanity was being denied."[12] The African American tradition in American popular music, in Bayles's analysis, finds its justification in the eternal affirmation of the human spirit (in language eerily reminiscent of the denunciation of rock in 1959 by Pablo Casals discussed earlier) and not in the exercise of the "radical autonomy" of art that she identifies with the legacy of Nietzsche: "The real break came in the late 1960s, when the counterculture went sour, and popular music began attracting people who were less interested in music than in using such a powerful medium for culturally radical purposes."[13] Although she maintains that Hornby would eschew the association, the two writers sound more and more alike the more carefully one listens to them. Their respective rejections of complex or ambitious rock in favor of pop, while arrived at by rather different routes (Bayles's philosophical and political, Hornby's narrowly personal), are in the end nearly indistinguishable. And both, I argue, consign rock & roll to a culturally subaltern role that would be fatal for today's musicians to accept. If it took either Hornby's or Bayles's advice, rock & roll really would be dead.

Few scholars have had a greater impact on the field of popular music studies than Simon Frith. In more than a quarter century of work, Frith has done as good a job as anyone in challenging the hegemony of the "mindless consumer/powerful marketing" explanation for the triumph of rock & roll and the perceived subsequent falling off of the music; marketing and marketing forces are always part of the equation for Frith, but they never quite explain the music's power in the life of a fan. In a representative recent statement, he writes, "It is certainly interesting to trace the commercial route that led Little Richard's 'Tutti Frutti' into my bedroom in a small town in North Yorkshire in 1956, but it is even more interesting—and rather more difficult—to explain why it instantly felt like music that made my life different."[14] Working (like Bayles) in full awareness of the work of the Frankfurt School critics but resisting their economic reductionism, Frith comes back time and again to the miracle of a highly mediated and commodified form of entertainment that somehow manages to be so—well, so entertaining, and at times perfectly transcendent.

Understanding that the history of rock & roll is full of contradictory threads, dead ends, and loose ends, Frith is a ready defender of a wide spectrum of musics—his most recent single-author book, *Performing Rites*, ranges from Ace of Base to X-Ray Spex—and preternaturally suspicious of claims that the rise of one kind of rock & roll, or the fall of another, signifies that "rock is dead."[15] In that study, for instance, Frith takes academic philosopher and music critic Roger Scruton to task for perpetuating simplistic, reductive pronouncements about contemporary popular music:

> Take this passage from Roger Scruton: "Consider modern pop music, and compare it with New Orleans Jazz and ragtime, and then with the folk music, African and American, from which both derive; you will see therein a tragic history of decline. Aggression and fragmentation have come in place of comfort and community."
>
> I find myself bristling at this not because of the aesthetic judgment involved (I'd happily argue for the value of aggression and fragmentation in art, certainly against comfort—and, given his brand of conservatism, "community" means something rather different to Scruton than it does to me), but because of Scruton's obvious ignorance of the musics mentioned. He presumes a high theorist can talk about the meaning of low music without listening to it at all.[16]

In important respects, Scruton's argument looks very much like that made by Martha Bayles (although, again, no one can accuse Bayles of not having done her homework, both listening and reading). By the same token, Scruton falls into the tired decline-and-fall narrative of popular music, wrought to its uttermost by Clarke, and like Clarke, Scruton seems to have come to his conclusions without suffering the mess and bother of actually listening to the music he dismisses. Of course, his criticism begs a real question: knowing "modern pop music" to be derivative and degraded, as Scruton (and Clarke) seems somehow intuitively to know, why would a man of wealth and taste waste his valuable time listening to it?

Frith is one of the senior statesmen of rock writers, born on the leading edge of the baby boom, and has been writing about rock & roll professionally for more than thirty years; he is currently teaching in the Department of Film and Media Studies at the University of Stirling, Scotland, and continues to write and lecture. Like Robert Christgau, Frith seems to have matured as a rock writer without having grown cranky. Indeed, it just may be that Frith is now more optimistic about the future of rock & roll than he was as a younger man. It's surprising, given his attack on Scruton, to find that Frith had, eight years earlier, fallen into just the same sort of "rock is dead" rhetoric that he's so keen at detecting in others. In the 1988 essay "Everything Counts," Frith wrote,

> I am now quite sure that the rock era is over. People will go on playing and enjoying rock music … but the music business is no longer organized around the selling of records or a particular sort of musical event to young people. The rock era—born around 1956 with Elvis Presley, peaking around 1967 with *Sgt. Pepper's,* dying around 1976 with the Sex Pistols—turned out to be a by-way in the development of twentieth-century popular music, rather than, as we thought at the time, any kind of mass cultural revolution.[17]

Few would disagree with Frith's clear-eyed assessment that rock & roll didn't change the world; those of us who had hopes that the 2004 "Rock the Vote" campaign might be effective in mobilizing young voters to effect "regime change" here in the United States were painfully reminded of this fact. But Frith was simply wrong to suggest that rock & roll is dead; if it didn't live up to the hype, neither, for the most part, did it participate in it. Sure, there are a handful of songs by performers like the Youngbloods ("Get Together," briefly parodied in the opening of Nirvana's "Territorial Pissings") and John Lennon ("Give Peace a Chance") suggesting, dewy-eyed, the revolutionary power of rock & roll; standing at the top of the world as young man is heady stuff, after all. But there are nearly as many powerful rock songs rejecting the idea out of hand: the Beatles's own "Revolution," for one, as well as R.E.M.'s "Revolution" (in which the band mocks both the Republican revolution and any facile equation of rock with revolt: "Your revolution is a silly idea, yeah").

The fact that the world today looks much the same as when rock & roll found it is not, ipso facto, evidence of the death of rock but rather evidence of a confusion about rock & roll's real provenance.

Robert Miklitsch, in one of the few truly thoughtful and scholarly considerations of the "death of rock," writes Frith off as one of the old guard who has thrown in the towel for rock: "For Frith as for Gillett, rock is now all but dead as a mass-cultural force because for all its revolutionary 'energy and excitement,' anger and anarchism, it has finally succumbed to those twin demons: capital and technology." "Frith's claim about the death of rock," Miklitsch continues, "also betrays, it seems to me, a not-so-residual romanticism where, as in the ideology of high modernism, the artist-as-rocker steadfastly refuses the Mephistophelian commercial temptations of late capitalism."[18] I argue, against Miklitsch, that Frith's position has actually shifted away from the simplistic version of rock history sometimes suggested in his earlier work. The two instances in Frith's work that Miklitsch points to are, first, the passage from "Everything Counts," the preface to his 1988 *Music for Pleasure,* quoted earlier, and, second, Frith's disillusionment with Bruce Springsteen's 1985 live album, articulated in that same volume. Miklitsch is certainly right to suggest that Frith is among that company who has declared the death of rock & roll, but when he writes that "for Frith … rock is *now* all but dead," he misrepresents the trajectory of Frith's work. As Bob Dylan sang back in 1964, "I was so much older then, / I'm younger than that now."

Miklitsch brings us back to the most significant of academic "rock is dead" writers, Lawrence Grossberg. If Miklitsch doesn't quite give Frith fair treatment, his critique of Grossberg is exact, and I think devastating; in some ways, it obviates the need to deal with the large volume of Grossberg's writing over the years touching on the death of rock & roll. In just a few pages, then, I'd like to discuss Grossberg's claims and Miklitsch's critique, and to suggest a few nuances that it seems to me Miklitsch might have missed.

Grossberg has written more, and thought more carefully, about the "death of rock" than any other writer. He has also frequently discussed the notion of "authenticity." These two concepts are closely related, because the perceived loss or waning of authenticity most often leads to the music being declared dead; certainly this formula holds true in most of Grossberg's own writing.[19] The "death of rock"—for Grossberg, as for me, always placed in scare quotes, although with varying degrees of acceptance or endorsement—has been an ongoing subject of scholarly investigation for more than twenty years now. Such a serious engagement calls out for an equally careful reading.

The first essay in which Grossberg entertains in a serious way the prospect that rock might be dying, or already be dead, is "Another Boring Day in Paradise: Rock and Roll and the Empowerment of Everyday Life," from 1984. Grossberg's rhetoric and perspective are measured; he writes, for instance, of rock & roll as "a historically locatable event," and one with an inevitable teleology: "changes in the contemporary context of everyday life," in other words, "raise the question of the impending 'disappearance' of rock and roll."[20] In this, the essay's first attempt to broach the subject, the "death of rock & roll" isn't an empirical fact, or even an opinion, but something like a syllogism: all historical events come to an end; rock & roll is a historical event; rock & roll must come to an end. This is presented as a neutral fact, to be neither celebrated nor mourned.

As the essay continues, it turns out that not only does rock & roll have a history but also rumors of the death of rock have a history:

> The rhetoric of the possible death of rock and roll has become increasingly common, entering the pages of such prestigious rock journals as *New York Rocker* and *New Musical Express;* it has become a common topic of conversation among rock and roll fans as well.
>   This is not the first time that such rhetoric has appeared. It was common in the early sixties, only to be put aside by the arrival of the Beatles, and in the mid-seventies, again to be put aside by the arrival of punk. Yet there is something unique about the present moment [1984] and the challenge it poses to the affective power of rock and roll.[21]

Grossberg wrestles with a structural contradiction. If rock & roll is a historical event, it will end; yet, because the rumors of its demise have been around, by his estimate, for over twenty years at the time this essay was written, it begins to sound as if the predictions of its death have been a bit overwrought. The solution that Grossberg arrives at—confirmed, I think, in the essay's conclusion—is that rock has in some important sense died but that it appears to many of its fans still to be alive. The structure of this argument will, I hope, sound familiar; for what Grossberg describes, in skeletal form (no pun intended), is the figure of the rock zombie explored in chapter 2. In Grossberg's argument, rock & roll is still going through the motions, but it lacks "affective power"; rock looks alive, but it's dead at the center: a zombie.

Grossberg concludes the essay in an apocalyptic tone:

> Apparently, rock and roll no longer generally serves the affective functions I have described.... The result is that new alliances are being formed, and the cultural and political ramifications of this moment in the history of rock and roll may be as powerful and interesting as those that emerged with the "birth" of rock and roll in fifties. Whether it is the "death" of rock and roll remains to be seen.[22]

To be fair, I must say that Grossberg, in the end, suspends judgment: "There's something happening here," as Stephen Stills sang in "For What It's Worth"; "what it is ain't exactly clear." Certainly to Grossberg, it *feels* like the death of rock & roll; the "affective functions" performed by rock are functions Grossberg knows precisely because he has experienced them, has been fed emotionally by rock in these ways. The rules of the game, the structure of the "rock formation," seem to have changed: whether for good or ill, he cannot say, although certainly the essay ends with a note of foreboding—one that would only grow louder over the next twenty years.

Grossberg used the occasion of the Andrew Ross and Patricia Rose collection *Microphone Fiends* to revisit his earlier writing on the "death of rock." In this essay, he begins the project (later continued in his introduction to the 1997 collection *Dancing in Spite of Myself*) of making somewhat less personal, somewhat less partisan, his writing to date on the topic. He begins by frankly distancing himself from the "death of rock" rhetoric: "I want to address some questions about the current state of the rock formation in the U.S., and about the possibility not so much of the death of rock as of rock becoming something else. Or in other words, in what sense is it meaningful—and in what sense could it be true—to talk about the death of rock."[23]

In the course of this essay—as Miklitsch has astutely pointed out—Grossberg treats the "death of rock & roll" as a rumor he has heard somewhere, rather than one he had been actively involved in perpetuating, and he attempts to shift to the role of impartial social scientist:

> If the rock formation had a beginning, it is also possible that it has an end or at least, a trajectory of disappearance.... We have to acknowledge at least the possibility that, as the conditions themselves become so radically transformed so as to be in some sense unrecognizable, then the transformations of the rock formation may similarly become significant enough that we can no longer credibly speak about the resulting formation as rock, as if its continuities were more powerful than its discontinuities.[24]

Whereas the best of Grossberg's criticism is marked by a strongly personal voice, he shifts in this essay to strangely passive constructions:

> Of course, talk about the death of rock is not a new theme. There is a long history of such discourses which goes back almost to the emergence of rock in the 1950s. Traditionally such arguments are about the power of rock to change its audience and the world, a power which, it is assumed, can be measured in the sounds themselves, in the audience's social marginality or in the imagined uses made of the music.[25]

"Of course ..."; "There is ..."; "Traditionally ...": the openings of these three sentences evidence an active eschewal of any of the positions espoused in the writing. If talk of the death of rock & roll "is not a new theme," then Grossberg is not to blame for bringing it up; he's not pursuing an agenda, after all, but just examining history. It is a history that is "just there," apparently, rather than one constructed by the historian (Grossberg); it is associated with a "tradition" of judging the power of rock by its potential to shape social and political structures, change lives. Does Grossberg agree with these as criteria for evaluating the health of the "rock formation"? Heaven only knows; the writing here is giving nothing away.

Grossberg then presents a particularly unnuanced version of the narrative of rock & roll choked by money, one from which he effectively distances himself, while giving it air time all the same: "Rock is judged dead to the extent that the commercial interests, the co-opted music, seem to be in control, not only of the market but of the music and the fans as well (leaving only a few die-hard fans on the margins, fanning the embers of authentic rock). In a sense then, in this rhetoric, rock is never dead, but consistently in the process of dying or of being killed."[26] Rock, in other words, has lost touch with the sources of its power and energy, lost sight of what's real, become inauthentic: a litany that Grossberg, more than any other rock writer, has taught us to repeat. Yet here, strangely, it's the word on the street: without source or citation, it's a kind of common knowledge for which Grossberg is just audience, not author.

It's a pretense to disinterestedness, however, that Grossberg isn't long able to maintain. If it's unclear earlier in the essay whether he accepts the rock = rebellion equation, the mask is dropped at the essay's close: "I would suggest that there is almost a complete absence of any compelling, viable images of rebellion.... I am not claiming that the rock formation has disappeared, only that we may be witnessing its transformation;

or perhaps it is better to say that the rock formation is giving ground to something else."[27] This is a claim we've heard from Grossberg before, of course—way back in 1984—only here, the suggestion that it's not death but a passing of the baton that he's witnessing is even less believable. By the time of this essay's publication in 1994, Grossberg is unwilling to say that "rock is dead" only because he knows that the declaration is always already surrounded by invisible quotation marks. Instead, he emphatically puts the quotation marks on himself—"it is said that 'rock is dead'"—in a self-protective gesture that his own writing would dub "authentic inauthenticity."

In a last-ditch attempt to get ahead of this wave, Grossberg once again reframes his project in the introduction to *Dancing in Spite of Myself*. It has been plausibly argued that a book bearing such a title, and with a picture of Grossberg dancing on the cover, suggests no real desire to "spite itself"; few critics have been as deeply enmeshed in a conversation with themselves as has Grossberg over the course of his writing. Frankly confessing his own "obsession with the notion that rock is dead," Grossberg writes that he treats it "not as a judgment I want to make about particular musical practices or variants of rock culture but as a discursive haunting within the rock formation and, of course, as a possible eventual reality."[28] Yet by this point—and although I'm selecting quite ruthlessly from among Grossberg's voluminous writing on the subject, the effect, I hope, will still come across—it's hard to avoid the feeling that Grossberg is spending a great deal of time and energy putting down, or at least interrogating, a rumor that he is, at the same time, the single most active agent in perpetuating. For more than twenty years, Grossberg has been writing about the "death of rock & roll," and now—or from the start, really—a slightly different discourse runs alongside this first one, to wit, "Why does everyone keep talking about the 'death of rock & roll'?" Seemingly desiring to be both within and without this particular phenomenon, both participant and objective (even bemused) observer, Grossberg's position is finally too compromised and self-contradictory to provide any real guidance.

Grossberg's most recent (as of this writing) work on the "death of rock," or the "becoming-residual" of the "rock formation,"[29] as he now prefers to describe it, takes on one final, perhaps surprising, wrinkle. In his introduction to *Dancing in Spite of Myself*, he had written, "If I am right that the rock formation is coming to an end or at least being replaced by something different enough that it must be recognized as such, if I am right that the rock formation is no longer as powerful a site of agency and articulation as it has been for the past forty years, then both the terms for analysis and the political stake in such studies will have to be rethought." This is the affirmative argument that Grossberg has made, at times, for his "obsession" with the "death of rock" narrative. "My interest in the death of rock," he writes, "is actually an interest in the possibility of rock's becoming something else, in an attempt to ask what a new politics might look like and how it might be discursively constructed." As we'll examine in a minute, Miklitsch has a rather different explanation to offer for Grossberg's continuing fascination; but this certainly follows from the politics that Grossberg articulates in essays like "Rockin' in Conservative Times" (1992).

At this point, however, Grossberg makes a quite unexpected turn. He argues that the tectonic shift in the rock formation has resulted, indirectly, in a professionalization of popular music studies that (again, in a familiar pattern) Grossberg has participated in quite actively and now disdains: "I think this partly explains the increasing professionalization and disciplinization of popular music studies, a development with which, I must admit, I have limited sympathy and in which I have no interest."[30] This remark, when coupled with statements to the effect that popular music studies is making no real progress and lags far behind other cultural studies work, begins to suggest an unattractively self-involved last chapter to Grossberg's long and distinguished career. In his better moments, he is able to imagine a different kind of future for rock & roll than the kind he would have imagined as a young fan—or rather, not to imagine that future, but to imagine that there could be a future that plays out according to different logics and values than those with which he is familiar. He tries, for instance, at the conclusion of his 2002 essay "Reflections of a Disappointed Popular Music Scholar": "I suppose one could argue that this is a nonutopian yet integrative apparatus (unlike the older apparatus, which tended to be utopian and disintegrative)," he begins. But just one sentence into this project of empathetically imagining a different trajectory for rock & roll, it seemingly breaks down:

Yet it is also cynical: if those within this apparatus embrace commodification without illusions, it is because they cannot imagine an outside to or a way out of commodification. If they continue to seek a way to challenge everyday life, they can only imagine such a challenge within an economy of pure entertainment as an isolatable fraction of their lives. They are no longer "dancing all over their blues" but "for their right to party," for some claim to feel and care, usually about each other rather than about the music, and to reassert some sense of their own agency, even if it is within an extraordinarily constricted space within their own lives.[31]

While intellectually Grossberg recognizes that his own experience as a fan of rock & roll doesn't describe the horizon of possible musical experiences, his "rock formation" is so closely integrated with his own sense of self—his own autobiography—he finally can't imagine it going any other way: there is a complete failure of imagination (suggested, in part, by his misleading quotation from the Beastie Boys' "Fight for Your Right"). He wants, seemingly, to believe in other possible futures—the spirit is willing, but the flesh is weak. "To be honest, I have yet to figure out the politics of style, and the relationship between image and performance, in this apparatus," he concludes with disarming candor.[32]

Yet it's an honesty that quietly, surreptitiously, has the effect of reinscribing Grossberg's baby-boomer vision of the rock formation. Willing to grant, in theory at least, that there is a structure of feeling available in contemporary popular music that may fulfill some, if not all, of the functions with which Grossberg is familiar from the traditional rock formation, Grossberg in effect repeats the filmic Lester Bangs's words to William in *Almost Famous:* "too bad you missed rock & roll."[33] And as for the Bangs character, this is only half true, because both men are only half sorry. After all, they got there in time to see it, to hear it. As a result, they have a measure of (sub)cultural capital to which those following in their wake have no access.

Robert Miklitsch, too, has questioned Grossberg's affective investment in the "death of rock" project. "Bluntly," Miklitsch writes—and by the end of his essay, he does indeed become quite blunt—

> it will not do, on one hand, to ruminate about the death of rock and, on the other hand, to confess [as Grossberg has] that one has "given too little attention to the changing shape of the rock formation across space and over time." Given this performative contradiction, though, what, one wonders, is driving Grossberg's "obsession" with the death of rock?[34]

It is unfortunate, I believe, that Miklitsch has given too little attention to the changing shape of Grossberg's thought over time. While examining texts that range throughout Grossberg's long critical career, Miklitsch does not deploy a historical lens in looking at the ways in which Grossberg's thought has shifted, if only slightly, during those nearly twenty years.

Miklitsch's essay is an experimental hybrid of autobiography and cultural theory, and perhaps because of his own autobiographical investments, he makes a perceptive observation about the intersection of Grossberg's own personal history and his theoretical work on popular music. Grossberg taught his first class on popular music, Miklitsch reminds us, in the same year that James Miller says that rock & roll died; he uses this handy coincidence to delve into the hidden logics of Grossberg's project on the death of rock.[35] "Could it be," Miklitsch wonders out loud,

> given that Grossberg began teaching rock in 1977 (when, presumably, the corpse was still warm), that the historical claim about the death of rock is, as it were, auto-biological; that, not to put too fine a point on it, the mantra about the death of rock is merely a projection of the white male baby-boomer's rapidly aging body?[36]

We've already spent some time, in chapter 3, looking at the suspicious logic of baby boomers who would for their own reasons declare rock dead; that logic is very little different for scholars or journalists. There's more than a whiff of self-interest in the pronouncements of the death of rock as issued by these boomer critics: while by no means all the rock critics born in the decade 1943 to 1952 have gone sour on the music, the majority of those who think rock is dead—and who are busy publishing and popularizing this opinion—were born within five years of Wynonie Harris's "Good Rockin' Tonight." These critics are first-wave baby boomers and collectively have helped to create an influential myth about rock & roll that we see played out in broad strokes in films like *The Big Chill*. While there are many ways to tell the story of rock & roll, it is the boomers' narrative of rock as the authentic sound of freedom that remains dominant.

There's a lesson in all of this for all of us who do intellectual work. Archimedes famously declared, "Give me a place to stand and a lever long enough and I will move the world"; it's an attractive proposition, but for the critic, it's death. As cultural critics, we can't afford the luxury of standing still: the river of culture, as W.B. Yeats (echoing another Greek thinker, Heraclitus) reminds us, "changes minute by minute." If we establish a comfortable position on the bank, while pretending to be "down with" the river, we'll never really understand what's happening. Cultural historians might require that "place to stand" to do their work, but cultural critics must be willing, as the Limp Bizkit song has it (and the CCR song before that), to keep rollin', rollin', rollin'. It's a difficult task, but not impossible; the elder statesman of the boomer rock critics, Robert Christgau (b. 1942), has managed to keep listening, thinking, talking, and writing intelligently about the vital music that continues to be made.

Once public intellectuals have staked out their turf, and shaped and refined a lever—a style of reading, theoretical apparatus, thesis, habitual way of seeing—they can, if not move the world, at least accrue some measure of intellectual capital. One can ride a good, generalizable thesis about the functioning of culture for a full (if not entirely rewarding) career. The real challenge posed by a band like Radiohead, it seems to me, is to remain willing always to reexamine the ground beneath our feet and the appropriateness of the tools we'd employ. If rock is in fact about freedom, the paralysis of habitual styles of listening and thinking is perhaps our greatest outside threat.

5

DANCING ON ITS OWN GRAVE: THE STRANGE LOGICS OF THE "ROCK IS DEAD" SONG

It should come as no real surprise that competitors and critics insisted from early on that rock was dead; as we've seen, manifestos declaring the death of a new art form is a time-honored rhetorical strategy, almost a generational obligation, and rock's death is neither the first nor the most significant to have been shouted from the rooftops. But rock *is* perhaps the first popular form to take hold of the premature announcement of its demise and embrace it as a subject for its ongoing production—proving, with a perverse logic, that rock *isn't* dead because it continues to sing about its own death, feeding off its own corpse, rising phoenixlike from its own ashes.

Although there exists no systematic data on which to draw, I have for some time been collecting "rock is dead" songs—both those insisting that rock is dead and those insisting just as vehemently that rock can never die—and have cataloged well over two hundred, ranging from songs by the dBs and Todd Rungren, to the Corner Gnomes and Radiohead, Prince and Goldie, L.A. Style and the Deadlines, Rose Tattoo and Spybreak: songs from all across the popular music spectrum. Though we seem not to have noticed previously, after sex and drugs, rock's own death is one of its perennial themes. There is, of course, no small irony in this: the fact that much of rock's ongoing production sustains itself on the notion that there is no ongoing production. Such an observation dovetails nicely with arguments about the intrinsically ironic structure of much of rock music, and also with claims of rock's postmodernity.

A survey of the "rock is dead" genre of rock songs suggests at least eight different functions these songs can serve: eight distinct inflections of the phrase, eight different strategies for turning the putative death of rock into grounds for ongoing musical production. Dancing on its own grave, it seems, keeps rock eternally young, and, in the following pages, we'll attempt to sketch out a typology of these "rock is dead" songs, discovering, along the way, that each affirms by different means the continuing vitality of rock.

In the most literal-minded group of these songs, the phrase "rock is dead" often simply refers to the fact that a particular rock *star* is dead. Songs focusing on these deaths often take the form of a tribute: the genre of the rock elegy. To the extent that rock culture is a star culture, fetishizing Romantic notions of an individual genius—and given the degree to which, especially during its first decade, the viability of rock as a cultural form was tied directly to particular epochal figures like Elvis Presley—the death of these stars is understood to imperil the very future of the music itself.

Of these songs, the surreal archetype has to be Don McLean's "American Pie." That apocalyptic pop epic, of course, gave us the phrase "the day the music died," memorializing the death of the rising stars (or perhaps shooting stars) Buddy Holly and Ritchie Valens, along with the "Big Bopper," in a plane crash near Mason City, Iowa, on February 3, 1959.[1] Those deaths are linked in the song to nothing less than the decline of American culture and the triumph of evil over good (and, seemingly, bad music over good-time rock & roll): "I saw Satan laughing with delight / The day the music died." On another level—and radio listeners in 1971, when the album was released, were fascinated by the song's "levels"—McLean has constructed an elaborate allegorical tale about the decade between the death of Buddy Holly and the death of the youth culture at Altamont ("Now for ten years, we've been on our own").

Rock, it need hardly be pointed out, is as relentlessly obsessed with youth as any segment of contemporary American culture. Life begins at the hop and ends at around thirty: "Hope I die before I get old," Roger Daltrey (now in his sixties) swaggered in "My Generation." And many—far too many—did in fact die before they got old. In 1974, blue-eyed soul singers the Righteous Brothers had a number-three single with their cheesy evocation of a "Rock & Roll Heaven," a platitudinous tribute to dead rock stars Jimi Hendrix, Janis Joplin, Otis Redding, Jim Morrison, Jim Croce, and (bewilderingly, to contemporary sensibilities) Bobby Darin: "If there's a rock and roll heaven / Well you know they've got a hell of a band, band, band."[2]

Even while rock has celebrated youth, it has exhibited a morbid fascination with death, dating back to songs like "Tell Laura I Love Her," "Leader of the Pack," and "Dead Man's Curve." For those forever young, death seems merely an intriguing hypothesis; it's perfectly possible to toy with a fantasy version of death without taking its possibility seriously. There's no other way, perhaps, to explain the careers of Screaming "Lord" Sutch, Alice Cooper, Ozzy Osbourne, and Marilyn Manson. The frisson set up when young singers bring their audiences into a brush with death is no small part of the charge of rock, and part of the explanation of why claiming that rock is dead isn't, or isn't always, the same as trying to bury it.

The catalog of rock elegies is now quite extensive, and, as one might expect, the tone of these songs is far from uniformly reverential. Bill Drummond's "Julian Cope Is Dead" suggests, none too subtly, that death is a career move; System of a Down's sophomoric "The Ballad of Kurt Cobain" is just thirteen seconds long, announcing, simply, that the song's subject is dead. One perhaps doesn't expect elegiac beauty from a band called the Tits, and certainly we don't get it on their track "We're So Glad Elvis Is Dead," expressing their contempt for the star and happiness that he is no longer with us in these immortal punkish lyrics: "He was such a dick." The Cranberries, on their 1996 album *To the Faithful Departed,* included a first-person narrative from the perspective of Mark David Chapman, called "I Just Shot John Lennon," complete with sound-effects gunshots. It was intended as a courageous, not an opportunistic, song; but it just didn't work, for all kinds of reasons. Finally, and not too surprisingly, Iggy Pop ("the chairman of the bored") takes the air out of the entire genre in "Dead Rock Star": "I'm a dead rock star," he sings, after an instrumental intro built on the same chord progression as the Beatles' "Helter Skelter": "I took the hazing / They said 'amazing.'"

Many more, however, take the work of mourning seriously and think about the consequences for rock & roll when one of its titans is lost: especially a young titan, especially a male titan. From its earliest days, rock has also been morbidly fascinated with the story of the boy—and it is always a boy—who burns bright but burns out. James Dean, although no musician, nevertheless provides the early prototype—in the words of the Eagles, he was "Too fast to live, too young to die." Better to "burn out," wrap your sports car around a tree, than to slouch toward some midlife mediocrity: think Phil Collins ("Hope I die before I get old," indeed). Long before Dean was born, W.B. Yeats remembered the death of the son of his friend Lady Augusta Gregory in an oddly first-person elegy, "An Irish Airman Foresees His Death," which begins, "I know that I shall meet my fate / Somewhere in the clouds above." Although shot down in action in World War I, the Major Robert Gregory of Yeats's poem seems almost to have chosen his vehicular death, as James Dean was later to do: "I balanced all, brought all to mind, / The years to come seemed waste of breath." Rock & roll early on picked up on this romantic notion of the gifted young man who, in a world too coarse to appreciate what he has to offer, goes out instead in a blaze of glory, a narrative made famous in A.E. Housman's "To an Athlete Dying Young": "Smart lad, to slip betimes away / From fields where glory does not stay."

The image of the poet too delicate for this world—he who falls upon the thorns of life, and bleeds—is of course an invention of the Romantic era: Chatterton wasting away in his garret; Keats wasting away of consumption. Indeed, Keats's deathbed portrait, his head luminous in suffering, competes with Byron's posed portrait in Oriental garb for the best-known icon for the poetry of the period. There is a strong strain of this very Romanticism in early rock & roll, as Wallace Fowlie has demonstrated in the case of Jim Morrison.[3] According to a perverse logic, however, in many cases rock stars seem to have brought about their own demise—arranged their own deaths—because the death of a poet like Keats suggested quite powerfully the equation of beauty with suffering: to be a real poet, one must be willing to pay the ultimate price. Even, perhaps, if no one is seeking payment. And furthermore, in Shelley's "Adonais," his elegy for Keats, the poet is turned into the victim of social outrage, martyred for telling the truth to a people who would prefer not to hear. As Byron's Prometheus learns (in the poem of that title), the wages of (poetic) transgression is death. Atara Stein has argued persuasively that rock still identifies more closely with Romantic poetry than with the work of any other period or genre.[4]

The untimely death of rock stars, then, to some extent involves a confusion of cause and effect: because I died young, I must have been talented. Nothing succeeds like failure, and death is the ultimate career move. But surely this will no longer do; surely it's time to admit that most of rock's "martyrs" threw their lives away, died for nothing. There are of course important exceptions—those untimely rock deaths for which the star bears no responsibility: John Lennon, Dusty Springfield, Frank Zappa. But think of Elvis; think of Janis; think of Jimi: their given names alone suffice to recall the utter futility of their deaths. Like Keats, they were arguably "half in love with easeful death." This notion comes to infect even a rock critic like Lester Bangs, who seemed to believe that flirting with death was a strategy for "keepin' it real." On the other hand, Robert Christgau, whose writing career started before Bangs's, is still writing for the *Village Voice*. Now *that's* keepin' it real.

Like many of its biggest fans, rock is now middle-aged—fiftysomething—and increasingly has to deal with death and dying as an ordinary, rather than an extraordinary, occurrence. Rock is now old enough for its stars to have started to die of natural, in addition to spectacular, causes; I can't remember the last time I read about a rock star suffocating on his own, or, as with one of Spinal Tap's drummers, "someone else's," vomit. The obits for rock stars in both *Rolling Stone* and the *New York Times* are noticeably more frequent lately; and although it has taken many years, rock has now matured to the point where it can produce powerful, poignant elegies.

To follow this line of argument requires that I take minor exception with the most significant recent work on the modern elegy, Jahan Ramazani's *Poetry of Mourning*. In the opening paragraph of his important study—to which my thinking about elegy is greatly indebted—Ramazani dismisses popular music as a vehicle of true mourning: "We may need [elegies] now more than ever. For many of us, religious rituals are no longer adequate to the complexities of mourning for the dead. Insufficient too are the sentimental consolations of the funeral parlor, the condolence card, and the pop song." Surely the list of rock elegies contains many more poor songs than great ones; the same would have to be said, though, of the small proportion of poetic elegies that attain real transcendent power. And the best rock elegies, I maintain, have done precisely the work of the modern elegy as Ramazani describes it: they have "forged a resonant yet credible vocabulary for grief in our time—elegies that erupt with all the violence and irresolution, all the guilt and ambivalence of modern mourning."[5] A rock elegy, however, forges this resonant vocabulary in two different, though complementary, registers—the lyrical and the musical—giving it at least the potential to affect us more powerfully than words alone can ever hope to do.

The term *rock elegy* might be understood in at least two different ways, depending on whether "rock" is understood as standing for the elegiac subject or for the elegiac style, because rock has produced moving elegies both for those outside the rock world proper and for its own fallen soldiers. Kris Kristofferson's "Bobby McGee," definitively covered by Janis Joplin, is a deeply affecting elegy for a (presumably fictive) character who becomes real to listeners through the passion of Joplin's performance; our reaction to that performance is doubtless colored, moreover, by the knowledge that its singer would be dead at age twenty-seven. Eric Clapton's haunting elegy for his young son Dylan, "Tears in Heaven," leaves nary a dry eye; there too, the knowledge that the song's addressee is the guitarist's own child and of the tragic backstory to the song play on our emotions as much as does the song. In the realm of the political rather than the narrowly personal, Peter Gabriel's song "Biko" pays tribute to South African political martyr Stephen Biko and foreshadows Gabriel's movement into world music by employing native South African funerary music in the recording.

But arguably the music becomes more interesting, complex, even self-contradictory when rock begins to elegize its own: elegies about rock figures, figured in a rock idiom. While some would quarrel about her "rock" credentials (and his), Emmylou Harris's elegy for Gram Parsons, "Boulder to Birmingham," is to my mind one of the most beautiful elegies in rock. On the other hand, Puff Daddy's "I'll Be Missing You," his elegy for fellow rapper Notorious B.I.G., is one of the very strangest of rock elegies. The lyric is conventional enough, given the occasion, as Puffy pays tribute to Biggie's superior skills (and in this, surely, he does not dissemble). In an irony quite common to the elegy form, however, this tribute to his friend's gifts wound up being Puffy's biggest hit—bigger, too, than anything Biggie ever charted—the song by which, in the public mind, Puffy is best known. Elegy always betrays a nervousness that its act of tribute will slide imperceptibly into opportunism, the lesser poet seen to be riding the coattails—or, in the event, feeding off the corpse—of the late, great; as Ramazani writes, "Modern elegists are wracked by what

I call the economic problem of mourning—the guilty thought that they reap aesthetic profit from loss, that death is the fuel of poetic mourning."[6] The particular strangeness of "I'll Be Missing You," though, comes by means of the melody line, sampled from the Police's haunting "Every Step You Take," a song that unnervingly equates romantic devotion with stalking ("I'll be watching you"). Puffy changes the last line of the chorus to "I'll be missing you," but the substitution hardly suffices to drain away the song's menace.

Not surprisingly, perhaps, my reading of Puffy's elegy for Biggie is at odds with Nick Hornby's reading of the song. In *Songbook,* Hornby writes,

> Any musical response that you have to Puff Daddy's "I'll Be Missing You" is actually a response to the Police's pretty riff. You can admire that taste and the cheek, but not the creativity: to create music—to create any art—is surely to pull something out of thin air, to produce something where there was previously nothing.[7]

I haven't heard such an unabashedly Romantic theory of creativity pronounced by anyone but the greenest of undergraduate students in a very, very long time; it is not surprising, perhaps, that we'd hear it from a novelist, because creative writers are seemingly the last bastion of such thinking in the cultural marketplace (such sentiments would be laughed off stage by the great majority of bands now making records, but even going way back to the Stones, the Kinks, Elvis … how far back do you wanna go?). That philosophical difference notwithstanding, Hornby in effect says that this hip-hop track is reducible simply to its sampled loop; but what, one wonders, about its flow? The song's chorus is Sting's, but the verses, clumsy although they sometimes are, are Puffy's: clumsy, but oddly affecting.

It might make for an interesting top-five list, along the lines of those obsessively assembled by the Championship Vinyl staff in Hornby's novel *High Fidelity:* name the top five rock elegies, elegies *for* rock stars *by* rock stars. Any such list would have to include at least one song for the memory of Kurt Cobain; indeed, elegies for Cobain would threaten to monopolize the list, at least for those of us listening to music during the '90s and beyond. Because of his profound capacity for empathy—a quality that, rather grimly, he celebrates in his suicide note—Cobain's death meant a great deal even to some for whom his music was not especially meaningful. For American youth culture, the death of Kurt Cobain was *the* central death of the 1990s, just as that of John Lennon was for American boomers at the very start of the 1980s. Cobain was seen by many of his fans as a kind of sacrificial lamb, a scapegoat willing to suffer for the sins of a society that neither understood nor accepted him (nor, by extension, his fans); it was an image that he burnished in songs like "All Apologies," singing "I'll take all of the blame." In subsequent mythmaking, Cobain's death has been made to repeat Jesus Christ's; the ubiquity of those ultra-close-up photographs of his clear-eyed, beautiful, angelic face very clearly present Cobain as a type of grunge Messiah, and the overwhelming out-pouring of grief in response to his death, on a national and even interna-tional level, made it clear that his life had meant far more to millions of young fans than rational explanation could account for. In this sense that his life was somehow sacrificial, Cobain bears some resemblance to Jim Morrison, who self-consciously copped crucifixion poses in publicity photos and whose persona seemed, like Cobain's, to combine the erotic and the messianic in equal parts—but whose death, in retrospect, was less tragic than pathetic. Similarly, Elvis's death accomplished nothing for us: if fans lived vicariously through his rags-to-riches career, none wished to die with him, falling off a toilet in cardiac arrest, his system flooded with toxic levels of eleven different drugs.

Cobain was frequently referred to as the "voice of his generation," a designation that exasperated him while he was still around to object to it. One of the more eloquent fans for whom he seems to have served this function, the novelist Douglas Coupland, acknowledges both his reliance on Cobain and Cobain's explicit disavowal of any such role:

> I never asked you to make me care about you, but it happened—against the hype, against the odds—and now you are in my imagination forever.
>   And I figure you're in heaven, too. But how, exactly does it help you *now*, to know that you, too, as it is said, were once adored?[8]

Charisma is a notoriously difficult phenomenon to analyze, but on one level this is what we're talking about here: Kurt Cobain, disheveled and impatient, contemptuous of both his fame and often his fans, was para-doxically the most charismatic musical figure of his generation. His life and the integrity of his work suggested that one could live in this world, manage the terrible contradictions, deal with the pain, and survive; but his death necessarily suggested something much darker.[9]

Cobain's death was more difficult than most to mourn, and a more dif-ficult subject for elegy, precisely because it was suicide: back to the earliest days of the Western tradition, we've had no real idea how to deal with this kind of death. Jimi, Janis, and Jim may have indirectly taken their own lives, so heavy was their consumption of narcotics or alcohol, or both, but none of their deaths was ruled a suicide. Cobain, on the other hand—unless you believe the conspiracy theory of the week, which would improbably convict his ambitious wife of the murder—put the barrel of a shotgun in his mouth in the greenhouse of his Bellevue home, just months after taking an overdose of pills in Rome. (Nirvana's last studio album, eventually released as *Incesticide,* bore the working title "I Hate Myself and I Want to Die.") For his fans, the first suicide attempt in Rome was a kind of dry run at mourning his eventual death; again, Coupland evokes well what those hours, stretching into days, were like:

> Later that night there was *still* no real news. But at least it seemed as though you were out of your coma. But then a *new* dread emerged, one so bad that we couldn't even talk about it directly, as though the words would give the dread life of its own—the dread that you might emerge from the coma ... brain dead. So instead my friends and I talked about the weather. We tried to establish if, in fact, the sky that day had been sunny or rainy. It was such a close call that nobody could say for sure. Night had fallen before it could be made conclusive, before we could be totally sure that the sun had won.[10]

In mourning Cobain's death, young (and portions of middle-aged) America learned something very important—and not just about mourning the life of one who did not want to go on living. For Cobain's close and very public identification with the struggle for rights for the American gay and lesbian community meant that many looked, in his death, for a means to understand and work through the escalating toll being taken by AIDS. Cobain was vexed by the fact that the "heavy metal" sound of Nirvana's music meant that it attracted many unreconstructed metal fans to their shows, but Cobain and company wanted no part of heavy metal's dim-witted misogyny. As (again) many of the best-known photos help to suggest, Cobain was one of the softest of hard rockers, a feminist, pro-queer punk. He actively sought out opportunities to offend the macho sensibilities of both his fans and his detractors: giving a very friendly interview to the gay Bay Area magazine the *Advocate;* French-kissing bass player Krist Novoselic on stage years before Britney dreamed up her carefully choreographed stunt with Xtina and Madonna; appearing as Krist's "date" on MTV's "Headbanger's Ball" wearing a taffeta gown—"dressed for a ball," he insisted. Although the connections here are complicated, Cobain's efforts, in one of youth culture's most deeply homophobic arenas, were paying real dividends, making things just a little bit better for the gays and lesbians in his audience. "What else can I say? / Everyone is gay": although the rhyme is a bit trite, the sentiment (in the popular song "All Apologies") was powerful. And, in learning to mourn Kurt, we simultaneously found ways to mourn the mounting number of AIDS deaths—a number, as Mayor Rudy Gulliani said of the terrorist deaths on September 11, 2001, that is "more than any of us can easily bear."

The elegies for Cobain began to come quickly. A group no one had heard of before—and, to the best of my knowledge, no one has heard from since—For Squirrels, had a radio hit with "The Mighty K.C."; Hidden Agenda recorded a much less celebrated track, the bluntly titled "Kurt Cobain Is Dead." Vernon Reid, fellow guitarist from the then-defunct (and currently reunited) Living Colour, recorded "Saint Cobain"; a musician closer to Cobain, Nirvana's drummer Dave Grohl, formed a new band, Foo Fighters, and had a hit with "My Hero." Whether coincidence or no, neither the For Squirrels nor the Foo Fighters tribute, the two songs from this short list to have scored heavy radio play, mentions Cobain explicitly; this may be part of the price for elegizing suicide. (It might also be that they're simply better pop songs.)[11]

None of these early responses are particularly memorable as elegies: they range from the rather formulaic (Foo Fighters) to the truly forgettable. In time, however, more thoughtful responses appeared. Among the most interesting and challenging is Patti Smith's record *Gone Again*. The album's title, as well as its most haunting track "About a Boy," refer first and foremost to her husband Fred "Sonic" Smith, who died suddenly of a heart attack in 1994, aged forty-five. But both the album and "About a Boy" are also, paradoxically, for Kurt—both because Smith uses the death of Cobain to think through and come to terms with her own feelings of loss and because she knows that, inevitably, the album will be heard via the rock audience's still-open wound that Cobain's death had caused. Patti and Fred Smith had one of rock's few storybook marriages, having been married for fourteen years, until Fred's death; indeed, Patti had been criticized in some quarters for having been "domesticated" by marriage and family, and her work during those years was not particularly distinguished. Kurt Cobain and Courtney Love's marriage, famously, had nothing of this stability nor, one imagines, had Kurt lived would it have enjoyed the longevity of the Smiths'.[12] But Patti Smith, it seems, almost cannot understand, cannot come to terms with the death of her husband, except through the archetypal death of Kurt Cobain. Thus the central song of *Gone Again*, "About a Boy," takes its title from one of Cobain's (though not one he wrote for Courtney), "About a Girl." And in the lyrics, Smith allows for multiple identifications of that boy: he is, seemingly, both Kurt and Fred, any boy with genius and a generous spirit taken from us too soon. Smith knows these things about her husband, although, because he was never much in the public eye, the larger rock audience does not; but she can suggest what kind of man he was most effectively by invoking the ghost of a very much remembered Cobain. (In later titling his second novel *About a Boy*, Hornby productively remaps all this ambiguity once again, making the boy both Cobain and his young protagonist, Marcus.)

Kurt Cobain's death so completely dominated the consciousness of young America that, as Patti Smith seems to have realized, other elegies released around that time were often erroneously read as mourning his death, sucked into the vortex surrounding his suicide. One song that got a good deal of radio play at the time, Filter's "Hey Man Nice Shot," was written in response to the suicide, during a televised press conference, of Pennsylvania state treasurer R. Bud Dwyer; a quick look at the Internet shows, however, that many fans still believe the song to be an especially unsympathetic reaction to the news of Cobain's suicide, a reading that members of the band, in numerous interviews, have been at pains to put to rest. Another rock elegy that one might be forgiven for thinking was written for Cobain is Bikini Kill's "R.I.P.," on the album *Reject All American*. Cobain's Seattle-area riot grrrl neighbors include his ex-girlfriend Tobi Vail on drums; lead singer Kathleen Hanna screams in rage, "There's another boy genius who's fucking gone." This song is ostensibly not about Cobain, but about a gay/transsexual friend of the band: "This song is for Gene Barnes aka Portia Manson," say the liner notes, "who moved on to the 5th dimension on Oct. 9 after dying from AIDS-related meningitis. R.I.P. stands for rest in pissed-off ness." Yet the death of Cobain cast such a shadow over the music of the time, especially the music scene of the Pacific Northwest, that it's nearly impossible not to read Cobain into the song—nor, in all likelihood, would Bikini Kill argue against our doing so.

Two of the elegies from Cobain's friends carry especially complicated textual and emotional genealogies; in both cases, the songs of these musicians were "implicated," however tangentially, in Cobain's suicide. Biographer Charles Cross has suggested that Cobain pulled the trigger with

R.E.M.'s most ethereal and beautiful album on in the background: "The television was on, tuned to MTV, but the sound was off. [Cobain] walked over to the stereo and put on R.E.M.'s *Automatic for the People*, turning the volume down so that Stipe's voice sounded like a friendly whisper in the background—Courtney would later find the stereo still on and this CD in the changer."[13] Michael Stipe was deeply affected by Cobain's death; he has not spoken publicly about whether he knew of the role his music may have played in that grim final scene. The many situational ironies are deepened by the fact that *Automatic for the People* contains what is, by consensus, the most powerful and popular anti-suicide rock song ever recorded, "Everybody Hurts": "When you think you've had too much ... hang on."

When he got the news of Cobain's death, Stipe had just emerged from a prolonged period of grief and mourning for his friend River Phoenix. The band had returned to the studio and was halfway through the making of *Monster* (which is dedicated to Phoenix) when again, someone close to Stipe had died tragically, young—"another boy genius who's fucking gone." Stipe's response was to write "Let Me In," which he described to a *Newsweek* reporter this way:

Stipe: That's a song that I wrote to Kurt Cobain after he killed himself. [Pause.] I, um ... I should be able to do this without getting emotional. [Pause.] I lost a friend in October—River Phoenix was a very, very close friend of mine. And I've never suffered such a profound loss. I couldn't write for five months. We had started the record in September. I'd written two songs and then River died. And, having written Automatic for the People, I was not about to write another record about death and loss. So it took me five months to sit down and write again. Then, halfway through making Monster, Kurt died. At that point, I just threw my hands up and wrote "Let Me In."

Interviewer: So when you sing "Hey, let me in"—that's you talking to Cobain?

Stipe: That was me on the phone to him, desperately trying to get him out of the frame of mind he was in.... In the most big-brotherly way—God, I hate that term—in the most genuine way, I wanted him to know that he didn't need to pay attention to all this, that he was going to make it through.[14]

When Courtney Love heard the song, she gave Peter Buck Cobain's prototype light-blue Mustang guitar to perform it with, left-handed though it was; Buck regularly played the song with Kurt's guitar during R.E.M.'s 1995 world tour, playing it upside down, a sort of Jimi Hendrix in reverse.

If Stipe was on the stereo when Cobain ended his life, Neil Young was, even more publicly, in the suicide note; the story here is an even more complicated and interesting intertextual tale. Young's 1979 album *Rust Never Sleeps* is bookended with what are essentially two parts of the same song—"Hey Hey My My (Out of the Blue)" and "My My Hey Hey (Into the Black)." *Rust Never Sleeps* is not a "theme" or "concept" album, but one of its threads certainly is Young's renewed faith in the vitality of rock fueled by the punk explosion, and more specifically by the exuberant theatrical self-fashioning of John Lydon, aka Johnny Rotten. "The king is dead but he's not forgotten," Young sings on the closing track, "this is the story of Johnny Rotten." The king is dead, long live the king; Rotten is dead, long live Lydon. Young here is celebrating both the imaginative invention of and, just as important, the timely killing off of a stage persona; when Johnny Rotten "died," no one was lost—a persona was simply retired (like David Bowie's dramatic retirement of the Ziggy Stardust character, recorded in the final minutes of D.A. Pennebaker's film *Ziggy Stardust*). Young's admiration for Lydon's instincts is summed up in the song with the lines, "It's better to burn out / Than to fade away." This is the part of Young's complicated narrative that Cobain chose to quote, out of context, in his suicide note: "I don't have the passion anymore and so remember, *it's better to burn out than to fade away.*"[15]

Like Stipe, Young was devastated by the news of Cobain's death; like Stipe, Young had been worried about Cobain and had been in frequent telephone contact, suggesting that they work together and generally trying to help him pull out of his depression. To have those efforts fail—and, worse, to have his own song (and one that boldly proclaims, "Rock and roll can never die") quoted in Cobain's suicide note—has to have been unimaginably painful.[16] (It should be remembered, too, that Cobain's was one of the most public suicide notes in entertainment history: at the public memorial service for Cobain in Seattle, Courtney Love appeared via video feed and read large portions of the note to the assembled crowd, and photographic reproductions of the handwritten note are readily available on the Internet and elsewhere.) Young's response to this tragedy was, like Stipe's, to write a song, or rather, two: the title track and "Change Your Mind," from the album *Sleeps with Angels*. Lyrically, the songs are unfortunately rather undistinguished. "Sleeps with Angels" resorts to quite conventional imagery in the search for some kind of consolation ("He sleeps with angels / He's always on someone's mind"); what makes the song work, however—the real elegiac energy of the song—comes from the undisputable aural fact that Young's guitar is somehow channeling Cobain's. Neil Young is one of rock's most recognizable guitarists, yet on *Sleeps with Angels*, though not literally playing Cobain's guitar as Buck did on "Let Me In," Young captures the gritty intensity of Cobain's playing, and for the duration of the song the younger guitarist seems still to be with us.

The second Cobain track, "Change Your Mind," relies on much the same narrative as "Let Me In": the appeals of a concerned friend who feels cut off, cut out, during a time of crisis. To call "Change Your Mind" a "guilty" song greatly oversimplifies matters, but clearly Young is trying to work out some demons here, and not in an altogether logical fashion. To begin with, it is patently too late to be encouraging Cobain to change his mind—although, perhaps, the song might serve as a larger caution and comfort for those who share Cobain's despair (cf. R.E.M.'s "Everybody Hurts"). In successive verses, Young demonstrates that he understands well the pressures to which Cobain fell victim; his answer, though—while as profound as anything in human experience—finally feels inadequate to the occasion: "Distracting you from this must be the one you love."

Young maintains, in effect, that "all you need is love": true, perhaps, but not especially helpful as advice. Worse, the song clearly suggests that the love of a good woman should have been enough to stay Kurt's hand—"the one whose magic touch can change your mind." And even that solution is a temporary one: thoughts of suicide in the chorus seemingly have not been dispelled, but one is merely distracted from thinking about them (rather like the ultimately failed advice Lucrezia Smith is given by her doctors to stay the hand of her suicidal husband Septimus in Virginia Woolf's *Mrs. Dalloway*). In dealing with his own guilt over Cobain's suicide, Young shifts the blame—inadvertently, I have to believe—to Cobain's controversial widow Courtney Love—a woman who had more than enough of her own guilt to deal with.

The elegy for Kurt Cobain that means the most—even as messy, self-promoting, contradictory, and at times mean-spirited as it is—is the record *Celebrity Skin* made by Courtney Love's band Hole. The album was a long time in the making: Kurt's body was found on April 8, 1994, and

Celebrity Skin wasn't released until September 8, 1998. But Love's first public attempts at grieving were famously unsuccessful, and she might be forgiven an unusual degree of caution. First, in the public memorial service in Seattle, Love resolutely did not play the part of the grieving rock widow in the way that, for instance, John Lennon's widow, Yoko Ono, had done. In that gathering, Love interspersed snatches of Cobain's suicide note with sometimes quite caustic commentary, even persuading a bewildered audience to tell Kurt in unison that he was an "asshole." Grief expresses itself differently in each of us, to be sure, but this was by no means what Cobain's public had expected from Love; remember, too, that she already had a pretty imposing reputation as a self-willed, domineering wife and a heroin-shooting, neglectful mother.[17] Following Kurt's death and what was perceived by fans as a too-brief and inadequately grieved period of mourning, Love was quickly "linked romantically," as they say, to quite a roster of men, including Smashing Pumpkins front man Billy Corgan, whose sonic fingerprints are all over *Celebrity Skin.* Having her too-soon-taken lover produce the album made as a tribute to her late husband raised the inevitable questions: Has the woman no shame? Couldn't Kurt have been mourned without the Pumpkins' trademark kettledrum booming through?

Nonetheless, *Celebrity Skin* is the most successful of a genre that to date has not often been attempted in rock: an elegiac song cycle. The elegiac sequence allows the poet, or songwriter, to move through a number of stages of grief and mourning: not necessarily the pat sequence made famous by Elisabeth Kübler-Ross in her book *On Death and Dying,* but usually a messier, more conflicted sequence, giving free rein to all the complex and contradictory emotions of loss and grief. The very best elegies give voice to the ambivalence that renders loss so wrenching, and for obvious reasons, the elegiac cycle makes available a greater number of resources for the full exploration of this ambivalence, as for instance in Alfred, Lord Tennyson's *In Memoriam.* In music, the high-culture model for the song cycle that mourns those untimely taken from us is Gustav Mahler's *Kindertotenlieder,* "songs on the death of young children."[18]

I've taken rather a long digression here to talk in some detail about rock elegies, and the elegies in particular for Kurt Cobain, because following his death, we saw the most explicit example of how the death of a single star can be read as the very death of rock itself. The best place to find these analyses, not surprisingly, is the Internet, where one can quickly find many, many postings suggesting that Kurt's death was rock's own:

WE ALL LOVE YOU, MISS YOU ALWAYS, ROCK IS
DEAD—KURT DONALD COBAIN—NIRVANA—FOREVER
IN OUR HEARTS AND SOULS. PS: EAT SHIT COURTNEY,
HOLE FUCKING SUCKS! ALL NIRVANA FANS ROCK ON,
KEEP NIRVANA ALIVE! ... KURT DONALD COBAIN LIVES
ON, LEGENDS NEVER FADE!!![19]

It is too [*sic*] damn bad that Rock is dead. For me Rock died the day that
Kurt Cobain was murdered. I mean name me one really good rock
album that actually mattered since 1994.[20]

[Cobain] didn't invent rock and roll but it died with him. Grunge was
the last breath of original rock. When it died the genre died too. Currently the only innovative music out there is Techno or Trip Hop and
the rest is just re-heated microwave MTV leftover swill. I mean what is
cutting edge? Dixie Chix, Puff Daddy, and EMEMNEMEM?[21]

I don't know if Rock died when Cobain died, but I know it became less
important. The era which followed had no passion, it was cookie cutter
corporate music which is still the norm today especially on the wasteland
which is Radio.[22]

Kurt is dead; rock is dead. If James Miller seems callow to suggest that
rock died when Elvis did, his is just the boomer version of what turns out
to be a very familiar trope. For rock to soldier on bravely when its fair
prince is gone—whether that fair prince is Elvis, Janis, or Kurt—seems an
impertinence. It's the day the music should, in all decency, have died.

A second motif among "rock is dead" songs is the assertion that rock's
death is just a false rumor or bad dream: some sort of misunderstanding.
One good example of this genre is Rose Tattoo's song "The Radio Said
Rock 'n' Roll Is Dead"; the line that completes the couplet with its title
insists, "They don't know what they're sayin' must be outta their head."
Hence the large group of songs that assert not that "rock is dead" but,
conversely, that rock will, rock *can* never die: songs like Richie Blackmore's "Long Live Rock & Roll," seemingly covered by every metal band
ever to play a show, including the band Steel Dragon in the 2001 Jennifer

Aniston and Mark Wahlberg film *Rock Star;* songs like Ozzy Osbourne's quite reasonable ontological objection that "You Can't Kill Rock and Roll" (for how can one kill something that was never alive?). And a whole host of songs with soundalike names: "Rock 'n' Roll Will Never Die," "Rock 'n' Roll Is Here to Stay," "Rock Ain't Dead," "Rock 'n' Roll Is Still Alive," "Long Live Revolution Rock," "Long Live the Soul of Rock 'n' Roll," "Rock 'n' Roll (Still Alive and Well)"—well, you get the picture.

A handful of songs even asserts the ongoing viability with a title that asserts the converse: the Rubettes's "Rock Is Dead," for instance, plays with this paradox: "They said that rock would fade away / But I knew rock was here to stay." Aaron Macdonald's "Rock 'n' Roll's Dead" works according to a much more sophisticated logic, asking, "I want to know who said / Rock 'n' roll's dead." But the song actually constructs a dense network of allusions to other rock songs, reanimating them as it quotes them. The second verse, for instance, opens by quoting Simon and Garfunkel's "Homeward Bound" ("sitting in a railway station"), Buffalo Springfield's "Mr. Soul" ("hello Mr. Soul"), Joni Mitchell's "Carrie" ("well the wind is in from Africa"), Canned Heat's "Going Up the Country" ("the water tastes like wine")—and that's just for starters. For any listener who catches these allusions—and though many listeners would not catch them all, anyone who cares at all about music would notice quite a few—rock & roll is clearly not dead.

On one level, these songs establish their assertion quite effectively, proving the ongoing character of rock by participating in it. On the other hand, a cynic might say that, more often than not, they inadvertently prove rock to be moribund, if not medically dead: of all the examples I have culled over the years, Macdonald's "Rock 'n' Roll's Dead" is the only really innovative, challenging, genre-stretching example of a "rock ain't dead" song. Indeed, the more often the gesture is repeated, the flimsier the posture comes to seem. It may be just a personal prejudice, but hearing Richie Blackmore screaming "long live rock and roll" almost convinces me that the patient is beyond resuscitation.

It's tempting to think that this was not always the case; that the claim that "Rock and Roll Is Here to Stay" (as the title of the 1958 Danny and the Juniors hit had it) wasn't just a defensive rejoinder to a prior charge, wasn't riddled with anxiety; that there was a time back in rock & roll's early history when toasts to rock's power and vitality functioned as the spontaneous joyous shouts of those set free by it. Perhaps the first such song to celebrate the vitality of rock was Chuck Berry's "School Day"

(1957). As the song's narrative moves from the classroom and its drudgery to the juke joint and its license (and jukebox), rock & roll is held up as a real agent of teen liberation. It's one of rock's classic showdowns: the schoolroom's artificial discipline is ultimately unable to resist rock & roll's insistent rhythms. Thus rock has proved its primacy: "Hail, hail rock 'n' roll." School's not going away any time soon—not, at least, until it's replaced with the nine-to-five drudgery of a job. But rock promises to give the rhythm of the school day and workday a backbeat, leavening its monotony with something more exciting. Hence rock & roll is hailed as the new king, the new savior; the "hail" and "long live" formulae, as we'll discuss in this chapter's close, figure rock & roll as royalty.

But Berry's ode is not simply, as it is sometimes portrayed, a spontaneous and innocent testament to the life-affirming power of rock; instead it probably has to be heard, at least in part, as the sunny version of the story told, in such dour tones, by the popular movie *Blackboard Jungle* two years earlier. If "School Day" is the first song to narrate the story of students' liberation by rock, Bill Haley's "Rock Around the Clock" was—given the context within which it broke onto the larger public's consciousness—inexorably linked to the disruption of the school day by juvenile delinquents (JDs), fueled on some level by the disruptive rhythms of rock & roll.[23] Haley's anthem was the first "rock" song to be featured in a Hollywood film (although the reviewer for the *Washington Post*, clinging to an earlier terminology, called it "a nifty jump piece"),[24] and through a species of guilt by association, it came to represent the menace posed by the generation of JDs sensationally portrayed in the film.

Blackboard Jungle suggests that the school day was filled with ignorant violence, fueled by that new youth menace, rock & roll. Never mind that the JDs in Richard Dadier's classroom never heard the film's Bill Haley tune: audiences surely did, as the first and last thing to assault their ears in the theatre.[25] The sound of youth rebellion was all the more striking to theatergoers because of its volume, because the recording of Haley's song had not been compressed at the high and low ends, as was the custom in film music.[26] First-time viewers jumped right out of their seats; Glenn Altschuler quotes Frank Zappa on the sound track's salutary sonic assault:

> "It was the loudest sound kids ever heard at that time," Frank Zappa remembered. Bill Haley "was playing the Teenage National Anthem and it was LOUD. I was jumping up and down. *Blackboard Jungle*, not

even considering that it had the old people winning in the end, represented a strange act of endorsement of the teenage cause."[27]

In adapting Evan Hunter's novel for film, director and screenwriter Richard Brooks was faced with a uniquely modern problem: the rapid obsolescence of youth culture, its tastes and its fads, in the face of a burgeoning media culture. In the 1954 novel, as in the film, the "generation gap" (though the term was still a decade or more off) was represented most dramatically in the scene in which new teacher Joshua Edwards brings in his precious collection of jazz 78s to spice up his English class. Even without their titles attached, the shellac 78s, by 1954, stand as a quaint technological reminder of a different time: "Rock Around the Clock," of course, was issued as a vinyl 45. But by the time of the film's release, in March 1955, the semiotics of "hip" and "square" had already shifted significantly enough that Brooks had to do some substitutions to make plain the stakes in the classroom culture wars. In the novel, Edwards plays three records before all hell breaks loose: Bunny Berigan's "I Can't Get Started," the Will Bradley Combo's "Celery Stalks at Midnight," and Ella Mae Morse's "Cow-Cow Boogie." (Hunter suggests the taste gap between teacher and students in one of the unvoiced comments by our narrator: "Bunny Berigan? Who the hell is Bunny Berigan? What kind of crap is this, anyway? … Bunny Berigan. Sounds like a strip queen in Union City.")[28] By giving Edwards this playlist, Hunter casts him as a "moldy fig": Edwards's taste in jazz is ten to twenty years out of date; the Berigan side dates from 1936, the Bradley and Morse date from 1941 and 1942, respectively. His students hate the music, without really having listened to it; as one student asks, "You got any recent stuff?"[29] Edwards decidedly doesn't; indeed his introduction to the day's lesson seems calculated to alienate his students: "'No longhair stuff,' Edwards said."[30]

In his screenplay, Brooks puts poor Edwards even further out of touch: the Berigan, Bradley, and Morse of the novel may have been passé, but they were both passé and a bit recherché, and their symbolic significance too easily lost on an audience of moviegoers who were already rapidly losing touch with jazz history. In the film, Edwards gets only one chance with his students before they mutiny, and he blows it all with a really ancient side by a well-known performer, Bix Beiderbecke's "The Jazz Me Blues" (1927): the relatively subtle references of the novel are "dumbed down" for the film audience, made both more familiar and more clearly dated.

In the novel, the students reject Edwards's choices in favor of Joni James and Julius LaRosa, two pop crooners to whom time has not been kind but who were, for all that, very much up to date, widely popular at the film's moment: James's "Why Don't You Believe Me?" held the number-one position on the *Billboard* charts for six weeks in 1952 and her "How Important Can It Be?" hit number two in 1955, the year of the film's release. LaRosa, for his part, had a number of *Billboard* hits during the 1950s, and even appeared in the 1958 film *Let's Rock;* he was constantly before the public during the time of the novel and film and had been a regular from the end of 1951 through the end of 1953 on CBS's *Arthur Godfrey and His Friends*. The film substitutes Frank Sinatra for LaRosa in the student's taste—a solid, though unimaginative (and, for a classroom full of manual arts and high school boys, rather incredible) choice.

While in the film Edwards is made to seem even more out of touch, the classroom melee over his jazz records fails to suggest just what it would mean to be in touch with the cutting-edge current music scene. Brooks and producer Pedro Berman seem to recognize this shortcoming; as Martha Bayles has written, "the JDs aren't demanding rock 'n' roll; they're demanding *pop*."[31] Charlie Gillett, too, writes of the short interval between the novel's and film's appearance—only a number of months, but in cultural terms a whole generation:

> Hunter's book was published in 1954, and in the relatively short space of time between the date of publication and the release of the film in late [*sic*] 1955, the musical culture of the young had gone a step beyond the terms of the novel. In the film version ... it was the relentless rhythm of Bill Haley's "Rock Around the Clock" that emphasized the rejection of the relatively sophisticated "swing" of the jazz records played by the teacher. By late 1955, Tony Bennett and Perry Como were as obsolete as Bunny Berigan and Will Bradley, so far as the self-consciously youthful adolescents were concerned. The film version of *Blackboard Jungle* was a large success and a much discussed movie. What the presence in it of the music of Bill Haley, rather than Tony Bennett and Perry Como, helped to establish in the minds of both adolescents and adults was the connection between rock 'n' roll and teenage rebellion.[32]

Between the time MGM acquired the rights to *Blackboard Jungle* in April 1954 and the film's premier on March 21, 1955, something of real popular music importance had happened: Elvis Presley put a rock & roll face on American pop music. Rock & roll had become, de facto, the sound of young America.

A film released in the spring of 1955 suggesting that Joni James or Frank Sinatra was the "kids' music" risked being laughed out of the theaters: whether or not Elvis's ascendancy signaled the birth of rock & roll, his preeminence on the public stage required that the filmmakers somehow take notice. Rather than rewriting the classroom showdown over jazz—and perhaps unintentionally Gillett seems to suggest that Bill Haley enters the classroom scene, which he manifestly does not—Brooks and Berman settled on a cosmetic fix: having discovered Haley's 1954 top-thirty hit "(We're Gonna) Rock Around the Clock" through the offices of the teenage son of *Blackboard Jungle*'s star, Glenn Ford, Brooks tipped the music over the film's opening and closing sequences.

Although their license for the song allowed them unlimited use during the film, Brooks and Berman chose never to introduce it into the film proper—that is to say, into the high school: both times the song comes up in the film, teacher Richard Dadier is standing out in front of the school. Indeed, whereas the music of Bix Beiderbecke (and elsewhere, Stan Kenton) is intradiegetic to the film—the characters in the scene hear the music (and the students object to it), the music is "present" in the scene—"Rock Around the Clock" is only extradiegetic, laid over rather than laid into the film. We in the audience can hear the song—indeed, at that volume, we can't help but hear it—but the song doesn't figure, intradiegetically, in the film at all.

The movie does, briefly, suggest otherwise. In the opening sequence, the song begins as plainly extradiegetic and slowly shifts to a suggested intradiegetic role. As Mr. Dadier walks up to his new school, the music shifts its role from "movie theme" to, ostensibly, what the high school kids are listening to as they caper in the schoolyard before the opening bell. It's a rather unconvincing performance, however; the JD dance scene was shot long before the music to which the students supposedly are dancing was chosen, and there's a weird disconnect between their rockin' out and Bill Haley's rockin' around the clock. In realistic terms, there's no way for the kids to be hearing what we in the audience hear: as the abortive music lesson in Mr. Edwards's classroom later makes plain, there is simply no technology available that would allow "Rock Around the Clock" to boom across the schoolyard, and the invisible PA system is a significant interruption in the film's attempt to establish verisimilitude.[33] What we witness as Mr. Dadier approaches Manual High, then, is something like a reverse "hip synching": Haley's tune is synched more or less convincingly with the movements of the Manual High students as they wait for school. "Ring ring goes the bell," indeed.

The last-minute addition of Haley's song became, in many ways, the film's most memorable feature. Like the film, the theatrical trailer opens with Haley's music, with a solemn voice intoning, "You are now listening to 'Rock Around the Clock.' This is the theme music from MGM's sensational new picture, *Blackboard Jungle*. Many people said the story could not, must not, dared not be shown." In this promotional text, no rationale is given for the juxtaposition of Haley with the film's Manual High thugs (save, perhaps, for the telling description "sensational"); it is simply, without explanation, the "theme music" for juvenile delinquency. The half-conscious way in which the music was selected highlights the truth of Martha Bayles's claim that Hollywood wasn't yet "afraid" of rock & roll, because in fact "it hadn't yet made a mental connection between juvenile delinquency and rock 'n' roll—for the simple but forgotten reason that America's worries about juvenile delinquency predated rock 'n' roll by more than a decade."[34] The connection, as far as the film is concerned, is an almost accidental one; save for the facile plastering of "Rock Around the Clock" atop the finished film, *Blackboard Jungle* would have seemed to be arguing for Joni James and Frank Sinatra as the soundtrack to America's troubled teens.[35] And with Joni James an MGM artist, that never would have done.

It's important to point out, as many others have in the past, that "Rock Around the Clock" got a bad rap as a result of its association with the JDs of *Blackboard Jungle;* few, if any, among the film's early audiences seem to have paused to consider that the music did not have—indeed, cannot have had—anything to do with the violence portrayed in the film. Rock's most important early apologist tried to point out the arbitrary nature of the association, to no avail: "'It was unfortunate,' no less an authority than Alan Freed acknowledged, that Haley's song about having a good time had been used 'in that hoodlum-infested movie,' which 'seemed to associate rock 'n' rollers with delinquents.'"[36] The controversial film became even more notorious as teen audiences cut loose during the screenings, dancing in the aisles of theaters, singing along with the opening and closing sequences, even vandalizing theater property. *Time* magazine went so far as to suggest that *Blackboard Jungle* "undermined the American way of life, giving aid and comfort to Communists."[37] American cities tried to keep the film out; theaters turned the sound track down, or even off, during the incendiary opening and closing credits. *Blackboard Jungle* seemed, to those ready to have their suspicions confirmed, to provide ample evidence of the generalized suspicions about rock & roll prevalent in the 1950s. As Geoffrey O'Brien writes of both *Blackboard Jungle* and *High School Confidential:* "The story was overwhelmed by the noise. That in fact turned out to be the story."[38]

"As it entered popular discourse," Altschuler observes, "rock 'n' roll was a social construction and not a musical conception. It was, by and large, what DJs and record producers and performers said it was."[39] To Altschuler's list of influential cultural producers and middlemen, we must of course add movie producers: because, despite the fact that the movie had literally nothing to do with rock & roll, *Blackboard Jungle* de facto set the agenda for America's first reaction to rock & roll. Freed was a fixture well before *Blackboard Jungle,* and for a time afterward, before his inglorious fall from grace (for betraying the trust of precisely those cultural producers and middlemen); but in some ways, rock & roll never quite shook off the stigma, as well as the frisson, that quite accidentally attached to it owing to *Blackboard Jungle.*

In the conventional version of rock history that we have inherited, Chuck Berry is most often associated with an earlier, more innocent time in rock & roll; Bayles's description here is typical, when she calls Berry's music "a brief, high-spirited respite from the necessary routines of home and school."[40] But as I've just been at pains to argue, the fact is that the last-minute addition of "(We're Gonna) Rock Around the Clock" to the *Blackboard Jungle* sound track, as a sonic symbol of juvenile delinquency, meant that Berry was already fighting a losing battle. If not dead, rock already had a price on its head; "Long live rock 'n' roll," given the multitude of enemies it faced in the late fifties, can be understood only as wishful thinking. Danny and the Juniors' artless take on this theme makes the point even more explicitly: "Rock 'n roll is here to stay, it will never die / It was meant to be that way, though I don't know why." Hardly a reasoned argument, of course: this is a raspberry in the face of the forces of repression, and not a very effective one. One begins to sense that they—both Berry and Danny and the Juniors, as well as Bill Haley (in "Viva la Rock and Roll," a lame number set to the tune of "Viva La Compagnie")—protest too much. How much more so, then, the more recent song by the group Durango, "Rock & Roll Is Here to Stay," which is effectively just a punk updating of Danny and the Juniors: "Before my life just fades away, / Rock and roll is here to stay." Rock's vitality is rarely proclaimed except as a rejoinder to a (sometimes unspoken) claim that it's already dead. Rock's death is, it seems, a necessary precondition for its living.

One of the most popular recent songs to proclaim the death of rock is Lenny Kravitz's "Rock & Roll Is Dead," a song that belongs to a third distinct group: those in which the singer, implicitly or explicitly (which is to say either dramatically or rhetorically), announces himself as rock's savior: rock seems to be dead, but the star is able to bring it back to life through the sheer power of his own gifts. Kravitz's song is a pretty standard big, power-chord rock song, during which the singer intones again and again and again that "rock & roll *is* dead"; in the song's brief narrative, rock is pronounced a victim of its own success and excess: "You're living for an image / So you got five hundred women in your bed." The track plays heavily on the irony that here is a song that, in sonic terms, certainly rocks—but that, perversely, counterintuitively, argues that "rock is dead." Thus its musical logic runs something like this: Lenny's heard the news today, oh boy, and he's here to tell us, rock & roll is dead. But listeners are meant, I believe, to recoil in disbelief: "surely," we're to think, "if Lenny can play guitar like that, rock & roll is far from dead." If I were to suggest that Kravitz suffers from something like delusions of Jimi Hendrix, I'd hardly be the first; in "Rock & Roll Is Dead" he suggests—to paraphrase the Who—that "Hendrix is dead, long live Hendrix." In Kravitz's tune, then, and others of its ilk, the ironic declaration that "rock is dead" actually means just the opposite: that rock and roll is alive.[41]

Prince, a musician whose work seems to make trivial any kind of generic boundaries and distinctions, pulls off much the same feat, with a great deal more self-conscious humor and musical dexterity than Kravitz, on his B-side "Rock & Roll Is Alive (And It Lives in Minneapolis)." Rather than coyly pretending rock is dead, both medium and message in Prince's song are consonant: with wholly characteristic arrogance he suggests that he is the future of rock & roll. "Some people say it's dyin', but we don't wanna play that game / Rock 'n' roll is alive and it lives in Minneapolis! (Sing!)" Later in the song, Prince presents himself explicitly as rock's savior: "Sure as the land of a thousand lakes is sometimes made of snow / There'll always be another king 2 die butt-naked on the floor (Oh)."

Few have pulled off the performative irony Kravitz achieves with as much aplomb, though certainly it's a rhetorical strategy deployed in a large number of songs. The dB's "The Death of Rock," for instance, puts a rather straightforward death sentence ("This is the death / The death of rock") to vocals that sound like T. Rex's Marc Bolan and a bright, open guitar sound that is equal parts Bruce Springsteen and Peter Buck. The lyrics say rock is dead; the music makes us feel it's alive. Another interesting take on this genre is Madonna's swirling, synth-heavy 2000 remake of Don McLean's "American Pie." The song was a big hit for Madonna—and like many of her singles, a big hit on the dance floors of clubs across this country and the world. A club hit McLean's version never was, and in persuading young (and middle-aged) bodies to move to her abbreviated version of McLean's epic rock elegy, surely Madonna proved that for the moment, rock isn't dead. These songs, at a minimum, make hay of the paradox that they are rock songs singing about rock's death: a sort of ontological contradiction, like making a valentine to the death of love.

A fourth group of "rock is dead" songs differs only slightly from this third group—but that small difference makes all the difference. There are legions of songs that declare, simply and rather uninterestingly, that rock is dead, without providing any kind of either argument or evidence for rock's death and without any of the kind of performative irony we find in the Kravitz "Rock & Roll Is Dead." They're pretty uninteresting, individually and as a group. They seem to me to betray an almost complete lack of imagination; rather than feeling passionately either that rock is dead or that it can never die, these songs instead pick up "rock is dead" as a cliché and build formulaic songs around the trope. The less said here, perhaps, the better.

A fifth group of songs takes precisely the opposite approach to Kravitz in "Rock & Roll Is Dead": rather than posing as rock's savior, the musician announces himself as rock's assassin. Here the poster boy would have to be Marilyn Manson and the theme song "Rock Is Dead," his hit single from the *Matrix* sound track (as well, of course, as his own *Mechanical Animals*). Manson proclaims that rock is "deader than dead" precisely because he wants to be the guy who puts it out of its misery. The logic of Manson's manifesto is pithily summarized in the title of an instrumental track by a band called Organized Kaos: "Rock Is Dead Because I Killed It." Thirty years ago, Alice Cooper shocked parents everywhere (at least those who were paying attention to their kids' records) by singing about "Dead Babies"; now his epigone makes shock-rock out of the declaration that "Rock is deader than dead / Shock is all in your head." If rock is thought to be, in the familiar phrase, the music of youth revolution, Manson suggests that it was too tame and too pale by a good bit. The rock that comprises his inheritance is "ersatz dressed up and real fake," and he's here to give it to us straight. "Rock" is dead, but the music in which this diagnosis is pronounced, while eschewing the label "rock," is clearly, frighteningly alive, thank you very much.

Hence a sixth style of "rock is dead" song grows quite logically from the fourth form, and Manson's "Rock Is Dead" probably partakes equally of both strategies: songs and artists that insist that rock is dead because they do not consider themselves or do not want to be considered part of what Lawrence Grossberg calls "the rock formation." In this instance, celebrating the death of rock is tantamount to proclaiming the defeat of a powerful competitor, as well as the natural superiority of the music one proffers. When Marilyn Manson declares rock to be "deader than dead," he's both taking credit for the killing and suggesting that his music represents the superior evolutionary form that has come to replace rock. On her 2001 record *Britney*, Britney Spears covered Joan Jett's "I Love Rock & Roll" as a way of suggesting—rather unconvincingly—that she's not the Princess of Pop but the Goddess of Rock; in a structurally similar fashion, Manson sings that "rock is dead" to suggest that he's not rock but something much more bitchin' than that, whether Goth, or Industrial, or recycled Alice Cooper as produced by Trent Reznor. After all, rock is so … 1970s. As David Bowie sang on "Pretty Things," "gotta make way for the homo superior."

Under this same rubric, we would want to consider all those songs that attempt to kill off rock while themselves operating according to different generic conventions. Happy Apple have a track called "Long Live Rock & Roll," which consists of nothing but ambient instrumentals and transient noise bursts; the Frugals, in a song called "Long Live All That Is Rock," performs something of an archaeology of popular music, suggesting continuities rather than generic (or generational) differences; "They say rock is in but ska is dead," the song declares in a ska idiom, speaking to the way we tend to talk about the succession of styles in pop music by always using the metaphor of death. The 5000 Fingers of Dr. T announce, in the title of one of their instrumental tracks, "The Death of Rock 'n' Roll," but the track is trancy make-out music, seemingly unaffected by the death of rock & roll because it sees itself as standing apart, working according to an altogether different logic. Even a cover of a rock song can perform this kind of rhetorical killing, notwithstanding the fact that its title and lyrics contain no hint of such an agenda: a good example from the recent past was the Gourd's hilarious bluegrass version of Snoop Dogg's "Gin 'n' Juice." And of course the song that started the whole "rock is dead" campaign, discussed in chapter 1, works by this sort of stealth strategy: while the Maddox Brothers and Rose called their song "The Death of Rock and Roll," they were "America's favorite hillbilly band" and hoped to accomplish, rather than broadcast, rock's death through their cover of the Ray Charles hit "I Got a Woman."

Looking at the seventh and eighth categories of "rock is dead" songs, we'll be moving, in very short compass, from the sublime to the ridiculous. A seventh category comprises those songs that suggest, in one way or another, that "rock is dead" because it's killing itself: a category we might call "rock & roll suicide," after one of rock's great survivors David Bowie. Every time there is a literal rock & roll suicide, of course, a little bit of rock dies. As we have already noted, in a perfect, yet horrible, irony, the song in which Neil Young confidently declares that "rock & roll will never die"—his faith based on the raw energy and imagination that Johnny Rotten and the Sex Pistols brought to a largely moribund rock scene—is precisely the song quoted and badly misconstrued in the note left behind by the man who quickly became the archetypal rock & roll suicide, Kurt Cobain. The most representative song in this most disturbing category would have to be the Doors' weird and rambling, sixteen-and-a-half-minute odyssey "Rock Is Dead"; Jim Morrison makes explicit the equation of the death of rock and the death of its poet, proclaiming rock's demise as a way of announcing, or perhaps proleptically enacting, his own death: "As long as I got breath, the death of rock / Is the death of me, / And rock is dead." Here, the words of Lester Bangs (as portrayed, at least, in Cameron Crowe's film *Almost Famous*) are apposite: "The Doors? Jim Morrison? He's a drunken buffoon, posing as a poet." Certainly Morrison was a drunken buffoon on the night that this live track was recorded;

Morrison is stumbling toward something—sometimes he gets there, as in the haunting "The End," and sometimes he just stumbles, as here. We wait for him to tell us, as he promised to, about "the death of rock / And who killed it," but we crash into the egotistical sublime. Rock is dying, even as Morrison seems bent on his own destruction. Jethro Tull put it a bit more honestly, with a bit more self-awareness, in "Too Old to Rock 'n' Roll, Too Young to Die." Sometimes, within this category, a song will suggest that rock's death is not of its own making but due instead to larger, outside forces; the Buggles's "Video Killed the Radio Star" can represent all of those songs that suggest that commercial forces have killed whatever was vital in rock & roll.

Finally, I suggest an eighth thematic grouping within the "rock is dead" canon: those songs that invoke that old chestnut only to mock the very idea of rock's death. This is perhaps my own favorite thread, because it suggests rock's richly ironic resources, its self-consciousness, and its refusal (at its best) to take itself too seriously. In the Knack's "Pop Is Dead," Doug Fieger sings, over a big pop sound track: "Pop is dead / Please don't trouble me / While I'm watching TV." In King Missile's hilarious "Rock and Roll Will Never Die," John Hall screeches over a painfully self-indulgent '70s-style, feedback-laden guitar line that rock & roll will never die and adduces as evidence over-the-hill "death-in-life" bands like those John Strausbaugh chronicles in *Rock 'Till You Drop:* Def Leppard ("The drummer's got one fuckin' arm"), the Rolling Stones ("They've been around for 45 years"), and, most savagely, Guns n' Roses: "Need I say more?" In this version, of course, rock & roll will never die but really ought to. Like the Sibyl of Cumae in Petronius's *Satyricon,* rock has been blessed with eternal life but not with eternal youth: "When the boys asked her," Petronius writes, "'Sibyl, what do you want?' she responded: 'I want to die.'" Finally, take the Residents' truly sublime send-up of all the rock-is-dead hysteria, which it ridicules even in its punning title: "Bach Is Dead."

Not surprisingly, there is one final category of rock song that effectively anticipates my argument in this book: those songs that suggest that the very claims of rock's death are our most important evidence of its vitality. For every song bemoaning the fact that rock is "deader than dead," there's another boasting defiantly that rock can never die. Those songs, though few in number, betray a wisdom not often found in the "rock is dead" genre, and for that reason, we'll hold them over for discussion in our next and final chapter.

6

ROCK IS DEAD: LONG LIVE ROCK

Insistence on its own morbidity is rock & roll's "strange necessity": rock seemingly must believe itself dead if it is to continue to be what it has always been. Early rock & roll, later just "rock," defined itself primarily as "not pop": *not* Peggy Lee, *not* Mel Torme, *not,* despite his best efforts to the contrary, Pat Boone (his sublime late-career album *In a Metal Mood* notwithstanding). Having successfully, forcefully distinguished itself from its popular-music predecessors, however, as it entered its second generation, rock & roll faced something of a structural problem: What music do we rebel against *now*? One answer—an extremely unfortunate and destructive one, I believe—is that rock purists have come to insist on distinguishing "rock & roll" from all other popular musics that might reasonably be considered part of the rock formation, whether that music be called disco, techno, alt-country, or hip-hop. Lawrence Grossberg describes this as a kind of structural imperative:

> It is an essential sign of the popularity of rock and roll that it constantly marks its difference from other musical cultures, whether popular or not. Rock and roll is, from its own side, not merely a subset of "pop," and there must always be music that is not rock and roll. Such "other" music is "co-opted," "sold out," "bubblegum," "family entertainment," and so on.[1]

As Andrew Ross has pointed out, these exclusions often bear traces of both racism and homophobia;[2] "rock & roll," then, rather than the kind of ecumenical umbrella term for the wide variety of youth musics for which I have argued in my preface, has in some quarters become just another term for "music I like" or, even more callow, "music, the liking of which makes me unique." "I want to be different," John S. Hall of King Missile sings on "It's Saturday," "I want to be just like all the different people."

But another answer is that, in its need for perpetual rebellion, rock turns on itself, in a kind of autoimmune response: declaring rock dead enables rock to go on. This seems ironic, given the difficult time rock & roll fans often have in accepting the physical death of their heroes; hence the ongoing claims that dead rock stars are *really* alive. *Item:* In the video for 2Pac's song "Changes," he wears 1999 Air Jordans—shoes not available at the time of his death! *Item:* Celebrity psychic Kenny Kingston has given up on chatting to Doors rocker Jim Morrison from beyond the grave—because he's convinced Jim's not dead! *Item:* Elvis was seen last week at a truck stop in Bradenton, Florida! (All of these remarkable claims can be verified quickly on the Internet.) While finding confirmation of rock's death in some of the most unlikely places, American culture is almost equally obsessed with proving that actual dead rockers are still alive. The heart of this paradox may lie in the hope that, by refusing to accept the real death of a rock star, the passing from center stage to margin of one type of music, and the triumph of the new, can equally be denied. And it's often precisely the success of the new that proves to the fan of the old that "rock is dead." Clearly, we're dealing with some end-of-life issues here.

In the final analysis, the group most likely to declare that "rock is dead" isn't rock journalists, critics, musicians, or even rock "haters" from among the Right or the Parents: it's rock fans, the most fickle and traitorous of all popular entertainment consumers. In the mouth of a fan, or in her letter to *Spin* or *Rolling Stone* (often in the most artless of ways), the phrase "rock is dead" signifies a sense of betrayal: a band or performer that one has identified with the ongoing vitality of rock has, for one reason or another, fallen from grace in the fan's eyes. And to the monomaniacal fan, nearly anything can signal the death of rock: Creed appearing on the cover of *Rolling Stone;* the commercial success of Radiohead's last three studio albums; the White Stripes appearing on the Video Music Awards; and Moby's commercial licensing of every track on *Play.*

This death is experienced by the fan as the collapse of the various forms of rock (metal, rap, alternative, punk) into the vast, undifferentiated no-man's-land of "pop": pop is the place old rock goes to die, a kind of sanitarium for rock & roll that's lost its edge, drive, and power. So the fan believes, for example, that Metallica was an authentic heavy-metal band *before* they lost their original bass player Cliff Burton, but now they're too "poppy." But "pop" is an ill-defined and moving target; rock fans must always worry that the music they love isn't really rock & roll but merely pop, as those in the know will quickly realize—and they'll be outed as a fan of the dread "bubblegum" about which Grossberg writes. (The best current example of this danger is the phenomenally successful British power-balladeers Coldplay, who seem, on the release of their third album, *X & Y*, to have been declared by the rock press to be treacly pop.)[3] In this worldview, rock is a very fragile thing, unable to fight off even the weakest of infections, the predations of popular taste; hence the all-too-familiar narrative of the performer or band fighting valiantly to preserve artistic integrity and authenticity against evil, corporate forces pressuring for a sellout, a topic we dealt with in some detail in chapter 1.

Of all the cultural forces poised to make the death of rock a reality, the most threatening is an unarticulated "divide and conquer" logic that encourages fans and critics to fetishize minute distinctions between various members of the rock family. "I don't like rock & roll," for instance; "I only listen to alternative." "Divide and conquer" makes a lot of sense from a marketer's perspective; all sectors of American culture are now subject to "narrowcasting," and those 175 genres of rock & roll—so finely discerned at the allmusic.com website—enable advertising executives to fine-tune their message and "hone in" on specific audiences for the maximum return on the buck. For real music fans and real musicians, however, these labels and artificial barriers erected in what is finally a seamless continuum of popular musics seem far less important—deleterious, even.

Just one example of the danger of categorization is the guitarist and singer Junior Brown. His allmusic.com profile pegs him as "country," and that's right, so far as it goes. Junior is most famous, perhaps, for playing his "guit-steel," a twin-necked guitar of his own design that's half electric guitar, half steel; and in terms of aural clichés, nothing says "country" like a steel guitar. I went to see him a few years back when spending some time with a friend in New York; my friend Jon is a guitarist and had heard of Brown and heard too that he put on a good show. Given my suburban Los Angeles upbringing, and congenital dislike for country music, I can't say I was enthusiastic, but I was a houseguest, and live music in a small club is almost always a good thing.

I went along to that show, and I have to admit now that it fundamentally changed the way I think about contemporary popular music. Junior Brown is a delightful player to watch: joyous, technically proficient—and that guit-steel, corny though it may be, does allow him to do some pretty amazing things. As a writer, his forte (if it can be called that) is really the novelty song: probably his best-known composition is a narrative about a former girlfriend with the infectious title and refrain, "You're wanted by the po-lice / And my wife thinks you're dead."

Junior Brown is a dazzling guitarist (dubbed "the unbelievable Junior Brown" by *Guitar Player* on their March 1997 cover), but there are a dispiriting number of dazzling guitarists out there. What's most impressive about Junior is the way he absolutely demolishes the boundaries between ostensibly discrete and distinct genres of popular music. His set that night included, besides his own compositions and some familiar country standards like Hank Williams Jr.'s "Free Born Man" (played at blistering speed), Johnny Rivers's 1966 hit "Secret Agent Man," played in a surf-guitar style reminiscent of Dick Dale; Jimi Hendrix's "Foxey Lady," rendered as a stylistic homage to the Master of the Stratocaster; even "Lovely Hula Hands," with his steel guitar taking on the accents of the islands. His sets are instinctively ecumenical; even more so individual songs, in which Brown makes effortless acoustic allusions to songs and players from all across the popular radio dial, many flitting by so quickly they're hardly noticed. Walking into that nightclub sure I wasn't going to like what I heard, because I didn't "like country," I walked away both elated and ashamed of myself. Looking now at Junior Brown's website, I discover that my reaction wasn't an unusual one: "A lot of people tell me they don't like country music, but they like what I am doing," Brown says there; "I hear that line more than anything else." He continues,

> Just about the time they label me as some old time honkytonk singer, I throw something new in there that surprises them. And then they'll appreciate the traditional styles of country music too. Do something to wow them without ruining the roots of country and they end up accepting the music that they would have been prejudiced against.[4]

Whether we call him country or, as his website does, "the soul of country and the spirit of rock n' roll," Junior Brown makes music dedicated to the anarchic, democratic spirit that has kept rock & roll alive and fresh past its silver anniversary.

When we insist on policing too-strict generic boundaries that hem in rock & roll, we risk robbing it of what's most important and vital about it. The problem is not with the labels but with their reification: when the labels come to seem more real than the music they were meant to describe. Chuck D gets at this dynamic; when asked whether rock & roll is dead, he responded, "Rock and roll, when it calls itself rock and roll—that's when it has its problems.... When the music expands, that's when it tends to do better. The same thing with rap."[5]

The border skirmish that's currently doing the greatest damage to rock & roll involves the captious distinction between rock & roll and the form that has, for the past decade and more, been rock's most innovative as well as commercially successful venue: rap. Today, rap is the litmus test: if one is willing to acknowledge that rap is a forward advance of the rock formation, is in fact *a part* of rock & roll, then it seems to me there's no logically coherent way to argue that rock is dead. If, on the other hand, one insists that rap is no part of rock & roll—well then, rock is in a bit more trouble (though still vital in some very interesting pockets, I'd argue). As Lawrence Grossberg writes,

> Some locate rap within rock, positioning it as the new internal site of authenticity (reproducing the structure of rock verses pop). Others, claiming that rap is not part of the rock formation (usually by drawing a sharp distinction between white and black musical formations) nevertheless position rap as the heir to rock's vitality and potential as a nascent act of resistance.[6]

In his memoir *Tha Doggfather,* Snoop Dogg makes a point of distinguishing the music he makes from rock & roll. His logic for this distinction is never articulated in great detail, but it seems that declaring rap's independence from rock & roll is, for Snoop, something of a boast (and thus something he's rather good at). For instance, he claims, "There's a reason hip-hop music outsells rock & roll two to one,"[7] a statistic rather hard to substantiate, especially when its terms are so porous. And again: "Check it out—today, hip-hop music sells more records than R&B or soul ever did; it sells more than country and Latin and jazz combined; it sells more than motherfucking *rock&roll,* and that's no bullshit."[8] While claiming to be the Dogg*father,* there are clearly some Oedipal dynamics in evidence here, and Snoop (and many other rappers with him) is eager to show how rap has overcome *its* father, rock & roll.

If Snoop wants nothing to do with rock & roll, clearly large segments of the traditional rock audience want nothing to do with him. On one webpage dedicated to the "death of rock & roll," for instance, Snoop is listed as one of the seven sure signs that the music in question is *not* rock & roll:

> You say Rock and Roll will live forever? Why not take my simple Rock and Roll challenge? It's fun, it's easy, and you can take it in the privacy of your own home. My challenge to you is to name just one Rock and Roll song. Your song will be disqualified if it matches the following criteria:
>
> A) The song does not contain a guitar solo.
> B) The song has been played on an "Alternative" radio station.
> C) The song has been played on a Top 40 Pop radio station.
> D) The song has been played on an Adult Contemporary radio station.
> E) One of the song's principal instruments is a Blues harmonica.
> F) The song is performed by Snoop Doggy Dogg.
> G) All of the above.
>
> If you can find a recent song that fails all of these conditions, by all means let me know, I'd like to be the first one to attempt CPR on Rock and Roll.[9]

Others from the worlds of rock and rap, however, are more thoughtful about the mutually beneficial, synergistic relationship between the two. As Robert Miklitsch has incisively commented,

> The point is, from Afrika Bambaataa, one of the seminal old-school Master of Ceremonies, to Run-D.M.C. and "new school," pre-"Walk This Way" rap-'n'-rock tunes such as "Rock Box" (1984) and "King of Rock" (1985) to, most recently, Sean Combs and his Police-inspired ode to the Notorious B.I.G., "I'll Be Missing You" (1997), rock has been part and parcel of that eclectic mix that is rap, a musical mélange forever memorialized in the lyrics of "Payoff Mix": "Punk rock, new wave and soul / Pop music, salsa, rock & roll / Calypso, reggae, rhythm & blues, / Master, mix those number-one tunes."[10]

Miklitsch stays for a moment with the (then current) example of Sean "Puffy" Combs, aka Puff Daddy (later, P. Diddy, and now just Diddy), quoting from an interview in *Rolling Stone:*

Rolling Stone:　What bands do you like now?
Puffy:　　　　Radiohead.[11]

Given the mercurial pace of change in rock & roll, I know that (like Miklitsch) my "current" example will be dated by the time this book is read; but a song just starting to get airplay as this goes to press, Kanye West's "Diamonds (From Sierra Leone)," seems to me (in part) an eloquent response to the rock & rap rivalry. West's first album, *The College Dropout,* won Grammys for Best Rap Album, Best Rap Song, and Best R&B Song and was glowingly discussed as signifying a kind of renaissance for rap. On "Diamonds (From Sierra Leone)," the first single from the follow-up album *Late Registration,* West sings, "The Roc is still alive every time I rhyme." A listener (rather than a reader of lyrics) might be forgiven for hearing "rock" for "Roc," and interpreting West as saying that the best of rap both affirms and contributes to the vitality of rock & roll, of which it is a vital part.

In his pun, West is first and foremost celebrating the commercial success of his record label, Roc-A-Fella Records, founded by Jay-Z and Damon Dash. But the very name of this most successful of rap labels inevitably sounds the name of rock every time it is pronounced. Roc-A-Fella Records starts with "rock" and with the goal to rock a fella; and the rhyming of Kanye West (and Jay-Z, for that matter) serves as a glorious affirmation that rock is still alive. At the very worst—and this hardly seems a bad thing—something like "classic rock" may now have passed on the crown to hip-hop. But hip-hop and rock & roll are part of the same royal family; rap is the heir apparent to rock's throne. At moments of accession like these, the only thing to do is to affirm, as the British do with the crowning of a new monarch, in the words of the Who: "Rock is dead they say / Long live rock!"

One thing that rock critics, rock's critics, and rock fans all have in common is that they deploy (usually rather unreflectively) the rhetoric of "rock is dead" to describe what a more neutral observer might not call "death" but change, or even evolution. Both rock's musical and cultural critics are made nervous by an object of study (or in the case of the cultural Right, an object of careful surveillance) that refuses to keep still, and the rock fan's ire is raised when a beloved band, performer, or scene—in spite of his plea, "don't ever change"—changes. There are those, of course (David Bowie and Madonna preeminent among them), who believe that change is the very essence of rock & roll; rock's "dinosaurs," in this model, like real dinosaurs, die when they can't adapt—when they're too old to rock & roll but too young to die.

Asked whether the Lester Bangs character that he created for *Almost Famous* was right to insist that rock was dying, Cameron Crowe told an interviewer,

> Yes, he was right, but rock dies every year. Rock is dying this year.... And the debate over rock being dead happened in the late '80s. Someone was trying to get me to do a cover story for *Esquire*, "Rock is Dead, Elvis Costello is the only living remnant." And shortly after that, Kurt Cobain wrote "Smells Like Teen Spirit" and the whole thing was alive again.[12]

Rolling Stone veteran Ben Fong-Torres makes the same point, while pushing the origin of the rumors even earlier. He recalls an interview he did with Jim Morrison of the Doors back in 1971, where the "death of rock" was a topic of conversation: "It seems that from the late '60s on, the recent death of rock and roll has been a recurrent subject. Rock and roll is always dying."[13] Rock has been on its deathbed, as we have seen, not just since the late '80s, or even the late '60s, but since the mid '50s—within a year or two of its being born.

The birth and death of rock aren't just coincident—they didn't just happen at practically the same moment: they are, in fact, two different ways to talk about the very same thing. Whenever and wherever art protests its unwillingness to serve as simple entertainment, it will be resisted and suppressed. They only say it's dead—they only want to kill it—because it's so obviously, threateningly, joyously alive.

NOTES

Notes to Preface

1. Joyce 2004, p. 315.
2. Arnold 1993, p. 3.
3. Crosby 1956b, p. 63.
4. Gillett 1983, p. 3.
5. In the introductory note to "Another Boring Day in Paradise," Grossberg writes, "Please note that I use the term 'rock and roll' [in my case, 'rock & roll'] to include all postwar, technologically dependent youth music. The attempt to distinguish 'rock and roll,' 'rock 'n' roll,' and 'rock' would only confuse the argument I am trying to make" (Grossberg 1997, p. 286).
6. Bakhtin 1981, p. 262.
7. Ibid., p. 263.
8. Michael Holquist, "Introduction," in ibid., p. xxxii.

Notes to Chapter 1

1. Quoted in Gilbert and Gubar 1988, p. 156.
2. In a fittingly symmetrical gesture, Pete Seeger is reputed to have wanted to cut the power cables to Dylan's equipment. In a 1999 interview, Seeger both effectively denied and confirmed this rock legend, explaining that when Dylan and his band began to play, "it was so loud you could not understand the words. I was backstage, and I ran over to the person in charge of the controls, and I said, 'Clean up that sound so we can understand the words,' and they shouted back, 'No, this is the way they want it.' I said, 'Goddamn it, if I had an ax, I'd cut the cable.' I was really furious" (Whitehead and Stancui 1999, n.p.).
3. Barth 1984, p. 72.
4. Menand 2005, p. 82.
5. Marzorati 1998, p. 38.
6. Giddins 2004, p. 40.

7. Two volumes of Larkin's collected jazz writings have been published. *All What Jazz: A Record Diary* (1985) is the more dyspeptic of the two; a reviewer on Amazon.com calls it "diary of a sourpuss." The second collection, *Larkin's Jazz: Essays and Reviews, 1940–1984* (2001), is more balanced.
8. Giddins 2004, p. 42.
9. For a brief critique of the central role of "authenticity" in rock writing, see the Introduction to Dettmar and Richey (1999) and the essays collected in that volume.
10. Giddins 2004, p. 43.
11. Ibid., p. 44.
12. www.allmusic.com, accessed March 3, 2005.
13. Giddins 2004, pp. 45–47.
14. Ibid., pp. 50–51.
15. Eliot 1975, pp. 38–39.
16. Giddins 2004, p. 55.
17. Samuels 1958, p. 19.
18. This recording was actually made at the Free Trade Hall in Manchester and was long available on bootleg LPs and CDs before Columbia issued the "official" bootleg, Bob Dylan, *Live 1966*, Columbia/Legacy C2K 65759.
19. A song from the summer before, the summer between the Summer of Love and Woodstock, seemed to some to telegraph the same message: Iron Butterfly's "In-A-Gadda-Da-Vida," from the recording industry's very first platinum album, was misheard by some, including *The Simpsons'* Reverend Lovejoy, as "In the Garden of Eden."
20. Baudrillard 1988, p. 166.
21. Andrew Ross points out that the "Disco Sucks" movement was about more than just aesthetic preferences and instead "was partly homophobic, partly racist, and partly an expression of the counterculture's distaste for studio-produced synth music" (Ross 1994, p. 10).
22. Denby 2003, p. 105.
23. Ross 1994, p. 3.
24. DeCurtis 1994, p. 8.
25. For a more complete examination of the contradictory logics of alternative rock, see Hibbett 2005. "Alternative" now seems to mean almost nothing, if ever it meant something. For example, when (in August 2004) I visited the webpage of Mississippi Nights, a St. Louis club where Nirvana played a legendary gig in October 1991, the separate links for upcoming "rock" and "alternative" acts took me to exactly the same listing of events.
26. Wilco does a wonderful send-up of this kind of thinking on "Late Greats," the closing track on their 2004 album *A Ghost Is Born:* "The best band will never get signed / They never even played a show."
27. Fricke 1994, p. 54.
28. Azzerad 1994, p. 202.
29. Fricke 2001, p. 77.
30. Ibid., p. 122.
31. Accessed August 7, 2001.
32. Quoted in Diehl 1999, p. 128.
33. Mick Jones of The Clash does a nice shaggy-dog version of this pun in a Q & A session with reporters, included in the *Clash on Broadway* trailer that opens the DVD *The Essential Clash:*

Interviewer: Under what circumstances does a group sell out? What does that mean to you?

Jones: Well when we come to Bolton, right, and we announce we're going to play some dates, right? And a lot of people queue up in the morning, right? To buy their tickets, right? And there's no further tickets available, right? That constitutes a sell-out.

34. Bordowitz 2004.
35. *On the Beach,* 1974, Reprise 9362–48497–2.
36. Harrington 2002, p. 556.
37. "Excerpts from Speech by Minow," *New York Times,* May 10, 1961, p. 91.
38. Harrington 2002, p. 556.
39. Clarke 1995, p. 403.
40. Horkheimer and Adorno 2000.
41. Clarke 1995, p. 494.
42. Harrington 2002, p. 58.
43. Whether rock & roll is in fact dominated by a modernist or postmodernist ethos is a live question, and one perhaps not to our purposes to pursue here. One good place to start investigating the competing claims is Richey and Dettmar (2001).
44. Cable 1977, p. 199.
45. Strausbaugh 2001, p. 192.
46. Pareles 1999, p. B9.
47. Ibid., p. 27.
48. Klosterman 2001, p. 13.
49. Strausbaugh 2001, p. 23.
50. Robert Miklitsch compares the two halves of his essay to two sides of a 45: one side dealing with the birth, the other the death, of rock & roll. The metaphor suggests that the birth and death of rock & roll are "two sides of the same coin"; see Miklitsch 1999, ¶ 1.
51. Dawson and Propes 1992.
52. September 29, 1956, Columbia 4–21559. Nick Tosches (1985) seems to have been the first to make this identification.
53. Whiteside 1997, p. 157.
54. Tosches 1985, pp. 34–35.
55. Whiteside 1997, p. 157.
56. Ibid.
57. Charles cut the record on November 18, 1954; it hit number two on the R&B charts on March 16, 1955.
58. Guralnick 1994, pp. 178, 238.
59. Whiteside 1997, p. 157.
60. Ibid., pp. 157, 158.
61. Jerry Butler, interviewed in Jones, Meyrowitz, Salzman, and Solt 2004.
62. Guralnick 1986, p. 50. Despite the large number of performers to have recorded the song, I can find no evidence to support Gillett's claim that Alex Bradford waxed it for Specialty. If this were true, it would make for an even more interesting odyssey, the song having been recorded on Little Richard's label.
63. Garofalo 1997, p. 118.
64. Baudrillard 1988, p. 166.

Notes to Chapter 2

1. Quoted in Koskoff 2001, p. 355.
2. See Lutz 1991.
3. Martin and Segrave 1988, p. vii.
4. Ibid., p. 3.
5. Altschuler 2002, p. 100.
6. Harrington 2002, p. 3.
7. Guest 2001.
8. Martin and Segrave 1988, p. 35.
9. "'Rock 'n' Roll' Stage Show Frantic, Noisy" 1955.
10. Altschuler 2002, p. 3.
11. Ibid., p. 99.
12. Martin and Segrave 1988, p. 43.
13. "Rock-and-Roll Called 'Communicable Disease'" 1956.
14. "They Agree on This" 1955.
15. "Pepper ... and Salt" 1956.
16. McLemore 1956.
17. Crosby 1956b.
18. Bracker 1957.
19. "Rock 'n' Roll Music Is Tops with Teenagers" 1956.
20. "Rhythm and Rumble" 1956.
21. Quoted in Frith 1996, p. 129.
22. Quoted in Garofalo 1997, pp. 172–73.
23. Martin and Segrave 1988, pp. 18–19. See also Garofalo 1997, p. 169.
24. Marsh 1993.
25. Nuzum 2001, p. 214.
26. The best study of the social guidance films is Smith 1999. Many of these films can be viewed at Rick Prelinger's Prelinger Archive website, http://www.panix.com/~footage/
27. Martin and Segrave 1988, p. 38.
28. Coleman 1956.
29. *Encyclopedia Britannica Book of the Year* 1955, p. 470.
30. Gillett 1983, p. 60.
31. For a thorough account of the payola scandal, see Altschuler 2002, pp. 142–60.
32. Coleman 1956.
33. "Rock 'n' Roll Will Soon Be Only for Rowboats, Songwriters Think" 1956.
34. Wolters 1957.
35. Townsend 1958.
36. McDonough 2005.
37. Crosby 1956a.
38. Leonard 1957.
39. "Songs by Machines" 1957.
40. "Gorilla Digs Rock 'n' Roll" 1960.
41. Lieber 1959.
42. Sanjek 1972.
43. Bayles 1994, p. 145.
44. Ibid.

45. Perhaps the most staggering example of the genre is Constantine (2000). However, the imprint of Feral House publishers, dubbing themselves a "publisher of high-quality books on forbidden topics," raises a red flag from the outset, as does Constantine's dedication: "For the victims of Operation CHAOS and COINTELPRO."
46. "Rock 'n' Roll Opponents Are Due for Big Break" 1958.
47. Altschuler 2002, p. 4.
48. Nuzum 2001, p. 216.
49. Ibid., p. 221.
50. Wolters 1958.
51. Page 1958.
52. Gillett 1983, pp. 24–25.
53. Coyle (2002) provides the best discussion of this phenomenon.
54. Ibid., p. 17.
55. Quoted in Guralnick 1994, p. 293.
56. Siegel 1988.
57. Rogin 1987, pp. 238, 245.
58. Quoted in Rogin 1987, p. 259.
59. Ibid.
60. Goldwater 1962.
61. Kirsch 1955.
62. Murphy 1962.
63. "Red Infiltration Will Be Described to GOP" 1961.
64. Siemers 1954.
65. "Coming to Life," *Washington Post*, May 17, 1960, p. A18.
66. "Live Students," *Washington Post*, February 17, 1962, p. A10.
67. Davis 1951.
68. Lieber 1959.
69. Talese 1957.
70. "Leader of White Councils Lays Integration to Reds" 1956.
71. Adorno 2002, pp. 470–96 (p. 475).
72. "Yeh-Heh-Heh-Hes, Baby" 1956.
73. Nuzum 2001, p. 171. While providing a handy compendium of the resistance to rock & roll since its inception, Nuzum's book plays rather fast and loose with the definition of *censorship* and borders on paranoia in its identification of coherent, secret plots to rub out the music.
74. Ibid., p. 232.
75. Bracker 1957.
76. Gelb 1961.
77. Stinson 1961.
78. Warren 2002.
79. Topping 1962.
80. "Rock•'n' Roll Mimed" 1960.
81. "Moiseyev Dancers Plan Spoof on Rock 'n' Roll" 1961.
82. "Yevtushenko Defends Rock 'n' Roll and Twist Despite Red Denunciation" 1962.
83. Liner notes, the Zombies, *Zombie Heaven*, Big Beat/Ace Records, 1997, p. 9.

Notes to Chapter 3

1. Gillett 1983, p. 65.
2. Ibid., pp. 167–68.
3. Ibid., p. 189.
4. The entire rhetoric of "roots music" seems ripe for cultural studies analysis, an attention that, to the best of my knowledge, it has not yet received. One interesting place to start is with the title of Nick Spitzer's punningly titled NPR radio program "American Routes," suggesting that routes into the future, rather than (heavily mythologized) "roots" in the past, is where the real action is in American popular music.
5. Clarke 1995, p. 364.
6. Ibid., pp. 401, 492.
7. Ibid., p. 427.
8. Ibid., p. 489.
9. Ibid., p. 493.
10. Ibid., p. 500.
11. Ibid., p. 498. Klosterman's (2001) book is an intelligent and eloquent evocation of what heavy metal music means in the life of its fans. Among more scholarly works Walser's (1993), Waksman's (1999), and Weinstein's (2002) books have helped to illustrate the sometimes prodigious musical intelligence that undergirds this unapologetically "stupid" music.
12. Clarke 1995, p. 557.
13. Bloom 1987, pp. 74–75.
14. Bérubé 1999.
15. Though I believe he uses the term *censorship* a bit freely, even inaccurately, Nuzum's (2001) book is the best we have on the topic, and he gives special attention to the controversy over "Darling Nikki" (see pp. 21, 27).
16. Journalist Richard Pachter (2000) has identified the secret power of Bangs's name: "Lester Bangs. What a name! Better than Wolf Blitzer. It's a declarative sentence!"
17. Crowe 2000.
18. Bangs 1988, pp. 45–46.
19. Ibid., p. 8.
20. Ibid., p. 224. According to Robert Christgau, Richard Meltzer agreed with the 1968 date: "Meltzer started with the rock-is-dead shit in 1968. Young people scoff when I tell them this, but although he flirted with country and fell for punk and remains an avant-jazzbo, Meltzer repeats the date many times in *A Whore Just Like the Rest*—all but 18 pages of which were published 1969 or later" (Christgau 2000).
21. Bangs 1988, p. 327.
22. Fetishically "old school" though they certainly are in their very public eschewal of all trappings of the rock industry, the White Stripes brilliantly send up this kind of simplistic equation in their blues-based "The Big Three [i.e., record companies] Killed My Baby" (*The White Stripes*, 1999, Sympathy for the Record Industry 577).
23. Goodman 1997, p. xii.
24. Ibid., pp. 353–54.
25. Nehring 1993.

26. Review by "jpcii" posted on July 10, 2000 at http://www.amazon.com/exec/obidos/tg/detail/-/0684865602/ref=cm_cr_dp_2_1/103-6112256-3499835?v=glance&s=books&vi=customer-reviews
27. Miller 1999, p. 353.
28. Arnold 1997.
29. Miller 1999, pp. 16–17.
30. Ibid. Miller's comment echoes, inescapably (if unconsciously), Kurt Cobain's explanation for his "retirement" from the world of rock—in his suicide note: "I haven't felt the excitement of listening to as well as creating music along with reading and writing for too many years now.... The fact is I can't fool you. Any one of you. It simply isn't fair to you or me. The worst crime I can think of would be to rip people off by faking it and pretending as if I'm having 100 percent fun.... I don't have the passion anymore and so remember, it's better to burn out than to fade away" (quoted in Cross 2001, pp. 338–39). Presumably because he arrived on the scene long after rock was officially dead, Cobain is dismissed in two sentences in *Flowers in the Dustbin*—described as a screaming disciple of Janis Joplin and dismissed as an "avatar of excess consecrated by the rock culture industry" (pp. 266, 347). Cobain warrants no mention whatever in Fred Goodman's *Mansion on the Hill.*
31. Miller 1999, p. 19.
32. Ibid., p. 311.
33. Ibid., p. 317.
34. I am neither the only nor the first to level these kinds of charges against *Flowers in the Dustbin.* Strausbaugh (2001) points out, for instance, "In Miller's chronology, David Bowie is the beginning of the end: the first overtly ironic reflection of rock's hype and its tropes back on itself" (p. 24). He goes on to quote Jim DeRogatis, "a younger rock critic," who sums up Miller's thesis this way: "'It wasn't me who changed, it was the music.' ... Yet another Baby Boomer refuses to grant that the sun doesn't shine out of his ass" (p. 25). Finally, Gerald Marzorati (1999) puts the point quite bluntly in his *New York Times* review: "He ends the book sounding like a rock neocon."
35. Gerald Marzorati (1999) suggests, "It is with the release of 'Sgt. Pepper's Lonely Hearts Club Band' on June 1, 1967, that 'Flowers in the Dustbin' reaches its apogee."
36. Miller 1999, p. 321.
37. Though his purview is very different, the argument that Leonard Diepeveen makes in *The Difficulties of Modernism* (2002) is apropos here: the modernist revolution in the arts (of which rock & roll is the beneficiary, if not the dutiful inheritor) turned difficulty in art from a liability into an asset.
38. Miller 1999, p. 352.
39. Ibid., p. 354.
40. Hornby 2000.
41. For an attempt to articulate precisely what's triumphant and transcendent about the music of Radiohead, see Dettmar 2005, pp. xiv–xx.
42. Bérubé 1999.
43. Hornby 2002.
44. Ibid., pp. 13–14.
45. Ibid., p. 30.

46. Ibid., p. 64.
47. Strausbaugh 2001, p. 238.
48. Hornby 2002, p. 66.
49. Ibid., p. 76.
50. Ibid., pp. 91–92.
51. Hornby 2004.
52. One letter writer to the *Times* touched on another of Hornby's (2004) unexamined prejudices, suggesting that no one who had been listening to any rap could complain of "the suffocatingly airless contemporary pop-culture climate" (*New York Times,* Editorials/Letters, May 25, 2004, p. A26).
53. Carlyle 1831.
54. Richey and Dettmar 2001.
55. Hornby 2004.
56. *New York Times,* Editorials/Letters, May 25, 2004, p. A26.

Notes to Chapter 4

1. Grossberg 1994, p. 52. A version of the talk Grossberg gave at Duke has been published (Grossberg 2002).
2. Grossberg 2002, p. 47. He adds, in a note to this passage, "This description is based on ethnographic research I conducted with a group of high school students during summer 1995 in Illinois."
3. Waugh 1916.
4. Larkin 1985.
5. Quoted in Miller 1999, p. 169.
6. Andrew Ross (1994, p. 9) writes, "Baby boomers often consider their experience of youth to have been uniquely definitive, and consequently have made this experience into an object of both envy and resentment for their children."
7. Christgau 2004, p. 35.
8. Miklitsch 1999.
9. Bayles 1994, pp. 3, 13, 12. While treating her here as a scholarly critic of rock & roll—and certainly her scholarly credentials and her scholarship are impressive—her placement here has the unfortunate effect of blurring her intellectual sympathies with neocons like Allan Bloom (thanked in the acknowledgments to her book), whose influence on popular rock writing is treated in chapter 3.
10. Dettmar 2001.
11. Bayles 1994, p. 3.
12. Ibid., p. 391.
13. Ibid., p. 12.
14. Frith 2004, p. 22.
15. Frith 1996.
16. Ibid., pp. 252–53. The Scruton passage comes from Scruton 1995, p. 197.
17. Frith 1988, p. 1.
18. Miklitsch 1999, ¶ 26, 27.
19. Much of this writing for the period 1984 to 1994 is collected in Grossberg (1997), which can be supplemented with the more recent pieces in Grossberg (1994, 2002).

20. Grossberg 1997, p. 32.
21. Ibid., p. 61.
22. Ibid., p. 63.
23. Grossberg 1994, p. 41.
24. Ibid., pp. 41–42.
25. Ibid., p. 42.
26. Ibid.
27. Ibid., p. 55.
28. Grossberg 1997, p. 17.
29. "The [rock] formation that had been central (albeit not exclusive) in my own work, which emerged in the 1960s to become the dominant U.S. cultural formation of 'American' youth at least until the mid 1980s, had, by the end of the 1980s, been displaced. I believe this apparatus is 'becoming-residual'" (Grossberg 2002, p. 45).
30. Grossberg 1997, pp. 20–22.
31. Grossberg 2002, pp. 48–49.
32. Ibid., p. 49.
33. Miklitsch (1999, ¶ 32) rather elegantly suggests an example of a new style of musical consumption that may in fact recapture some of the rebelliousness that Grossberg associates with the traditional rock formation: "Beavis and Butt-head … represent, in however twisted or demented a form, the continuing vitality of rock. That is, if Beavis and Butt-head can be said to dramatize the demise of what Grossberg calls the 'ideology of authenticity,' it's pretty obvious that for all their benumbed, dumb-and-dumber behavior, they can hardly be said to be affectless when it comes to the subject of rock."
34. Ibid., ¶ 50.
35. Grossberg mentions that he "began teaching classes on popular music in 1977" in the first endnote for *Dancing in Spite of Myself.*
36. Miklitsch 1999, ¶ 65.

Notes to Chapter 5

1. While it is traditional to talk of the three rock stars lost in that crash, I simply cannot bring myself to call the man who recorded "Chantilly Lace" a rock star. For the definitive treatment of this event, see Lehmer 1997.
2. The song was brilliantly parodied in a December 9, 2000, *Saturday Night Live* sketch, "VH1: Behind the Music," in which Val Kilmer reprised his portrayal of Jim Morrison from the 1991 Oliver Stone film *The Doors.* Back in 1961, Tex Ritter had a hit with "I Dreamed of a Hill-Billy Heaven," perhaps the paradigm for this type of song, in which Tex is greeted at the pearly gates by Will Rogers and introduced to Carson Robinson and "the Mississippi blue yodeler" Jimmie Rodgers.
3. Fowlie 1994.
4. Stein 1999.
5. Ramazani 1994, p. ix.
6. Ibid., p. 6.
7. Hornby 2002, p. 140.
8. Coupland 1996, pp. 98–99.

9. For an imaginative exploration of the effect of Cobain's death on two British teenagers, see Hornby 1998.

10. Coupland 1996, p. 98.

11. I cannot hope to discuss all of the Cobain elegies here, and the number is in all likelihood not yet complete. Among other notable tributes to Cobain not discussed here are the Red Hot Chili Peppers' "Tearjerker"; Coyote Shivers' "I'm Secretly Jealous of Kurt Cobain"; and Hidden Agenda's "Kurt Cobain Is Dead."

12. For a sensationalistic version of their relationship, see Bloomfield 1999.

13. Cross 2001, p. 337. In his notes, Cross writes, "The events of Kurt's final hours are pieced together from police reports, forensic evidence reports, and pictures of the scene" (p. 364).

14. Giles 1994.

15. I have explored the connection of rock and suicide more thoroughly in Dettmar 2000.

16. And Cobain wasn't the only gifted singer–songwriter to misinterpret Young's song; in an interview with David Sheff, John Lennon said about the couplet, "I hate it. It's better to fade away like an old solider than to burn out. If he was talking about burning out like Sid Vicious, forget it" (quoted in McDonough 2002, p. 534). Again, Young certainly wasn't talking about Sid Vicious: he was talking about Johnny Rotten, the stage creation of John Lydon.

17. For an analysis of the media's portrayal of Love, in tandem with that of Madonna, see Manners 1999.

18. For a thorough analysis of *Celebrity Skin* as a rock & roll elegiac cycle, see Dettmar 2005.

19. Posted by Freakdine@aol.com at "The Breakdown of Nirvana" pages, www.geocities.com/SunsetStrip/Booth/8166/Nirvana1.html, accessed February 1, 2005.

20. Posted by "Jake," October 7, 2002, www.iwilldare.com/archives/002878.php, accessed February 1, 2005.

21. Ibid.

22. Posted by "Ketut (Keith)," October 8, 2002, www.iwilldare.com/archives/002878.php, accessed February 1, 2005.

23. The best study of the relationship of the movies to youth culture during the period remains Doherty's (1988).

24. Coe 1955. About the music in the film, Coe writes more fully, "There is a corking good jazz score, highlighted by a nifty jump piece, 'Rock Around the Clock,' which terrific as it is, only heightens the frantic, emotional whizbang."

25. Actually, this is a bit of an oversimplification: the first sound in the film plays while a text expressing the filmmakers' concern over the rising tide of juvenile delinquency scrolls across the screen. That text is accompanied by dramatic, martial drumming; in a rather nifty production trick, then, that drumming segues quite nicely into the famous opening drumbeats of "Rock Around the Clock," the song's opening made even more menacing by this preface.

26. Donald Clarke (1995, p 382) summarizes the comments of Milt Gabler: "Film soundtracks were usually 'pinched' at the top and bottom of the frequency range, to save the ears of the people in the front rows from the noise

of the huge speakers and amplifiers used in big cinemas; but *The Blackboard Jungle* soundtrack was processed wide open."

27. Altschuler 2002, p. 32.
28. Hunter 1954, p. 168.
29. Ibid., p. 169.
30. Ibid., p. 167.
31. Bayles 1994, p. 117. Although I take issue with Bayles's larger argument elsewhere in this book and disagree with some of her conclusions in the case of *Blackboard Jungle* as well, hers is our best analysis of the film's importance for the development of rock & roll and the importance of Haley's song for the film.
32. Gillett 1983, pp. 16–17.
33. And how much more threatening the youth become, years later, when technology does allow them to set up their own portable sound systems for producing their own B-boy mayhem: think of Spike Lee's *Do the Right Thing* (1989), for instance.
34. Bayles 1994, p. 117.
35. The fact that the theme music was a very late addition is confirmed by Peter Ford, son of the film's star Glenn Ford:

> On Thursday January 13, 1955 my dad went to a screening room at MGM to see a rough cut of *Blackboard Jungle*.... About two weeks later, the final version was complete and a sneak preview was scheduled. Dad knew that I would like it and told me to expect to hear "that song" somewhere during the film. All dad knew is that they laid in a music track for the first time and that "my song" was going to be in the film somewhere.... The theater grew dark, and I remember very clearly my thoughts as the first scene opened on the empty blackboard as the credits rolled by: Wow! Not only were they playing "Rock Around the Clock," the song that dad had borrowed from my record collection and given to Mr. Brooks, but it was so loud—just like I played it at home. (Peter Ford, "'Rock Around the Clock' and Me," http://www.peterford.com/ratc.html, accessed November 17, 2004)

36. Altschuler 2002, p. 33.
37. Ibid.
38. O'Brien 2004, p. 99.
39. Altschuler 2002, p. 23.
40. Bayles 1994, p. 261.
41. To complete one more turn of the screw, one might reasonably ask if sonic recreations of Jimi Hendrix's guitar playing are evidence of the vitality or the morbidity of rock; Hendrix (d. September 18, 1970) had been dead almost twenty-five years to the day when Kravitz's album *Circus* was released on September 12, 1995.

Notes to Chapter 6

1. Grossberg 1997, p. 38.
2. Ross 1994, p. 11.

3. One other complicated response to this phenomenon is the notion of the "guilty pleasure": yeah, I know that Guns n' Roses (or Coldplay) are crap, but I like them anyway: they're a guilty pleasure. This, too, seems a mode of betrayal best left to one side by real fans; as my friend Jennifer Wicke says, for any form of popular entertainment that gives real joy, real pleasure, there's no guilt. We need, instead, critics who are willing to do the hard work of explaining *why* they value the music that others want to write off as pop—this is an important and compelling critical project. Call it the Celine Dion problem, perhaps.
4. See http://www.juniorbrown.com/biography.asp, accessed June 8, 2005.
5. Chuck D, interviewed in Jones, Meyrowitz, Salzman, and Solt 2004.
6. Grossberg 1997, p. 104.
7. Snoop Dogg 1999, p. 6.
8. Ibid., p. 45.
9. Webpage, Jason Harland, "The Death of 'Rock and Roll'" (1997); page now offline.
10. Miklitsch 1999, ¶ 38.
11. Ibid., p. 38; quoting Sean Combs, "Puff Daddy," interview with Anthony Bozza, *Rolling Stone* 776/777, December 25–January 8, 1998, p. 78.
12. From an interview by Shawn Levy in *The Oregonian,* September 22, 2000, http://cameroncroweonline.com/press/famous/oregonian.htm, accessed February 1, 2005.
13. David Templeton, "Crazy Days: Ben Fong-Torres on the Death of Rock and Roll," Metro-Active Movies (webpage), http://www.metroactive.com/papers/sonoma/10.05.00/talk-pix-0040.html, accessed November 8, 2004.

BIBLIOGRAPHY

Adorno, Theodor. (2000). "On Jazz," in *Essays on Music*, ed. Richard Leppert, trans. Susan H. Gillespie. Berkeley: University of California Press, pp. 470–495.

Altschuler, Glenn C. (2002). *All Shook Up: How Rock 'n' Roll Changed America*. New York: Oxford University Press.

Arnold, Gina. (1997). *Kiss This: Punk in the Present Tense*. New York: St. Martin's.

———. (1993). *Route 666: On the Road to Nirvana*. New York: St. Martin's.

Azzerad, Michael. (1994). *Come as You Are: The Story of Nirvana*. New York: Doubleday.

Bakhtin, M. M. (1981). *The Dialogic Imagination: Four Essays*, ed. Michael Holquist, trans. Caryl Emerson and Michael Holquist. Austin: University of Texas Press.

Bangs, Lester. (1988). *Psychotic Reactions and Carburetor Dung*, ed. Greil Marcus. New York: Vintage/Random House.

Barth, John. (1984). "The Literature of Exhaustion" (1967), in *The Friday Book: Essays and Other Nonfiction*. New York: Pedigree/Putnam, pp. 62–76.

Baudrillard, Jean. (1988). "Simulacra and Simulations" (Orig. pub. 1981.), in *Selected Writings*, ed. Mark Poster. Stanford: Stanford University Press, pp. 166–184.

Bayles, Martha. (1994). *Hole in Our Soul: The Loss of Beauty and Meaning in American Popular Music*. Chicago: University of Chicago Press.

Bérubé, Michael. (1999). "The 'Elvis Costello Problem' in Teaching Popular Culture," *The Chronicle of Higher Education*, August 13, pp. B4–B5.

Bloom, Allan. (1987). *The Closing of the American Mind: How Higher Education Has Failed Democracy and Impoverished the Souls of Today's Students*. New York: Simon & Schuster.

Bloomfield, Nick, dir. (1999). *Kurt & Courtney* (1997). WinStar TV & Video DVD.

Bordowitz, Hank. (2004). *Turning Points in Rock and Roll: The Key Events That Affected Popular Music in the Latter Half of the 20th Century*. New York: Citadel.

Bracker, Milton. (1957). "Experts Propose Study of 'Craze'," *New York Times*, February 23, p. 12.

Britannica Book of the Year. (1955). Chicago: Encyclopedia Britannica.

Cable, Michael. (1977). *The Pop Industry Inside Out*. London: W.H. Allen.

Carlyle, Thomas. (1831). "Characteristics," in *The Edinburgh Review* LIV (December), pp. 351–83.

Christgau, Robert. (2004). "U.S. and Them: Are American Pop (and Semi-Pop) Still Exceptional? And By the Way, Does That Make Them Better?," in *This Is Pop: In Search of the Elusive at the Experience Music Project*, ed. Eric Weisbard. Cambridge, MA: Harvard University Press, pp. 26–38.

————. (2000). "Impolite Discourse." *Village Voice,* July 4, p. 78.

Clarke, Donald. (1995). *The Rise and Fall of Popular Music.* New York: St. Martin's.

Coe, Richard L. (1955). "Tiger Twisted in This Jungle," *Washington Post and Times Herald,* April 22, p. 48.

Coleman, William A. (1956). "After Rock 'n' Roll, What? Will Tunes Get Even Jumpier or Is Cornball Coming Back?," *Washington Post and Times Herald,* July 8, p. AW4.

"Coming to Life." (1960). *Washington Post,* May 17, p. A18.

Constantine, Alex. (2000). *The Covert War against Rock: What You Don't Know about the Deaths of Jim Morrison, Tupac Shakur, Michael Hutchence, Brian Jones, Jimi Hendrix, Phil Ochs, Bob Marley, Peter Tosh, John Lennon, the Notorious B.I.G.* Venice, CA: Feral House.

Coupland, Douglas. (1996). *Polaroids from the Dead.* New York: Regan Books/HarperCollins.

Coyle, Michael. (2002). "Hijacked Hits and Antic Authenticity: Cover Songs, Race and Postwar Marketing," in *Rock Over the Edge: Transformations in Popular Music Culture,* ed. Roger Beebe, Denise Fulbrook, and Ben Saunders. Durham, NC: Duke University Press, pp. 133–157.

Crosby, John. (1956a). "Could Elvis Mean End of Rock 'n' Roll Craze?," *Washington Post,* June 18, p. 33.

————. (1956b). "Melody on Way Back Even without Puritans," *Washington Post and Times Herald,* March 30, p. 63.

Cross, Charles R. (2001). *Heavier Than Heaven: A Biography of Kurt Cobain.* New York: Hyperion.

Crowe, Cameron, dir. (2000). *Almost Famous.* Hollywood, CA: Columbia/Dreamworks.

Davis, Sid, prod. (1951). "The Terrible Truth." Sid Davis Productions, 10 mins.

Dawson, Jim, and Steve Propes. (1992). *What Was the First Rock 'n' Roll Record?* Boston: Faber and Faber.

DeCurtis, Anthony. (1994). "Kurt Cobain, 1967–1994," in *Cobain,* ed. the Editors of *Rolling Stone.* New York: Rolling Stone Press, p. 8.

Denby, David. (2003). "Private Worlds," rev. of *A Mighty Wind,* in *New Yorker,* May 5, p. 105.

Dettmar, Kevin J.H. (2005). "Foreword," in *The Music and Art of Radiohead,* ed. Joseph Tate. Aldershot: Ashgate, pp. xiv–xx.

————. (2004). "*Wunderkindtotenlieder*: On Dying Too Young in Rock," *The CEA Critic* 66: 2–3, pp. 1–20.

————. (2001). "Is Rock 'n' Roll Dead? Only If You Aren't Listening," *Chronicle of Higher Education,* May 11, pp. B10–11.

————. (2000). "Ironic Literacy: Grasping the Dark Images of Rock," *Chronicle of Higher Education,* June 2, pp. B11–12.

————, and William Richey, eds. (1999). *Reading Rock & Roll: Authenticity, Appropriation, Aesthetics.* New York: Columbia University Press.

Diehl, Matt. (1999). "Pop Rap," in *The Vibe History of Hip Hop,* ed. Alan Light. New York: Three Rivers Press, pp. 121–133.

Diepeveen, Leonard. (2002). *The Difficulties of Modernism.* New York: Routledge.

Doherty, Thomas. (1988). *Teenagers and Teenpics: The Juvenilization of American Movies in the 1950s.* Boston: Unwin Hyman.

Eliot, T.S. (1975). "Tradition and the Individual Talent," in *Selected Prose of T.S. Eliot,* ed. Frank Kermode. New York: Harcourt Brace Jovanovich, pp. 37–44.

Fowlie, Wallace. (1994). *Rimbaud and Morrison: The Rebel as Poet.* Durham, NC: Duke University Press.

Fricke, David. (2001). "The *Rolling Stone* Interview: David Grohl," *Rolling Stone,* September 13, pp. 77, 122.

————. (1994). "In Utero," in *Cobain,* ed. the Editors of *Rolling Stone.* New York: Rolling Stone Press, p. 54.

Frith, Simon. (2004). "'And I Guess It Doesn't Matter Anymore': European Thoughts on American Music," in *This Is Pop: In Search of the Elusive at Experience Music Project,* ed. Eric Weisbard. Cambridge, MA: Harvard University Press, pp. 15–25.

———. (1996). *Performing Rites: On the Value of Popular Music.* Cambridge, MA: Harvard University Press.

———. (1988). "Everything Counts," in *Music for Pleasure: Essays in the Sociology of Pop.* New York: Routledge, pp. 1–8.

Garofalo, Reebee. (1997). *Rockin' Out: Popular Music in the USA.* Boston: Allyn & Bacon.

Gelb, Arthur. (1961). "Habitues of Meyer Davis Land Dance the Twist," *New York Times,* October 19, p. 37.

Giddins, Gary. (2004). "How Come Jazz Isn't Dead?," in *This Is Pop: In Search of the Elusive at the Experience Music Project,* ed. Eric Weisbard. Cambridge, MA: Harvard University Press, pp. 39–55.

Gilbert, Sandra M., and Susan Gubar. (1988). *No Man's Land: The Place of the Woman Writer in the Twentieth Century.* Vol. 1: *The War of the Words.* New Haven, CT: Yale University Press.

Giles, Jeff. (1994). "Everybody Hurts Sometime" (interview with Michael Stipe), *Newsweek,* September 26, p. 61.

Gillett, Charlie. (1983). *The Sound of the City: The Rise of Rock and Roll,* rev. and expanded ed. New York: Pantheon.

Goldwater, Barry. (1962). "Unions Foster Zombies, Robots," *Los Angeles Times,* October 16, p. A4.

Goodman, Fred. (1997). *Mansion on the Hill: Dylan, Young, Geffen, Springsteen, and the Head-on Collision of Rock and Commerce.* New York: Vintage.

"Gorilla Digs Rock 'n' Roll." (1960). *Christian Science Monitor,* February 6, p. 4.

Graff, Gerald. (1992). *Beyond the Culture Wars: How Teaching the Conflicts Can Revitalize American Education.* New York: Norton.

Grossberg, Lawrence. (2002). "Reflections of a Disappointed Popular Music Scholar," in *Rock over the Edge: Transformations in Popular Music Culture,* ed. Roger Beebe, Denise Fulbrook, and Ben Saunders. Durham, NC: Duke University Press, pp. 25–59.

———. (1997). *Dancing in Spite of Myself: Essays on Popular Culture.* Durham, NC: Duke University Press.

———. (1994). "Is Anybody Listening? Does Anybody Care? On 'The State of Rock'," in *Microphone Fiends: Youth Music and Youth Culture,* ed. Andrew Ross and Tricia Rose. New York: Routledge, pp. 41–58.

Guest, Val, dir. (2001). *Expresso Bongo* (1959). Guest Productions, 1959; Kino Video DVD.

Guralnick, Peter. (1994). *Last Train to Memphis: The Rise of Elvis Presley.* Boston: Little, Brown.

———. (1986). *Sweet Soul Music: Rhythm and Blues and the Southern Dream of Freedom.* New York: Harper & Row.

Harrington, Joe S. (2002). *Sonic Cool: The Life and Death of Rock 'n' Roll.* Milwaukee: Hal Leonard.

Hibbett, Ryan. (2005). "What Is Indie Rock?," *Popular Music and Society* 28 (1): pp. 55–78.

Horkheimer, Max, and Theodor W. Adorno. (2000). *Dialect of Enlightenment* (1944), trans. John Cumming. New York: Continuum.

Hornby, Nick. (2004). "Rock of Ages," *New York Times,* May 21, p. A27.

———. (2002). *Songbook.* San Francisco: McSweeney's.

———. (2000). "Beyond the Pale," *New Yorker,* October 30, p. 97.

———. (1998). *About a Boy.* New York: Riverhead Books.

Horowitz, Joseph. (2005). *Classical Music in America: A History of Its Rise and Fall.* New York: W. W. Norton.

Hunter, Evan. (1954). *The Blackboard Jungle.* New York: Simon & Schuster.

Jones, Quincy, Bob Meyrowitz, David Salzman, and Andrew Solt, prods. (2004). *The History of Rock 'n' Roll,* Vol. 1. Time-Life/Warner Bros. DVD 34991.

Joyce, James. (2004). *A Portrait of the Artist as a Young Man and Dubliners,* ed. Kevin J.H. Dettmar. New York: Barnes & Noble.

Kirsch, R. (1955). "The Book Report," *Los Angeles Times,* September 28, p. A5.

Klosterman, Chuck. (2001). *Fargo Rock City: A Heavy Metal Odyssey in Rural North Dakota*. New York: Scribner.

Koskoff, Ellen, ed. (2001). *The Garland Encyclopedia of World Music, Vol. 3: The United States and Canada*. New York: Routledge.

Larkin, Philip. (2001). *Larkin's Jazz: Essays and Reviews, 1940–1984*. New York: Continuum.

———. (1985). *All What Jazz: A Record Diary*. London: Farrar, Straus and Giroux.

"Leader of White Councils Lays Integration to Reds." (1956). *Washington Post*, June 16, p. 3.

Lebrecht, Norman. (1996). *When the Music Stops: Managers, Maestros, and the Corporate Murder of Classical Music*. New York: Simon & Schuster.

Lehmer, Larry. (1997). *The Day the Music Died: The Last Tour of Buddy Holly, the "Big Bopper," and Ritchie Valens*. New York: Schirmer.

Leonard, William. (1957). "You Can Have Rock 'n' Roll!," *Chicago Tribune*, February 3, p. F42.

Lieber, Leslie. (1959). "Pablo Casals Says: Down with Rock 'n' Roll!," *Los Angeles Times*, May 17, p. J19.

"Live Students." (1962). *Washington Post*, February 17, p. A10.

Lutz, Tom. (1991). *American Nervousness, 1903: An Anecdotal History*. Ithaca, NY: Cornell University Press.

Manners, Marilyn. (1999). "Fixing Madonna and Courtney: Sex, Drugs, Rock 'n' Roll Reflux," in *Reading Rock & Roll: Authenticity, Appropriation, Aesthetics*, ed. Kevin J.H. Dettmar and William Richey. New York: Columbia University Press, pp. 37–71.

Marsh, Dave. (1993). *Louie Louie: The History and Mythology of the World's Most Famous Rock 'n' Roll Song*. New York: Hyperion.

Martin, Linda, and Kerry Segrave. (1988). *Anti-Rock: The Opposition to Rock 'n' Roll*. Hamden, CT: Archon/Shoe String Press.

Marzorati, Gerald. (1999). "Where Have You Gone, Sgt. Pepper?," *New York Times Book Review*, September 5, p. 8.

———. (1998). "How the Album Got Played Out," *New York Times Magazine*, February 22, p. 38.

McDonough, Jimmy. (2002). *Shakey: Neil Young's Biography*. New York: Random House.

McDonough, John. (2005). "Looking Back at 'Your Hit Parade'," in *All Things Considered*. Washington, DC: National Public Radio, broadcast April 20.

McLemore, Henry. (1956). "The Lighter Side," *Los Angeles Times*, April 20, p. 30.

Menand, Louis. (2005). "Gross Points," *New Yorker*, February 7, p. 82.

Miklitsch, Robert. (1999). "Rock 'n' Theory: Autobiography, Cultural Studies, and the 'Death of Rock'," *Postmodern Culture* 9 (2); http://www.iath.virginia.edu/pmc/text-only/issue.199/9.2miklitsch.txt.

Miller, James. (1999). *Flowers in the Dustbin: The Rise of Rock and Roll, 1947–1977*. New York: Simon & Schuster.

"Moiseyev Dancers Plan Spoof on Rock 'n' Roll." (1961). *Los Angeles Times*, June 13, p. B26.

Murphy, William S. (1962). "A Frightening Satire," *Los Angeles Times*, November 4, p. A15.

Nehring, Neil. (1993). *Flowers in the Dustbin: Culture, Anarchy, and Postwar England*. Ann Arbor: University of Michigan Press.

Nuzum, Eric D. (2001). *Parental Advisory: Music Censorship in America*. New York: Harper Perennial.

O'Brien, Geoffrey. (2004). "Interrupted Symphony: A Recollection of Movie Music from Max Steiner to Marvin Gaye," in *This Is Pop: In Search of the Elusive at Experience Music Project*, ed. Eric Weisbard. Cambridge, MA: Harvard University Press, pp. 90–102.

Pachter, Richard. (2000). "Almost Lester," *Miami Herald*, October 25; reprinted at http://www.wordsonwords.com/reviews/ AlmostLester.html, accessed April 19, 2005.

Page, Don. (1958). "Whittinghill, Foe of R&R, Succeeds," *Los Angeles Times*, May 11, p. G19.

Pareles, John. (1999). "From Rock On to Rock Is Dead," *New York Times*, August 26, pp. B9, 27.

"Pepper ... and Salt." (1956). *Wall Street Journal*, January 18, p. 14.

Ramazani, Jahan. (1994). *Poetry of Mourning: The Modern Elegy from Hardy to Heaney*. Chicago: University of Chicago Press.

"Red Infiltration Will Be Described to GOP." (1961). *Los Angeles Times,* August 6, p. OC26.

"Rhythm and Rumble." (1956). *Washington Post,* June 6, p. 14.

Richey, William, and Kevin J.H. Dettmar, eds. (2001). "Rock and the Condition of Postmo-dernity," Special Issue of *Genre* 34 (3/4), pp. 169–178.

"Rock 'n' Roll Mimed." (1960). *New York Times,* December 8, p. 44.

"Rock 'n' Roll Music Is Tops with Teenagers." (1956). *Washington Post and Times Herald,* June 24, p. F1.

"Rock 'n' Roll Opponents Are Due for Big Break." (1958). *New York Times,* January 13, p. 49.

"Rock 'n' Roll Stage Show Frantic, Noisy." (1955). *Los Angeles Times,* November 4, p. B9.

"Rock 'n' Roll Will Soon Be Only for Rowboats, Songwriters Think." (1956). *Los Angeles Times,* July 29, p. B15.

"Rock-and-Roll Called 'Communicable Disease.'" (1956). *New York Times,* March 28, p. 33.

Rogin, Michael Paul. (1987). *Ronald Reagan, the Movie: And Other Episodes in Political Demon-ology.* Berkeley: University of California Press.

Ross, Andrew. (1994). "Introduction," in *Microphone Fiends: Youth Music and Youth Culture,* ed. Andrew Ross and Tricia Rose. New York: Routledge, pp. 1–13.

Samuels, Gertrude. (1958). "Why They Rock 'n' Roll—And Should They?," *New York Times Magazine,* January 12, p. 19.

Sanjek, Russell. (1972). "The War on Rock," in *Downbeat Music '72 Yearbook.* Chicago: Maher.

Scruton, Roger. (1993). "Notes on the Meaning of Music," in *The Interpretation of Music: Philo-sophical Essays,* ed. Michael Krausz. New York: Oxford University Press, pp. 193–202.

Siegel, Don, dir. (1988). *Invasion of the Body Snatchers* (1956). Republic Pictures Home Video.

Siemers, Ida Turner. (1954). "Saving the World Again," *Chicago Daily Tribune,* April 28, p. 20.

Smith, Ken. (1999). *Mental Hygiene: Classroom Films, 1945–1970.* New York: Blast Books.

Snoop Dogg. (1999). *Tha Doggfather: The Times, Trials, and Hardcore Truths of Snoop Dogg.* New York: William Morrow.

"Songs by Machines." (1957). *Los Angeles Times,* August 11, p. B4.

Stein, Atara. (1999). "'Even Better Than the Real Thing': U2's (Love) Songs of the Self," in *Reading Rock & Roll: Authenticity, Appropriation, Aesthetics,* ed. Kevin J.H. Dettmar and William Richey. New York: Columbia University Press, pp. 269–86.

Stinson, Charles. (1961). "More Science Fiction Films on Local Screens," *Los Angeles Times,* September 2, p. A7.

Strausbaugh, John. (2001). *Rock 'Til You Drop: The Decline from Rebellion to Nostalgia.* London: Verso.

Talese, Gay. (1957). "Wrestling Fans Rival Rock 'n' Roll Addicts," *New York Times,* March 10, p. S4.

"They Agree on This." (1955). *Los Angeles Times,* April 10, p. F7.

Topping, Seymour. (1962). "Moiseyev Scorns Rock 'n' Roll as 'Disgusting Dynamism'—Calls for Russian Works," *New York Times,* April 29, p. 4.

Tosches, Nick. (1985). *Country: Living Legends and Dying Metaphors in America's Biggest Music.* New York: Scribner.

Townsend, Dorothy. (1958). "Rock 'n' Roll on Way Downhill," *Los Angeles Times,* January 4, p. B6.

Waksman, Steve. (1999). *Instruments of Desire: The Electric Guitar and the Shaping of Musical Experience.* Cambridge, MA: Harvard University Press.

Walser, Robert. (1993). *Running with the Devil: Power, Gender, and Madness in Heavy Metal Music.* Middletown, CT: Wesleyan University Press.

Warren, Jerry, dir. (2002). *Teenage Zombies* (1957). Alpha Video DVD.

Waugh, Arthur. (1916). "The New Poetry," *Quarterly Review,* p. 226.

Weinstein, Deena. (2000). *Heavy Metal: The Music and Its Culture,* rev. ed. Boulder, CO: West-view.

Whitehead, Jayson, and Tanya Stanciu. (1999). "Songs to Save the Planet: An Interview with Pete Seeger," *Gadfly,* July, n.p.; http://www.gadflyonline.com/archive/July99/ archive-seeger.html.

Whiteside, Jonny. (1997). *Ramblin' Rose: The Life and Career of Rose Maddox.* Nashville: Country Music Foundation Press and Vanderbilt University Press.

Wolters, Larry. (1958). "Rock 'n' Roll Has Had It on W-G-N Radio," *Chicago Tribune,* February 22, p. 14.

———. (1957). "Rock 'n' Roll's on Way Down, Say 3 Experts," *Chicago Tribune,* May 26, p. SW28.

"Yeh-Heh-Heh-Hes, Baby: Rock 'n' Roll." (1956). *Time,* June 18, p. 54.

"Yevtushenko Defends Rock 'n' Roll and Twist Despite Red Denunciation." (1962). *Washington Post,* May 27, p. A3.

Index